FLOATING THROUGH

Updated and revised version published by the author
in association with

www.lulu.com
2012

ISBN: 978-1-4710-4450-2

First published 2001 by Gopher Publishers UK. ISBN: 90-76953-30-9
Republished in 2006 by Librario Publishing Ltd. ISBN: 1-0904440-19-3

Further copies of this book can be ordered via the Internet

www.davisons-afloat.com
www.lulu.com
www.Amazon.co.uk

or by phone 0771 8351066

Floating Through France

(By Catamaran from the Channel to the
Carmargue)

by

Brenda Davison

The author and John sailing round Land's End, on
the first leg of their voyage

Dedicated to John,
without whom this trip would not have been possible and
to all the other *plaisanciers* we met during the trip.

About the author

Brenda Davison was born in Lancaster. She became a reluctant sailor when in middle life she married John who had been sailing all his adult life.

She now lives on the Wirral where she ran a busy training consultancy and wrote for business publications. Her first book *What's All This About Stress?* was published in 1999 and she continues to write and teach this subject.

She is a former University lecturer and has a background in the health service where she was, at different times, a training officer and an occupational therapist.

The theft and destruction of a boat that she and John had lovingly restored over several years made her realise how much she had come to love sailing and they bought another boat and began again. Their dream was to take the boat to the Mediterranean.

When she met John, Brenda was afraid of water, being a poor swimmer, unable to float and hating to get her face wet. She took swimming and sailing lessons so that she could fully appreciate the joys of sailing in the Greek islands and now says she is 'addicted to snorkelling'.

The first leg of their journey took them from Liverpool to Cornwall in 1999. This book describes the second leg across the English Channel and through the French canals. It describes their experiences, the places they visited, and the people they met and gives a picture of life on the French waterways.

They so enjoyed the journey through France that, after three years in Greece, they brought the boat back to England, where they sold her, and bought a Dutch canal boat, which they now keep on the French waterways.

Brenda has added further chapters to this book describing their journey back through France and the changes which had occurred since their first trip.

Acknowledgements

My grateful thanks go to Maureen and Steve of *Dolma*, to Lesley and Steve of *Gee Bee*, and Guy Lafleur of Langres, France, who kindly allowed me to use their photographs, and to Bill Else for the photograph on page 4.

Other photographs are the author's own.

Maps have been drawn by the author.

Contents

	Page
Introduction, *"Let's Go For It"*	11
Chapter 1, Entering St. Valéry, *The Odyssey begins*	23
Chapter 2, The Somme, *A French Salute*	37
Chapter 3, Canal du Nord, *Péniches – In Earnest*	51
Chapter 4, Compiegne, *Anacondas and Crocodiles*	63
Chapter 5, River Aisne, *Our Second Big City – Soissons*	75
Chapter 6, Reims – *City of Champagne and Coronations,*	
The Total Eclipse	87
Chapter 7, Vitry le Francois, *Locks, weeds and visitors*	101
Chapter 8, Canal de la Marne à La Saône, *The Spanish Cow*	111
Chapter 9, We Reach The Summit, *Two More Locks*	121
Chapter 10, The Saône, *Gare d'Eau*	135
Chapter 11, The Lower Saône, *Poste Restante*	149
Chapter 12, Lyon, *The Mighty Rhône at Last*	165
Chapter 13, Provence, *Camels and Llamas, Wine 'en Vrac'*	177
Chapter 14, Arles and Avignon, *The Bridge and The Bulls*	189
Chapter 15, The End of the Journey, *Mosquitoes*	203
Epilogue, *Port Napoleon Marina, Port-St-Louis-du-Rhône*	217
Update Chapter, *We return from Greece*	225
Final Chapter, Bringing *Chefren* home	235
Glossary and Information	245
Appendix, Addresses and Bibliography	250

List of Diagrams

(drawn by the author)

                                                      Page

Sketch Map of France and its waterways   10
Baie de Somme, showing buoyed channel as it was   22
St Valéry to Compiègne   38
St Valéry to Reims   64
Reims to St Jean-de-Losne   86
The Saône   134
Lyon to the Mediterranean   187

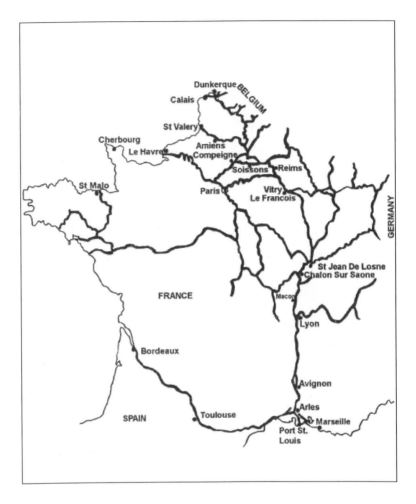

France and its waterways

INTRODUCTION

"Let's Go For It!"

Travelling through the French Canals to the Mediterranean had been a romantic dream that John and I had shared since the early days of our marriage in 1989. It was 'second time around' for both of us and, until that point, the most adventurous thing I had ever done was some cross country skiing.

John, however, had been sailing most of his adult life and when I met him he had an Elizabethan 29, a 29ft yacht called *Rally* which sailed like a dream and which he kept on a mooring in the river Mersey, a testing ground for yachtsmen where fierce high tides funnel into the river from the Irish Sea.

I had never sailed before, and in fact was very nervous of water, but since my divorce I had been determined to live a little and take any opportunities for adventure that life offered. Fortunately I had never suffered from seasickness, but the prospect of sailing on a small boat out of the sight of land filled me with terror. I wouldn't even swim out of my depth in a swimming pool; I hated to get my face wet and was too scared to try to float. But it's wonderful what love can do! John said that if I didn't like sailing he would sell his boat. After a statement like that, it would have been churlish of me not to give it a good try.

John initiated me to sailing gently. He refused to take me out in his boat until the weather and the tides were just right, and we then had several pleasant sails. Later that year he invited me to join him and some friends on a flotilla in the Mediterranean. This was a party of about twelve yachts, sailing between Sardinia and Corsica in clear, emerald-green waters, a cloudless blue sky arching above us, and in a warm climate instead of the wet and cold of Britain – and no tides. It was the closest I had come to Paradise, and I said: "If this is sailing you can count me in!" We also came back from

11

that holiday and made plans to get married – perhaps it was the effect of the sun and the sea?

Learning to sail with John, I discovered similar problems to those encountered by women whose husbands try to teach them to drive a car – trouble! So I took myself on a practical sailing course in North Wales. I was full of apprehension, expecting to be the oldest (I was in my fifties) and probably the only female, on board a small yacht where privacy would be at a premium.

For four days during a very wet May we sailed round the island of Anglesey. I was indeed the oldest of two females and three men but surprised myself by loving it, in spite of the cold, relentless rain. As a Girl Guide I had learned to 'tough it out' on wet campsites in the Lake District. I rediscovered some of that same hardiness and the companion-ship and teamwork made up for the discomfort.

On my 'test day' I not only had to be in charge of the boat but also had to contend with fog, but I passed, and the course helped my confidence enormously. I decided to learn navigation skills next, and persuaded John to accompany me to night school.

I also found a swimming coach for adults who taught me how to breathe properly and developed my confidence. Before very long I was swimming under water, floating and snorkelling. Who said you can't teach an old dog new tricks?

By this time we had sold *Rally* and, with the aid of a fortuitous legacy from an uncle, bought a beautiful 9-metre catamaran, which we called *Double Vision*. We had been able to buy her cheaply as she was in a neglected condition. Many man (and woman) hours were spent refitting and repainting. She was ready to make our dream a reality. Our plan was to take her in stages during the summer to the Mediterranean where we would use her for holidays, eventually returning to live more or less permanently on board once we had both retired. In the first year we would sail to the south coast of Britain, the next year the South of France, and so on.

Our plans suffered a setback in 1995 when *Double Vision* was stolen from her mooring in North Wales and discovered wrecked on a beach in Cumbria, her hull a shattered mess of fibreglass. She had been dashed to pieces on the shingle by the incoming tide. Alerted by the coastguard we hurried to Cumbria to find the remains of our personal possessions scattered over the wide beach, and the boat picked clean by scavengers. Sails had been removed, the anchor windlass unscrewed and removed together with all the ropes and halyards. Someone had even attempted to unscrew the gas water heater. I now understood the meaning of the phrase 'seeing red'. After my first sight of our wrecked dream, words cannot adequately express what I would have liked to do to the person responsible.

I found a wet and battered copy of 'The Cruel Sea' on the beach, which John had been re-reading. It seemed an unkind commentary. We were both devastated and I cried salty tears into my pillow for many nights to come.

The person responsible was caught and went to gaol and we received the insurance money. But none of this was any compensation for the immediate loss of our dream and all our hard work.

But one good thing came out of it. I realised how much I had come to love sailing. Until that point I felt I was going along for John's sake, but it was me who urged him to start looking for another boat.

We found the boat we were searching for in 1998 and, after spending three months getting her ready, we couldn't wait to begin our Odyssey and set off to sail her to the South Coast of Britain.

She is a 25-year-old Prout Snowgoose catamaran, 10m (35ft) long and 4.7 metres (15ft) wide, named *Chefren*. She is big enough to accommodate the two of us in comfort and three or four friends too. On the bridge deck, between the hulls, there is a large main cabin with a dinette aft and a sitting area forward. This sitting area doubles as our sleeping cabin, converting to a double berth, and is curtained off at night. In the starboard hull there is a galley separating a single cabin forward and another aft. The navigation

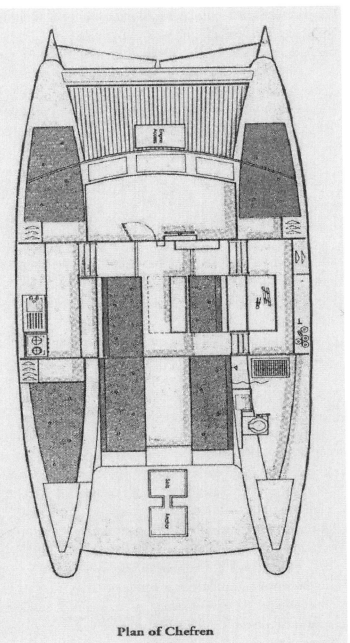

Plan of Chefren

area with a chart table and sailing instruments is in the port hull, with 'heads' forward and another single cabin aft, which John has claimed as his 'tool shed'. She has a rear cockpit with lockers to sit on, where the steering position is, and from where the sails are handled. Aft of the cockpit there is a wooden, slatted platform where we stow gear on passage, but where we can also sit and enjoy the sun.

The sails are easy to handle. We have a roller furling foresail and an in-boom roller furling main sail. [A glossary of sailing terms is included at the end of the book.] By the time we set off John had already taken early retirement but I was still working for myself running a training consultancy and had just published my first book. However, I decided that the time had come to wind the consultancy work down and concentrate on sailing and writing, a sort of partial retirement. Life is more than work and we believed it was time for me to stop 'living at work' and for both of us to start 'working at life'.

We sailed out of the river Mersey in July 1998 in the worst weather conditions we had experienced during our sailing years together. We were tossed by choppy seas and lashed by heavy downpours and on several occasions were to be found sheltering in a harbour waiting for storms to abate. Everything inside and outside the boat was wet. It reminded us of why we were taking the boat to the Med and not sailing in Britain.

The worst experience of the trip came when I was standing in the cockpit by the open cabin. As *Chefren* pitched forward our bow scooped up a foaming wave which washed over the foredeck, continued over the cabin top and caught me full in the face, sending streams of icy seawater down my neck and depositing a couple of gallons into the cabin, all over my beautiful blue carpet.

Our trials and tribulations were more than made up for when some twenty bottle-nosed dolphins joined us as we crossed the Bristol Channel. They swam and played with us for four hours, cresting our bow wave, slip-streaming, diving under the boat, shooting between the hulls, playing 'chicken' across our bows, or simply swimming alongside looking up at us with a knowing eye, which seemed to say, "What do you think of that then?" We felt very privileged to have their attentions.

Our sail to the south coast highlighted several problems that we would need to put right before leaving Britain. One of the worst was that *Chefren* was taking in water. She wasn't in danger of sinking, but the protective rubbing strake around the outside of the boat was leaking where it was bolted through the hull. Over the years the bolts had worked loose and some of the wood had rotted, letting water in from the outside into the lockers. All our efforts to fill the boltholes, and replace the rotted timber hadn't cured the problem. Rainwater and some seawater were still getting in. Filling the holes and fitting a completely new rubbing strake seemed the only answer.

We also decided that we needed a fridge. We believed that in the warmer climate of the Mediterranean, where we might be away from shops for several days at a time, a larger fridge would be a necessity. (It would also be useful for cooling the beer and wine.)

Reaching Cornwall, we found a small marina-cum-boat yard where we laid up *Chefren*, returning the following spring to live aboard and tackle the necessary work, before setting sail for France.

We were laid up alongside another catamaran which was being extensively re-built by the owner who was also living aboard on his own for large periods of time. We shared tools and expertise, not to mention cups of tea and fish and chips, and were soon firm friends. When we finally set off he came with us to crew across the channel and into the canals where his wife also joined us, after travelling across on the ferry. As his name was also John, I'll refer to him by his surname, Hobbs, to save confusion. He was a multi-talented man who had spent most of his life working on the docks, but early redundancy had enabled him to discover other talents, including enormous skill in working with wood. He had created many huge tree sculptures using a chain saw and was rapidly making a name for himself. He had a great sense of fun and we enjoyed having him along. His infectious grin, underneath a shock of blonde, curly hair often lightened a tense moment.

Hobbs helped us to fit the rubbing strake, attaching this to the outside of the boat with epoxy resin – a good choice for Britain but one that gave us some problems in the extreme heat we were to encounter later.

We had seen a fridge unit at the London Boat Show that year. It consisted of a top opening, polypropylene box, made to fit the shape of the hull, and a condenser unit to fit inside it. These would give us a bespoke fridge for the space available. It would run off the batteries, but a sintered bronze shoe fitted to the outside of the hull and cooled by the seawater, made it very economical.

To fit the fridge we had to re-build the galley around it. We also fitted a wind generator to keep the batteries charged for running the fridge, my computer and our on-board washing machine as well as a miniature vacuum cleaner.

We tried to obtain paid help with some of the other jobs, but found an extremely laid-back attitude in Cornwall. Another boat owner summed it up like this: "When a Cornishman says, 'Dreckly Zur' he means something like 'Mañana' but it's not quite as urgent." So rather than wait for the unpredictable Cornish labour we did most of the jobs ourselves and they took us several weeks. It was July before they were finished and all the cleaning and re-painting complete.

The reader might think that because John and I own a boat and were able to buy a fridge and other equipment for her that we are rich. Let me hasten to assure you that we are not. It has been said, 'a boat is a hole in the water into which you pour money'. This is only true if you have to pay other people to do the work for you, or pay expensive marina fees.

We are just ordinary people. John was an electrical technician and we have had to work hard all our lives, but we are both quite practical people and enjoy working with our hands. If anyone reading this has dreams of doing the same, it is possible to do it on a very limited budget. We do the majority of the work ourselves and buy our equipment second hand, mostly from 'boat jumbles'. Just occasionally we decide that something is sufficiently important to spend a larger amount of money on, such as the fridge, and we budget for this each year. Some of these more expensive items have been the wind generator, and a laptop PC powered by an inverter. We save money by avoiding marinas where possible, preferring to anchor in quiet bays or harbours where mooring is free.

My washing machine sounds good, but it is a very simple tub with an electrically operated agitator and has to be filled and emptied by hand and needs to be connected to shore power. It's only one step removed from hand washing but is very useful when there are no laundrettes near by. It was bought at a 'boat jumble' for £20.

Once we were ready to start we planned a route to cross the English Channel at the narrower end, from Newhaven to St. Valéry-sur-Somme. We chose St.-Valéry because we were told that the Somme is very beautiful and unspoilt, and so it is. We wanted to cruise through pleasant scenery on quiet rivers, enjoying the countryside and the wildlife, missing as many big cities as possible.

The majority of boats seem to choose Le Havre and travel up the Seine, which is tidal as far as the first lock, very industrialised and used by big ships. This didn't appeal to us.

From the Somme we would be able to use some of the lesser known waterways initially, join the Rhône at Lyon and go from there to the Mediterranean coast, where we would look for a secure marina in which to leave the boat for the winter.

We felt we were embarking on a big adventure. When we told friends of our plans, many were surprised to hear that you could travel through France by boat, especially in one as wide as ours. Not only can you do this, but you also have a choice of routes. It would be possible to go to Belgium, Holland or Germany, or even right across Europe coming out in the Black Sea.

The French inland waterways have been used commercially since the 16th Century when a system was created to link the Loire with the Seine, and the Saône with the Rhône, creating the first highway between the Channel and the Mediterranean. The canals reached their heyday in the 19th century, and then began to decline. Recently there has been an increase in traffic, both commercial and pleasure. In conjunction with local Chambers of Commerce, the Voies Navigable de France (VNF) spends a lot of time, money and effort creating facilities for pleasure boats. They are putting down pontoons, sometimes with water and electricity provided (often free), and issue licences to use the canals.

The width of the European waterways is greater than that of English canals, although on the route we chose many of the locks were only 0.3 metres (12in) wider than *Chefren*, and in places the canal was very shallow. We often had to manoeuvre with great care.

We bought ourselves several books to help with route planning. We read articles in the sailing press and talked to others about our plans. A good idea you might think, but we almost gave up the idea because of all the horror stories we heard and read.

Our sailing friends told us horror stories of fierce sluices in locks; of being harassed by *péniches* (huge commercial barges) who would hold us up in the narrow canals, and ram us in the locks; of rude anglers; unhelpful lock keepers; and locks with sloping sides where it was difficult to attach a rope. As in Britain the canals are often used for dumping rubbish and we would need to look out for supermarket trolleys and the like, but hopefully would not suffer the same fate as a boat, whose owner we had met whilst sailing in Greece, who had his keel ripped off by a submerged Volvo saloon Articles in the sailing press always tell you about disasters. They wouldn't make interesting reading otherwise, would they? Did we really want to tackle this we wondered? More importantly, were we up to it?

We were a little daunted by what seemed to be a mass of regulations - we would need a licence to use the waterways, obtainable only in France and one of us would need an Overseas Certificate of Competence. If we remained in France for more than six months it seemed that we might need an import licence, and so on[1].

Then there was the boat itself. One sailing book categorically stated that a catamaran would not be a suitable boat for inland waterways, presumably because of its size. But, having obtained the dimensions of the canals and the locks, we were sure we could choose a route which *Chefren* could negotiate.

We were also well used to locks, and their hazards. We had wintered a previous boat in a boatyard in Northwich and sailed her down the river Weaver to the Manchester Ship Canal on our way to the sea. On our very first trip I was standing on the after-platform to throw a rope ashore in the first lock when I lost my balance. I still had the rope in both hands, and had looped it over the bollard, but I ended up dangling on the end of the rope, up to my waist in the filthy, murky water of the lock. To make matters worse no one saw me go! I was hauled out, none the worse for my encounter. Fortunately the lock gates were still open and the sluices not in operation or it might have been a different tale. But I now have a healthy respect for locks.

Non-sailing friends questioned us about safety equipment on board, and wanted to know whether the Channel would be rough. What would we do if we sank and did we carry a life raft? Once upon a time I might have shared their fears but now I felt confident that *Chefren* was seaworthy and her crew competent.

We already knew about the traffic separation zones in the Channel, rather like a dual carriageway for big ships, where we would need to cross at right angles in order to be clearly seen. We had also read in our pilot book about the difficulties of entering the Baie de Somme with its ever-shifting sand banks and a buoyed

---

[1] No longer needed

channel which had to be regularly up-dated. We were cautioned not to enter without local knowledge.

Finally we were advised to be wary about the French people who were reputed to hate the English, and whose accents were so varied we wouldn't be able to understand them.

Whilst we took careful note of all the advice our minds were made up and we decided to go for it anyway.

This book is the story of that journey; how we, two sixty-somethings, faced up to and overcame the difficulties which we did encounter. I hope you, the reader, will enjoy travelling the French rivers and canals with us in this book, being introduced to some of the people we met, visiting with us some of the out of the way places as well as some of [he well known ones, witnessing with us the eclipse of the sun, and the bull running in Arles.

We ended the trip fitter, with many new friends, and an added bonus was that John, whose only previous visit to France had been a week-end in Paris, left England as a Francophobe; not very fond of 'fancy' French food and wine; and believing that all French people hated the English, and ended it a confirmed Francophile, having discovered the delights of French cuisine and wine. The French people were charming, warm and friendly and we will definitely be going back.

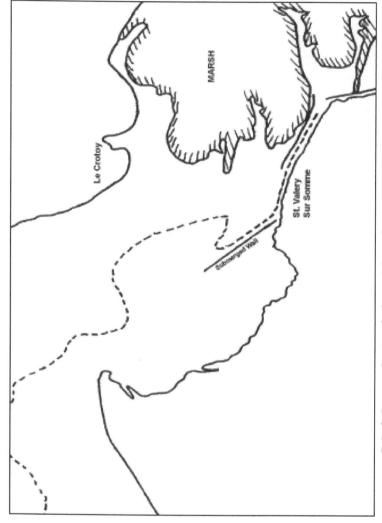

Baie de Somme, showing the buoyed channel as it was on the day we arrived

CHAPTER 1 – Entering St. Valéry

The Odyssey begins

It was a sunny Saturday afternoon when we sighted the coast of France. A cloudless sky arched above us and the sea was calm, as it had been all through the trip. We were tired, having been up most of the night, but exhilarated to have made landfall without mishap. We congratulated ourselves that our first obstacle was over.

Chefren at sea

On board *Chefren*, were myself, my husband John, and our friend Hobbs. Hobbs was a blonde haired giant of a man whose many talents proved very useful as the trip proceeded, and his quirky sense of humour added greatly to our team spirit.

We'd sailed from Cornwall to Newhaven and from there to France, taking it in turns to sleep during the night, arranging the watches so that there were always two people on deck. We left before midnight to catch the tide and arrive in France during daylight, on a rising tide.

The trip was not without event. While off the Isle of Wight I was asleep down below. I was disturbed by a change in the note of the engine. We were slowing down. Trouble, I thought, and quickly pulled on my sailing jacket and shoes. It was early dawn, as I appeared, bleary-eyed, on deck, in time to see Hobbs leaning over the guardrail, with a boat hook in his hand.

"Got it, John!" he called, and began to pull something on board. A body? A fish? My sleep hazed mind worked overtime. It was a deck chair, washed out to sea from one of the many beaches on the south coast. It had suffered from its time in the ocean, but proved a useful addition to our boat's equipment.

Another heart-stopping moment had occurred as we left Newhaven marina at 23h30 to enter the narrow harbour channel. Heading for the open sea we could see lights ahead of us, and some of those seemed to detach themselves from the rest and move towards us. The terrifying blast of a ship's siren alerted us to the fact that a huge Superseacat ferry was entering the harbour. Pulling into the side to give her a wide berth reminded us that we hadn't called the port radio station to let them know we were on the move. They would have warned us of the approaching ferry. Black marks all round.

Half an hour out, under sail, enjoying a cup of steaming coffee, and with the auto helm steering our course, a noise disturbed our complacency. It was the warning beep, beep, beep of the auto-helm. The drive belt had snapped, we were thrown off course and lost the wind from our sails. For the next few miles we went back to steering by hand; no problem really, just a little boring at that time of night, especially as the wind was constant. Eventually the ever-resourceful Hobbs made a temporary repair using some duct tape and staples, which lasted until daylight.

Otherwise the crossing was uneventful, the wind was on the beam, blowing steadily all night, and we used the engine as well to increase our speed. Overhead the moon's kindly beam gave us enough light to steer by and we made good progress.

It was an exhilarating experience to feel the gentle breeze on my face, to look up at the graceful curve of the sails outlined against the midnight sky and see the stars winking reassuringly. We were really on our way.

We needed to cross two busy shipping lanes and whilst we were concerned about this we knew the procedure. Hobbs and John had a lifetime of sailing experience, but I was a comparative newcomer with only 11 years of sailing to my credit. However the credentials I had

24

obtained, which allowed me to obtain the Overseas Certificate of Competence, made me (laughably) the most qualified sailor on board.

In the event, the horror stories about heavy traffic had no basis. We only saw two other ships all night – another Superseacat and a fishing boat. Maybe we were just lucky.

We didn't have a life raft on board, but we did have an inflatable dinghy which we carried ready inflated in davits, and all the usual safety equipment. During the night we wore harnesses when we were on watch, securing us to the boat, and self-inflating life jackets attached to our wet weather jackets which we wore all the time.

In the Baie de Somme, as well as the ever-changing buoyed channel, there is a submerged sea wall that is covered at high tide. To get local knowledge is sound advice for inexperienced sailors, but as we have sailed regularly in and out of the Mersey and also over the Caernarfon bar, we are familiar with buoyed channels.

We had planned to arrive on a rising tide so that if we did go aground on a sand bank we would be sure of floating off again as the tide came in. Like all good sailors we also had an alternative course to another harbour planned should conditions be unfavourable.

There are 50 buoys marking the channel that winds tortuously across the wide bay to St. Valéry at the mouth of the Somme. Realising that these might be inaccurate we approached with healthy caution, looking for the cardinal buoy marking the entrance and hoping to see a local boat that we could follow into the river estuary.

As we approached we could see that the bay was alive with boats. Craft of all shapes and sizes were taking advantage of the summer sunshine and the light airs, many with brightly coloured spinnakers, creating a kaleidoscope of shape and colour on the sparkling blue water. No one as far as we could see was keeping to the buoyed channel, and we were tempted to do the same and head straight for where we judged the estuary to be but, we were British and the Brits stick to the rules. The pilot books told us to keep to the buoyed channel, and keep to it we did, carefully threading our way from one buoy to the next, avoiding the sailing boats which were taking advantage of the fact that 'power gives way to sail'.

It took us at least an hour to negotiate the channel and we were at buoy 32, well in sight of the line of marks indicating the submerged sea wall, when a local fishing boat appeared from the direction of Le Crotoy on the north side of the bay and we followed it into the river mouth.

We then motored down a wide channel bordered on each side by marshes, where it's possible to pick samphire grass and marsh lilies. Amongst the marshes we saw distant figures with shotguns slung over their shoulders. No doubt the local duck population was being decimated that day. It was the first day of the six-month hunting season, which various bodies are now campaigning to shorten in order to preserve French wildlife.

Reaching the outskirts of St. Valéry, we motored along, admiring the rather opulent residences edging the quay. They were all different shapes and sizes, with ornate balconies and steep roofs. They reminded me of the sea front houses that were part of the Jacques Tati film, '*M. Hulot's Holiday*'. We learned later that they had been built by former ship owners who made their fortunes exporting salt.

Suddenly we found ourselves surrounded by boats. A marina had been built in the river itself, presumably because this was as far as one could go before the lock into the canal. On our right, finger pontoons protruded into the river where motorboats, yachts and canal boats, from the opulent to the downright scruffy, filled every conceivable space. On our left was a single long pontoon a little way out from the shore, which turned out to be the visitors' pontoon. A young Frenchman in a dinghy appeared from nowhere to greet us and escort us to a berth. He took our lines and made them fast then welcomed us by shaking each of us by the hand and showing us the whereabouts of the *Capitainerie*. He spoke no English and I had to exercise my rusty French, being the only one on board with any knowledge of the language.

I had taken a French O level forty years before and had used it little since, except for the few holidays I had had in France in my thirties. I was greatly reassured to find that as the trip progressed fluency returned and I was able to understand and be understood in most situations, with only one or two hiccups. French teachers out there take heart, some of us do learn what you teach and it stays with us – well mine has.

The visitors' pontoon was on the opposite side of the river from the *Capitainerie* and there was no bridge, instead a fleet of little orange fibreglass dinghies with outboard motors were provided, but at that stage we had no idea that these were for our use. Instead we launched our own dinghy and rowed ashore.

St. Valéry Marina

At the *Capitainerie* we were given a *Releve de Balisage* - a chart of the bay with the positions of the buoys updated on the 2nd July, only two weeks previously. It is issued by the *Direction Departementale de l'Equipement de la Somme*, and would have been invaluable to have in advance if we had known of its existence.

Having reported in and paid our dues, we could relax. We sat on a wide veranda outside the marina bar, overlooking the water, basking in the warm sun, surveying the other boats, and taking stock. We were still a little apprehensive, a long trip was ahead of us in unknown territory, but we had successfully negotiated the channel crossing and the Baie de Somme so we felt that a congratulatory refreshing drink was in order, and allowed ourselves to savour our arrival in France.

In addition to the bar, which also served meals, the marina provided water, electricity, rubbish collection, toilets, free showers and hot water. All of these very modern facilities were housed in an attractive wooden building situated above the pontoons on the steep bank of the river, approached by a floating walkway. It was one of the best marinas we encountered on the trip.

The toilet block was unisex. This is often a shock to those coming to France for the first time, but the French take these things very much for granted and it is all very proper.

We discovered a notice, in French, about the little orange boats. It asked users to ensure that there was always one boat left on the pontoon at each side of the river. This posed some difficulties when only one boat remained. It reminded us of the puzzle about the fox, the hen and a bag of grain that need transporting across a river. We worked out a solution involving all three of us and two boats, causing a lot of hilarity as we ferried backwards and forwards. Especially when the motor stopped half way across and the two boats started drifting down river!

We never saw any French people doing this. The French have a healthy disregard for rules and regulations and for authority generally. This seems to be a legacy from the Revolution when the people executed the aristocrats who had previously exercised the authority. Was it because we were British that we went to such pains?

There was an air of festivity in the town which was thronged with holidaymakers wandering along the quayside and taking trips on the *petite train* that seems to be a feature of all tourist towns. A small white engine pulling two open carriages ran along the road, giving visitors a guided tour of the local sights. As well as this there was a real 'Puffing Billy', which was 100 years old. Its railway line ran along the quay and it occasionally announced its presence by a blast on its whistle, encouraging pedestrians to get out of the way. The route of the train was over the bridge spanning the river just before the lock gates, and its route took passengers to *Le Crotoy* and to the war museums of the Somme.

Overhead light aircraft circled, trailing banners advertising *Specialité Les Plongeurs Fous*, which seemed to be a reference to mad divers, and verbal announcements of other attractions were made by loudspeaker vans touring the streets. My ear was insufficiently tuned to the new language to distinguish just what they were advertising.

Having a French meal was our next priority and on Sunday evening we ventured into the little town in search of a suitable establishment. We were surprised to find that most of the restaurants were closed by 20h00 and had to search hard to find one that was still open. Perhaps it was because it was Sunday and this was only a small town?

Eventually finding a restaurant, we treated ourselves to the 'whole hog' – appetisers, three courses and wine. John was keen to try *Pastis Ricard*, which he remembered from his previous visit to France. I tried, for the first time, a *kir*, white wine with cassis (black-currant liqueur) which was to become my favourite drink during the trip.

The meal was memorable, not only for the food but also for the service. When the young, rather nervous, trainee waiter brought our food he clumsily knocked over a carafe of water into John's lap. Fortunately John's trousers were drip-dry, suitable for life aboard, and the water made little impression other than dampening his spirits! The embarrassed waiter provided napkins to mop it up, but I thought he could have been a bit more apologetic. Perhaps it was the language difficulty? Later, the same waiter was pouring our wine, and the *maitre d'hôtel* (female) came across and lightly tapped his forearm to make him raise the bottle just a little higher, avoiding drips. Well, they don't mind drowning their guests with water, but it wouldn't do to splash the wine, would it?

The next day dawned bright and clear, the sun beat down from a cloudless blue sky and the night had been warm. We were eager to finish equipping the boat and begin our trip. We visited a chandlery across the road from the marina to buy a new belt for the auto-helm. It was about 11am, but while we were there they began to pull down the shutters and close for lunch.

Most French establishments close for two hours in the middle of the day and stay open later in the evening. We were not surprised by this, nor the turning away of customers, but we were surprised that they should be doing it so early. Walking on into the town we found the *Office du Tourisme* also closed. This caused us to stop and think. We remembered the restaurants which had been closing early the previous evening, the chandlery closing early and now this. Peering through the door at their clock we realised our mistake. French time is one hour ahead of English time and we hadn't put our watches forward. I wondered what other gaffes we'd make before our trip was through?

A visit to the *supermarché* to fill the galley shelves with 'goodies' for our trip was next on the agenda. After obtaining instructions (in French) from the marina staff we set off down a little flagged street of typically French houses huddled together. These were the fishermen's cottages in the heart of the town, single storey with coloured shutters and flowers in window boxes and tubs at the door. We walked a long way and there was still no sign of the *supermarché*. I took my courage in both hands and asked a knot of people who were chatting at the roadside. I could just about manage: *"Est-il un supermarché pres d'ici, s'il vous plait?"*

We gathered from their reaction that we had walked in the wrong direction and the *supermarché* was a long way back. Our faces fell and, as we turned to retrace our steps, they called us back and offered us a lift. I had just enough French to thank them effusively for their kindness and to introduce us but that was about all. This was our first encounter with ordinary French people and we felt we were going to enjoy getting to know their compatriots.

Something had gone seriously wrong with my translation of the directions we had received and I didn't discover what it was until much later in the trip when I made the same mistake.

St Valéry itself is an ancient town, founded around 611 by an apostle from Luxeuil in the south. The little black and white chequered brick chapel, dedicated to St. Valéry, was visible from the marina, looking like a gingerbread house. This building, which was rebuilt in 1878, is said to commemorate where the saint lived and is buried. The main event for which the town is famous is that it was from here in 1066 that William (the Conqueror) set off for Britain.

It's a picturesque little place and in 1837 Victor Hugo wrote that it was "charming at dusk, the moon which went down an hour after sunset, descended slowly towards the sea, the sky was white, the earth brown and portions of the moon leapt from wave to wave like balls of gold in the hands of a juggler".

We stayed for two nights and were wondering whether to remain another day to do some sightseeing, but made a hasty decision to leave, late on the Monday, when we realised that if we didn't go on that particular tide the sea lock might not be open to traffic the following day, as the tide would be too late in the afternoon. When we saw other boats casting off and disappearing up river we decided to follow.

At this stage we still had our mast in position and had been told we could have it removed once we were in the canal. There was a very anxious moment when we realised that we needed to pass through a swing bridge into the lock. All the other vessels, motorboats without masts, had already passed under it. I had to use the radio and ask for the bridge to be swung for us. I couldn't understand what was said in reply, but at the point when we were about to turn back, the bridge opened and we were able to pass through into a wide basin where the other boats were already waiting for the lock gates to open.

When the level of the tidal river reached that of the river on the landward side we went through into a short stretch of canal, which disappeared under another bridge. This was not a swing bridge, and there was no way we could pass through until we had had our mast removed. The boatyard was here at the Quai Jules Verne on the right bank, but it was closed. We would have to wait until morning. The other boats had already disappeared. We had to find somewhere to tie up, but the only available pontoon was fully occupied by French canal boats. On the bank near the pontoon were several dogs and children, whilst the Dads were fishing alongside. The general impression was of a group of boats sailing in company, and we felt we would be intruding if we rafted alongside.

On the opposite bank a huge barge was tied to a small quay and at that moment a dark-haired middle-aged woman, in a turquoise sweater, appeared on its deck and spoke to us in English. She explained that we wouldn't be able to go any further without having our mast taken down (that much had become obvious), but if we liked we could moor alongside their barge, named *Maja*, until the boat yard opened in the morning.

We were glad to take up her offer and later clambered across their barge (taking care to only use the foredeck, as is sailing etiquette), and scaled up to the rather steep quay using their ladder. Once on shore we looked at the crane in the boatyard and discovered where to moor the following day.

The occupants of the barge were an English couple, Audrey and Tony, who lived permanently on the French canals. Their beautifully kept boat was an old commercial barge decorated with tubs of flowers and with lace curtains at the windows, and a piece of equipment resembling an old fashioned mangle on the foredeck for raising the anchor.

The following day they had visitors who also lived on the canals. We invited them aboard *Chefren* and they told us about life on the waterways. We were to meet many such expatriate couples, living in France, full of enthusiasm for the French country and its people, not to mention its food, its wine and even its health service.

Going ashore to make arrangements at the boatyard, we were shown by *le patron* where to tie up, in a little 'cut' alongside the main quay. He warned us to be careful as we entered because the river current was very strong and there was a breeze blowing from up-river. Both of these factors would affect the behaviour of our boat. Tied to the main quay were a number of very smart yachts and motorboats, probably in for storage or repair.

Le patron was concerned that we might damage one of these if we were not careful and emphasised his instructions (in French) with hand signals.

John is quite used to handling boats in similar circumstances and had weighed up what he needed to do as we approached, compensating for current and wind. Suddenly one of the employees of the boatyard appeared on the quay, shouting and gesticulating. Whilst we couldn't understand what he was saying, we did understand his body language and his shouts of: "*Non, non!*" as he waved us off. We were very puzzled and tried to explain that *le patron* had instructed us to go there, but he was insistent.

We backed off and immediately were caught by the wind and the current, and found ourselves being taken sideways downstream towards the lock gates. John began what should have been a three-point turn to make another approach but discovered that the boat would not answer the helm and continued its sideways progress. We were not in any real danger but the whole thing was becoming very embarrassing as he attempted to turn the boat around under the scornful eyes of the employee.

Hobbs and I watched helplessly, making ourselves ready with boat hooks and fenders to keep us off other boats and the bank. Hobbs didn't realise that there was a problem with the steering and was itching to get his hands on the wheel. I think he thought John was inexperienced. A couple of days later he had an opportunity to discover the problem for himself. *Chefren* has an inboard engine, but an out-drive steerable leg. This leg was changing direction of its own accord. In addition, when the engine was put into reverse, the leg was lifting out of the water instead of remaining locked down. What a way to start our trip. Further down the canals we met two other catamarans with similar problems, but at this stage we had no idea what was happening.

After much filling and backing, and revving of the engine, not to mention colourful language, John got the boat round and headed back to the boatyard, feeling very embarrassed. We discovered that the employee had wanted us to tie up at a quay around the corner so that he could warp us round using ropes only, not under engine. He was very concerned about the strength of the current and the possibility of us being swept down onto other boats. In fact, he put the other boats in greater danger by chasing us off as he did.

Getting from the quay to the cut became a major performance. After much throwing of lines, reversing, swearing and English/French translation we eventually managed it. It took us two hours, and by this time it was 12h00 and everything went quiet as they knocked off for lunch. So we did the same, sitting in the cockpit in the sunshine enjoying the fruits of our trip to the *supermarché* - pâté, cheese, salad and French bread, washed down with a bottle of Cabernet Merlot which had cost us 150FF (£1.50). We were enjoying this.

On the dot of 14h00 we heard the engine of the crane start up and there was *le patron* with two of his staff ready to remove our mast. He drove the crane while the two men set about dismantling the mast. They were two very different individuals. The employee who had warned us off was a typical dark-skinned, good-looking Frenchman, with a long lean body displayed to advantage in shorts and immaculate T-shirt. In contrast his mousy-haired companion had missed out in the good looks stakes and had done nothing to assist nature. He was clad in a purple T-shirt and ragged jeans, and had allowed his wispy hair to grow well below his ears. A drooping moustache framed a mouth filled with stained teeth and many gaps.

They leapt nimbly about our deck and took down the mast very quickly and efficiently. We were pleased by the cost too - 300FF (about £30). Later on in our trip we heard tales of charges up to 900FF at other marinas.

It took us the rest of the day to secure the mast safely to the top of the cabin, supported by the davits at one end, and the guardrails at the other. It was then too late to set off and we remained tied up at the boatyard that night.

It was at this stage we realised that we had not needed to undergo any customs formalities. We hadn't been asked for our passport or my certificate of competence - nothing. We were two weeks into the trip before anyone asked for papers of any kind. We later learned that EU boats are not required to pass through customs, and an import licence is no longer required.

When I opened my eyes the following morning, the day was already bright, although it was still early. I found it hard to believe that at last we were on our way into the French waterways and our dream was starting to come true.

With every fender we possessed tied to the outside of the boat ready to protect us in the locks, we got underway and passed under the first bridge and into a tree lined canal. *Chefren*, deprived of her mast, was looking like a graceful swan that had turned overnight into an ugly, ungainly duckling.

The sky was cloudless, the birds were singing and our spirits were high, although it was not without some apprehension that we anticipated our next lock. What would it be like? Would we be bounced around by the sluices; would we have enough rope for the depth of the lock; did we have enough fenders to protect our hull? But the lock was 15 km away and we had some time to relax and enjoy the scenery.

This canalised section of the River Somme stretched straight as an arrow before us, lined with leafy chestnuts on one side, and fields and distant villages on the other.

We found that all the canal banks throughout the trip were lined with trees, planted to absorb moisture and prevent the banks from softening and caving in, and each area has a different type of tree. The rivers we used, like the Somme, had been canalised by building locks, straightening out some of the curves and strengthening the banks.

There were four swing bridges to negotiate on the first stretch. The first was opened for us and we passed through without incident. The next gave us quite a scare because we did not realise that it would swing, although we could see that it was very low, and we passed under it. As we did we realised that we had very little clearance, and in fact the top of the Dan buoy scraped the bridge, and our crosstrees which were still attached to the mast on top of the cabin cleared only by a matter of inches. We set about removing the Dan buoy and the crosstrees thinking that this was a possible height for canal bridges. It was only on reading the guidebook later that we realised our mistake. No wonder the bystanders looked interested!

The Dan buoy is a floating marker with a little red flag attached that you throw into the water if someone falls overboard, to mark the spot. We found this was very useful lashed to the starboard forward rail, so that whoever was on the helm could judge the position of the starboard bow when we entered the locks.

The English couple on *Maja*, had advised us to buy *Navicartes*[2], or *Guides Vagnon*. These are detailed guidebooks to the French waterways which give a map of each waterway, showing possible hazards, and the bridges, locks, quays, with distances, heights, depths of locks etc. They even tell the reader whether a lock is automatic or manual and list the services available at each tying up point. We didn't manage to obtain any of these until much further on, although we did have a couple of very comprehensive guidebooks to the waterways, which provided excellent information but were insufficiently detailed. We could have obtained *Navicartes* in Britain had we known of their existence, and I would recommend their purchase to all would-be travellers on the French canals.

If we had had a *Navicarte* we would have avoided the next little incident which occurred at Abbéville...

---

[2] Now Fluviacarte

CHAPTER 2 – The Somme

A French Salute

Alittle wiser from our encounter with the low bridge we motored on between fields of ruminating Charolais cattle and scattered hamlets, arriving eventually at a sleepy town where a long, high quay fronted a row of shops and houses. This was probably Abbéville but we could see no sign of the *supermarché*, or the

Chefren without her mast

restaurant boat we had been told was moored at the quay. Moreover our onward passage was blocked by a very low concrete bridge. It was so low that even we couldn't think of trying to get under it, and it didn't swing or lift. Closer inspection showed that it bore a rather faded 'No Entry' sign - two red horizontal stripes. We had clearly gone wrong somewhere. To cover our embarrassment and give us time to take stock, we nonchalantly tied up and brewed a cup of coffee. I volunteered to climb the ladder to the top of the quay where I found a passer by, exercising his dog.

I asked: *"Qu'est que le nom de cette ville?"*

He confirmed that this was Abbéville. Consulting a guidebook again we discovered the following passage, "there is a sound quayside mooring at the northern end of the non-navigable branch of the river"! We must have missed the lock cut that bypasses this part of the town; an easy thing to do as there had been no signs indicating that the canal deviated from the river.

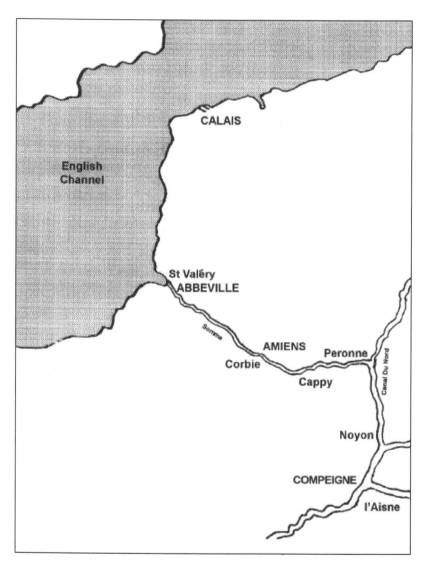

St Valéry to Compiegne

Before we retraced our route I took a walk on the quay, to look for any sign of the lock-cut, and also to gain an impression of the town. The quay was high and wide here, and had been recently covered with fine red gravel, making a pleasant open space, where tubs of flowers added a riot of colour. But one thing ruined the whole aspect and we were to find this again and again in France. The local inhabitants used the quay for their own promenade and for exercising their dogs. No attempt was ever made to clean up the mess which the French call *crottins de chien*. There was the ever-present hazard of transferring the filthy stuff to the boat on the soles of one's shoes. In fact Hobbs had already done this in St. Valéry, much to his disgust. Fortunately he didn't bring it aboard.

Retracing our route we found a tiny lock cut about half a kilometre back overhung with trees and greenery and giving the impression of a tiny tributary, perhaps for private boats. We took a chance and turned in. Sure enough it widened out and there was our first canal lock looking very welcoming in the morning sunlight with a young *éclusier* ready to assist us. He was probably a student, as lock keeping is one of the seasonal occupations offered to them.

It was an easy lock, in the sense that it was not too deep and was manually operated so no enormous learning curve was needed. It was 38.5m long and 5.80m wide, which would have comfortably accommodated three buses, end to end, and two abreast. We were ascending but, as its depth was only 1.80m, it was comparatively easy to attach our lines, especially with Hobbs to help. Once we were secure I jumped ashore and went ahead along the towpath to take some video film.

From my vantage point on the towpath I could see *Chefren* in the lock, and was able to watch the activity of closing the gates and opening the sluices. I was also able to look about me. The quay where we would tie up was visible from here, shaded by slender poplar trees. On this side of the waterway was an overgrown park, accessed once upon a time by an ancient metal gate which had not been used for a very long time. It was rusting and green with age, but constructed in an intricate design of a bygone era. Beyond the trees on the other side of the canal a row of terraced houses drowsed in the sunlight, whilst a black cat stretched itself lazily on a doorstep.

Turning my attention back to the lock I was surprised to see one of the upstream gates still closed and nothing happening. I could see from my vantage point that the young *éclusier* was struggling with the operating mechanism. There was obviously a problem. I then saw John leave *Chefren*, approach the *éclusier* and offer something. Some sign language, and a nod, and John bent down to the mechanism. A few moments later the gate opened and *Chefren* was on her way. The *éclusier* had chained down the handle which operates the gate and it had become jammed. John had cut it free with a pair of bolt-cutters.

We proceeded to the new town quay where we saw the promised restaurant barge. We pulled in and made ourselves fast.

We had been looking forward to Abbéville because we had been told that there was a large *supermarché* and a filling station a short walk away. These *supermarchés* are one of the delights of France. They sell everything from vegetables to video recorders.

We were starting to feel confident using them, having mastered the fact that you weigh your own fruit and vegetables on the scales provided, selecting it for yourself from the produce on display. Above the scales is an electronic board, bearing pictures of the fruits and vegetables available. You press the appropriate picture and a ticket is delivered showing the amount to pay, which you attach to your purchase. This seemed an admirable method and the only difficulty we experienced was in differentiating between, for example, four varieties of tomatoes - plum, grape and beef, as well as the common or garden ones. Since our return home I've found this system in one or two British supermarkets.

We were also impressed by the dual currency cash registers – French francs and Euros. All the goods were marked with prices in the two currencies and the total amount shown on an indicator enabling us to see how much we should pay.

We wandered round the shop for over an hour marvelling at the sheer choice of foods exhibited for sale – patés, meats, pies, cheeses, fresh fish and wines, as well as a huge variety of ready made up dishes, and all at such reasonable prices. We had been told that France was expensive but what we were finding was that whilst eating and drinking out in café-bars and restaurants was sometimes dearer than in Britain, the food in the *supermarchés* was very reasonably priced. We were able to eat well at no more than it would have cost us at home, often less.

Each *supermarché* was an experience of taste and smell. I was mesmerised by the cheese counter, a symphony of yellow from the palest cream to deep rich gold. I wanted to try them all. Often a few cubes of cheese would be laid out on top, or an assistant would be offering a particular variety for tasting. On one occasion an assistant discarded a piece of cheese and cut into a new whole one because the remaining slice was 'not good enough'. Food, to the French, is sacred, and always of the highest quality.

We lacked a table to use in the cockpit for *al fresco* meals and found that the *supermarché* at Abbeville was having a sale of damaged garden furniture. We were able to buy a small wooden table for only 20FF (£2). It needed some glue and a few screws to make it more stable but we had a bargain. When fixed it was also very useful to stand on when steering the boat. I am slightly smaller than John and needed a few extra inches to help me see over the mast, which was lashed to the top of the cabin.

Lunch that day was eaten in the cockpit. It consisted of a selection of French sausages; pork, beef and mutton, and herb, fried with garlic and onions, and eaten with fresh crusty bread and sliced tomato, accompanied by a bottle of Beaujolais. Mmmm...

After lunch and a siesta the two men took our spare fuel can, lashed onto an old 'granny trolley', to the filling station. They were an incongruous sight, in their shorts and T-shirts, as they joined a queue of cars at the checkout. They had no French to explain what they were doing and the cashier gave them a very penetrating look. To make their embarrassment worse John didn't have enough money on him and had to borrow from Hobbs. They then had to repeat this process twice

41

more before our tanks were full.

This cashier was, unsurprisingly, rather cool with them, but generally throughout the trip we found French people extremely courteous. In this instance the cashier may have been upset by what she thought was a lack of courtesy on their part, as they hadn't yet developed the confidence to say, '*Bonjour*' at the start of each transaction.

The French are unfailingly polite. Shop assistants always wished us "*Bonjour*" before serving us. Even complete strangers greeted each other in the street, and it would be unthinkable to them to meet someone they knew and not shake them by the hand, or kiss them on both cheeks. It was lovely to see even the teenagers greeting each other in this way when they met. Never did I buy anything in a shop, or use any services in France when the assistant did not greet me first, and say "*Merci, Au revoir*" when I was leaving. Having been to France before, I was prepared for this and it did oil the wheels of communication. French people tell me that the British have a reputation for being rude and I think this is because we don't greet people in this way, and rarely shake hands. Failing to shake hands is seen as discourtesy.

I believe this practice is to do with the respective sizes of our countries. Britain is a small island with a large population. The only way we cope with the press of people generally is to pretend they don't exist. Take travelling by underground – acknowledging the presence of other people is just not done. Even if they are pressed close against you whilst strap-hanging, you just don't look them in the eye. On the other hand when you go for walk in the open country other walkers will usually pass the time of day and exchange pleasantries in a way that would be unthinkable in the street.

In France there is more space. It is a large country with a smaller population and the proximity of other people is not a threat. The practice of acknowledging each other is still common but it is interesting to see that people in the larger cities are less polite than in the country. In Paris shop assistants can be downright rude.

Hobbs was in charge of the galley that evening and had bought a fresh salmon. I was very much enjoying having someone else in my galley, and he gave me ideas for meals and some cooking tips for use later in the trip. The boat smelled strongly of fresh garlic. Fortunately we all love it.

We also discovered that Hobbs had an unusual talent, a strong sense of remembered taste. Perhaps all good cooks possess this. He could think about a flavour, and then on the back of his tongue, in his imagination, blend other flavours with it until he had the ideal combination for something he was going to cook. This resulted in some memorable meals, in particular a pork casserole flavoured with John's favourite pastis Ricard.

There was only time for a brief walk into Abbéville before leaving next day. The town was reduced to rubble in 1940, but has been rebuilt and there is no longer any evidence of the conflict, apart from a ruined church, left as a reminder. Ruskin said of Abbéville that it was here that Gothic "got up and died". But we didn't have time to discover what he meant.

Taking stock, we noted we had passed through a sea lock and a canal lock, had had our mast removed, replenished our food reserves, and our fuel. We could safely say we were now on our way. But not before Hobbs had another visit to the *supermarché* – I think he just wanted to go and look. John and I found him standing in front of the wet fish counter, swaying from foot to foot, with a far away look in his eye as he contemplated the moist, aromatic wetness of the fresh mussels and the glistening scales of the fish in their bed of crushed ice.

That day we were hoping to reach Amiens and find a suitable mooring place where Hobbs' wife, Lynette, could join us.

We had seen very few other boats on this leg of the journey, a fact for which we were very grateful. We had had problems with our steering leg again at the first lock, where a fierce current was flowing at the point where the lock cut leaves the river. We couldn't immediately enter the lock, and there was nowhere to tie up, so we tried to hold the boat in the centre of the stream. The current was threatening to turn the boat around. Hobbs was on the wheel and was now able to appreciate the problems John had experienced when trying to turn the boat at St. Valéry. She just wasn't answering the helm as she should, and in the end we had to nose into the side.

When we finally entered the lock we discovered what people had meant when they warned us about fierce sluices. It was an ancient lock, with decrepit, weed-covered gates. We also felt the *éclusier* was not as careful as he might have been. When he opened the paddles the water rushed in very fast and *Chefren* was tossed about. We hadn't quite got our act together, so holding the boat steady on the ropes was a struggle. At this stage we were still learning and knew we would have to improve our technique.

Generally in a lock the strength of the sluices depends on the *éclusier* who, if he is very skilled, will open the paddles gradually, allowing the lock to fill more slowly. Others, as in this case, just open the paddles and let the water rush in. A Belgian motorboat joined us at the last minute and there was just room for the two vessels. The skipper of this boat looked apprehensively at our mast where it overhung our stern.

We were glad of the presence of this boat at the next lock. As we approached, we found that the canal divided and it wasn't obvious which way to go. We chose the widest channel but as we turned, a long blast on the Belgian's foghorn warned us this was the wrong one. We turned back, giving him a grateful wave.

This was another ancient lock, this time with sloping sides constructed of stone blocks, rather like a shallow pudding basin. The oldest locks were built in this way because it was the only known method of construction that would prevent the sides from caving in. The big drawback is that the boat is in the middle of the lock

A sloping-sided lock

44

and you can't reach the sides to get a rope onto a bollard. We were unprepared for this, but fortunately a workman who was painting the railings by the lock gate, saw our difficulty and took our line which he secured for us, and then walked across the lock gates to take another so that we were now held at the front by two lines and could hold ourselves, on the engine, against the flow of water.

This was the only sloping sided lock we encountered, although there are lots of them on the Burgundy canal. On reflection the best way to handle them would be to put a crewmember ashore outside the lock ready to take a line. A single-handed skipper might just have to get as far back in the lock as possible and hold the boat on engine only, as the Belgian boat did whilst sharing this lock with us. We came across many boat crews who held their boat on engine only, in straight-sided locks too, but this does contravene the regulations, which ask you to secure your boat at two points.

From now on the locks were straightforward and the *éclusiers* helpful and friendly. We also began to get our act together. Hobbs was well versed in techniques of lifting and handling (another of his many talents), having worked for several years on Swansea docks. When we stopped for lunch we had a discussion about the best way to tie up in the locks. He suggested a rope secured at a central point of both bow and stern. This would not only prepare us for mooring to either port or starboard, but a central purchase for a rope would give greater manoeuvrability to the boat. In fact we discovered that with one rope attached centrally at the stern we could hold the boat easily with this, together with the engine, against the flow of the water from the sluices. The bow line was just extra security that we rarely used when there were only two of us aboard.

Hobbs chose our longest and strongest warps and attached these centrally, fore and aft, and at each attachment point he also secured a shackle so that once the rope had been passed round the bollard it could be threaded through the shackle, giving extra purchase for whoever was holding the line. It is much easier to hold a boat steady when the line has been passed through a shackle or under a cleat.

Hobbs also gave me some lessons in how to throw a loop of rope over a bollard, a lesson that was to prove invaluable on many occasions throughout the trip. The technique is to estimate how much line you'll need to reach the bollard and come back to the boat. Divide this into two coils between your hands, leaving a loop between your hands and putting the rest of the rope in a coil on the deck, having secured the end to the boat. It's important that there are no tangles in the rope you are using. Then throw the rope, aiming to get the loop which is between your hands over the bollard, releasing the coils as you do so and holding onto the free end of the rope in your throwing hand. I got quite cocky about my rope throwing when I later saw crew members scaling lock ladders to attach their lines, whilst I merely stood on the cabin top and lassoed the bollard from there, usually in one easy movement, although I did occasionally miss, if I lost my cool. The other method is to pass a loop over the bollard using a boathook. I resorted to this method when the lock sides were very high.

We now felt more confident and better prepared as we set off again.

The next excitement was at Picquigny where the lady éclusier warned us that there was a péniche coming down. This seemed to be a big event and she gave us some instructions which we couldn't understand. Our acquaintances on Maja had warned us about the péniches, which ply along the canals, usually very slowly, and which always have precedence over pleasure craft. Fortunately the éclusier at the next lock, Ailly-sur-Somme, spoke excellent English and we were able to ask what the implications were. We wondered if perhaps we needed to tie up to the bank and wait until the péniche had passed, but he assured us that we should simply slow down and pull into the side.

The problem is of course that péniches, especially if laden, are constrained by their draft and must use the centre of the canal where it is deeper. Other craft have to give way.

From that point we all kept a keen look out for this monster, our first péniche, and when we finally sighted it on the approach to Amiens it was something of a relief. It was a live-aboard péniche, converted to living accommodation and no longer in use commercially. But it was still a giant, and we cowered into the bank until it was safely past.

All that day we travelled through wooded countryside where anglers patiently waited for a catch. Again we noticed the courtesy of the French people as they waved and gave us *"Bonjour"*. Some of them also gave us the Victory V sign when they saw our English flag, and an incident occurred just outside Amiens, which I treasured throughout the trip.

Two elderly anglers were fishing on the bank, seated on canvas folding stools. When they saw the English flag they stood up with one accord and raised their baseball caps, bowing to us, their faces wreathed in smiles.

The Battle of the Somme, a series of bitter campaigns conducted by the British and French forces against the Germans in the First World War, took a particularly heavy toll in the upper reaches of this river valley (1 million soldiers died), and it saw some of the bloodiest slaughter on the Western Front. There was very fierce fighting during both world wars and these two fishermen had obviously been grateful for the allies' contribution. I still feel emotional even as I write about it. That was a day on which we were very proud to be British.

On reaching the final lock on the outskirts of Amiens, imagine our surprise when we saw the *éclusier* waving frantically and telling us to back off. Our first thought was that there was another boat in the lock, but no, he called to us to ask what was the draft of the boat. When he learned that we drew just under 1 metre he waved us in. The lock had a concrete sill just inside the gates and he was concerned we might come to grief on it. There were in fact two locks on this stretch where we were asked about our draft, so this wouldn't be a good route for any boat which drew more than 1m, although the official depth is 1.80m.

I felt it was about time I learned to negotiate the locks, so I offered to take the helm and steer us out. Unfortunately I was a little enthusiastic, giving the engine too many revs as I turned the wheel to pull away from the lock side. John shouted a warning but it was too late. Chefren veered across the lock and collided with the gates.

Fortunately we had a fender tied at the strategic point, and, apart from puncturing it, I did no damage. But it shook my confidence a little.

We found a low quay on the other side of the lock where an American motorboat was already moored. This was the Quai St. Maurice. A road ran alongside the canal, beside a row of two-storey terraced houses and a café/bar, all shuttered against the sun. On the opposite side of the canal was a sign saying that drinking water was available. That decided it; we hadn't filled up with water since St. Valéry and we didn't know where we would next be able to get some. We hadn't yet learned that water is available at most locks, often with a hose pipe already attached to a tap, and all you have to do is open your tanks and fill up. You generally do this when you're at the same height as the quay and try not to hold up other boats as we did later on with alarming results.

The boats were the object of curiosity from the local children. We were unsure whether they were just interested, or looking us over to see if we had anything worth stealing. It may have been unnecessary but we were extra careful about security as a result.

Alongside the quay we found a boules pitch. As Hobbs had persuaded us to buy a set of boules in Abbéville, we spent the evening learning the rules and enjoying the game with a glass of red wine. We hoped some local people might come out to join us, but no such luck. As the houses were mostly shuttered we assumed that the inhabitants were away for the annual holiday.

We contemplated remaining here until Lynette joined us, and the next day went into the town so that Hobbs could enquire about car parking and obtain a map of the town. Before setting out I tried out my schoolroom French on the *éclusier*, asking him the whereabouts of the *Office du Tourisme*. He denied all knowledge of such a place, which was somewhat puzzling as we had an address on a leaflet given to us by the *éclusier* at Ailly, but without a map of the town we couldn't find the road indicated. Perhaps my French was so bad he didn't know what I was talking about.

As we were deciding which way to go, a voice hailed us from across the road. A smartly dressed lady asked us, in French, if we had need of anything. She had obviously overheard our discussion. I crossed the road and explained as best I could what we were looking for. She then gave us very clear directions, which was another example of the general politeness and helpfulness that we found amongst the French people.

We found the tourist office on a main street of the town, not too far from the splendid Gothic Cathedral of Notre Dame, which has become a symbol of the city. Having obtained the information we needed we were free to have a look at the town. We were delighted to discover that it was market day and Hobbs was again able to indulge his passion for food.

We strolled between rows of open stalls in the cobbled market square, displaying a tempting variety of country produce - shiny red apples, luscious golden melons, crisp green lettuce in abundance and some vegetables rarely seen in England, such as chanterelles, a mushroom which is something of a delicacy. There were live rabbits, guinea pigs and hens for sale – destined for the pot, not the garden hutch. We resisted the temptation (not hard) and settled for a chicken that was already prepared, a crisp white cauliflower and some earthy new potatoes.

Amiens is the capital town of Picardy and, because of the devastation of both World Wars, retains little of its ancient past as a wealthy cloth town, except for the cathedral. This is the largest in the country and the most impressive building to survive in this war-torn corner of France, where war museums, memorials and cemeteries abound. In 1918 Amiens bore the brunt of attacks and was set ablaze in 1940, with 60% of the city destroyed. This is almost impossible to imagine now, as it has been so well restored.

A charming quarter which survived the devastation is the district of St. Leu. This is the little Venice of Amiens (so named by Louis XI, who lived in the town after being kept prisoner in Peronne by Charles the Bald). It is a mediaeval workers' district of mills and small red brick terraced houses, huddled around a network of nine narrow canals. Nowadays it is full of craft and antique shops as well as cafés and restaurants, spilling onto the pavement.

Our wanderings around Amiens took longer than we planned, because we lost our way in St. Leu, and were relieved when we returned to *Chefren* to discover that she was undisturbed. However, we decided we were rather exposed here. As it was not a very picturesque spot at which to welcome Lynette, we decided to move on to the town quay the following day.

Empty péniche

CHAPTER 3 – Canal du Nord

Péniches – in earnest

We were now very low on drinking water and needed to replenish our tanks before leaving Quai St. Maurice. It was no mean feat. The tap across the waterway seemed to be designed for access by small boats only as the canal was very shallow and there was no tying up point. I was the one on the bank taking the lines, so I had to improvise, and secure our warps to some bushes. I was covered in nettle stings before we were through, but between the three of us we managed the operation. However we overlooked the fact that, when her tanks were full *Chefren*, would be lower in the water, and of course she grounded. It took all our efforts to re-float her and at one point we even wondered whether we might have to empty the tanks again. I was grateful we had Hobbs along; an extra pair of strong arms was very useful.

Arriving at Amiens town quay we were faced with a long row of *péniche*s and pleasure boats, nose to stern with not even space to tie up our dinghy. We were very disappointed as the quay was on a pleasant stretch of the river, very close to the town, the cathedral and the St. Leu quarter. On the opposite bank the tables of waterside cafes spilled out into the sunlight, shaded by colourful umbrellas.

We had been warned that the quay was often very noisy with traffic, mainly from light motorbikes which the teenagers in France are allowed to drive from the age of 14, without a licence. The youngsters love to find somewhere such as a long stretch of quay where they can race up and down with much revving of engines and scattering of gravel to impress their friends. We had been prepared to put up with this for a night or two but now had no choice. We decided to move on to a small town on the outskirts, called Corbie.

This stretch of the river was particularly pleasant, we passed along the edge of a district known as the Hortillonages, a green mosaic of market gardens and pleasure gardens, overhung with trees and separated by little canals. This is now a UNESCO world heritage site that can only be accessed by boat. Dotted along the banks we saw little summer houses, each with its own plot of land. Families were grouped around tables in the shade, or fishing on the bank, whilst children played in the sunshine. It looked idyllic, and I contemplated what it might be like to own such a cottage for summer use - perhaps if I ever get tired of sailing...

At a point where a rusting, half-submerged barge spoiled the scenery we came to another lock. The gates were firmly closed and we could see no sign of the *éclusier*. Until this point we had found that the lock gates usually opened as soon as *Chefren* came into view and we began to wonder if there was a problem. The bank was overhung with bushes and there was nowhere to tie up. A three cornered debate began. Should we pull right up to the steps at the lock gates and put someone ashore? Should we tie up to the submerged barge and wait? Should we just continue to stem the flow of the waterway and hope we didn't have to wait too long? Each of us had a different opinion.

Hobbs was at the helm and felt it should therefore be his decision. John, as skipper, disagreed and a contretemps ensued which was perhaps inevitable with two very experienced sailors in the same boat. I just tried to keep the peace.

Finally it was decided to put me, as the only French speaker, ashore to find out if there was a problem. We approached the wooded bank carefully and threw a rope round a bush to hold us temporarily, while I leapt ashore and transferred the line to something more substantial. My heart was in my mouth as I leapt from *Chefren* to the bank, but I made it. More nettles!

There was no sign of an *éclusier*, but in the lock was a Dutch canal boat. The occupants were calmly eating their lunch. Like most Dutch people they spoke some English, and told me that the *éclusier* had gone for lunch and given them permission to eat their lunch in the lock, which would open again at 14h00. It was then just after one.

We had already discovered that the French have a different attitude to work from the British. Not for them the frantic 'open all hours' of the British shops and supermarkets. Even the *éclusier* was taking the break to which she was entitled and everything else must wait.

Back at *Chefren* we decided the only sensible thing to do was to have our own lunch. Sure enough the lock began operations again on the dot of 14h00.

Further along the waterway we had an encounter with another *péniche*. We pulled into the side to allow it to pass, but the banks here were overhung with bushes which trailed over our decks as we did so. The flag of our Dan buoy, lashed to the starboard bow, was whipped off by a low hanging branch, and frustratedly we watched it disappear in the distance. This flag had been very useful as a marker when negotiating locks and bridges and we needed a replacement. I rummaged through the flag locker and found a multi-coloured fish windsock which we had bought to fly from the crosstrees in Cornwall and keep the seagulls off. We attached this to the upright of the Dan buoy and it became our mascot, and a talking point throughout the trip. We called it Roger.

At Corbie we found the quay just after the lock, but instead of the peaceful mooring we had been hoping for we found it was in the shadow of the local silo, and it was harvest time! From the moment we arrived until the small hours of the following morning a steady procession of tractors, pulling trailers loaded with grain, were driven at breakneck speed down the little road alongside the quay. It seemed that every member of the family, old, young, male and female, had been pressed into service. The grain they were delivering consisted of little round, hard pellets, and we never did discover what it was – animal feed, we think. With hindsight we might have preferred the motorbikes at Amiens to the constant roar of the tractors at Corbie.

However, we had little choice. By this time we had arranged for Lynette to join us here. Despite the tractors, it was a pleasant little town, again largely re-built since the war, with a chateau and some attractive buildings. Opposite the quay was a small riverside park where families picnicked and lovers lingered in the cool of the evening.

Our attention was caught by a red, British, telephone box by the lock, and we found more of these in other parts of France. It made us feel quite at home.

Lynette arrived the following day. I was full of admiration for her, having driven such a long distance from her home in south Wales to the ferry at Dover, and thence through France to Corbie, this last section being on the 'wrong' side of the road. She tackled the trip in the same way she tackled most things in life, with courage and determination. I was glad to have her on board.

Lynette left her car in Corbie and would return for it later in the trip. An unexpected encounter with the local chief of police in the tourist office gave her the information she needed. He reckoned it could be parked for about a week in comparative safety, and she found an on-street parking place outside the police station.

Another Dutch boat was moored behind us here. The occupants told us that when they arrived, a couple of days earlier, their entry into the lock had disturbed a body wedged behind the lock gates. It was that of an elderly lady who had become depressed and taken her own life. The young *éclusier* was very shaken. He said that it was the seventh to have been pulled out since his arrival. What is it about Corbie, I wonder, that depresses its inhabitants so?

We were not at all sorry to cast off the following day. We had tried to put up with the tractors with a good grace, they had to earn their living after all, but the noise was very wearing, especially coupled with the debilitating heat.

We motored on enjoying the countryside drenched in brilliant sunlight. The temperatures were climbing into the high twenties and we were starting to think of ways to keep cool. I had made a sun canopy from tent canvas in bright green (the only colour I could get). When we were sailing it would be fixed over the boom. Of course we had no boom now that the mast was down. We draped it over the mast as it lay at head height over the cockpit, and supported it at the sides with the deck brush and the boat hook. It didn't look very elegant, and had to be taken down when we were on the move, but it served a purpose.

The green colour proved to be a poor choice as it absorbed the heat. Next winter I'll make a white one which will reflect the sunlight and help to keep us even cooler.

We dug out our sun hats, and Hobbs fixed chinstraps to them so that we wouldn't lose them overboard in a gust of wind.

Sun tan lotion was a necessity and I had found one before leaving home, which incorporated a mosquito repellent. It was quite effective but sadly it didn't repel horse flies. On leafier parts of the waterway, these pests attacked us quite viciously.

The mosquitoes attacked ferociously in the evenings, particularly when trees overhung the mooring. Our choice was usually between an exposed quayside where the sun beat relentlessly down until quite late in the evening, or a shady spot shared with the mosquitoes. No matter how much repellent we used, and where we put it, there was always some part of our body unprotected and we had bites in the most private parts of our anatomies. John began to feel guilty because he was the only one of us seemingly immune to these attacks, but even this didn't last forever.

On these upper reaches of the Somme we found the locks were automatic, and we also began to encounter more boats, as there is a hire facility at Cappy, our next stop. There were no mooring bollards here and we secured the boat by hammering ronds into the bank, which is an acceptable practice, providing you don't stretch your lines across the towpath to obstruct pedestrians and cyclists.

This part of the river was particularly beautiful, surrounded on all sides by *étangs* (small lakes), which became more numerous as we neared the junction with the Canal du Nord. The countryside eventually became one big *étang*, dotted with small islands, rather like the Norfolk Broads, the river winding its way between them. Every so often a shout would go up as a flash of turquoise traced the path of a kingfisher. The river teemed with wildlife, solitary herons kept sentinel on the bank, waiting for a catch, and a variety of water birds such as moorhens, grebes and coots made haste to get out of our way as we approached.

We passed one part of the canal where a digger was repairing the banks. Back in Britain, when we had bought our licence, we had obtained a list of canal repairs and closures, known as *chomages*. This was one of the spots which had been closed to traffic a week or so earlier. We had had to plan our route with these *chomages* in mind.

The licence included a sticker which we would have to produce in the event of inspection. It had to be displayed prominently on the front of the boat, on the starboard side, visible from the outside. The licence was valid for 30 days travelling, and we had to sign and date one of 30 boxes on the reverse for each day of movement. The licence was never checked, but we did encounter others who had been inspected, and presumably the *éclusiers* were checking for the presence of this card. Ours cost us 1313FF in 1999, the price varying with the size of the boat.

We had now reached the end of the Somme and were about to enter the Canal du Nord, hoping to moor at the town of Péronne by the junction. This town too was almost entirely razed in 1916 and has been completely rebuilt. A sign on the approach to the *port de plaisance* here informed us that 'Port Taxies (sic) must be paid'. We inched our way in but it was very crowded and an ominous thud warned us that *Chefren* had touched the bottom. We decided to try the town quay round the corner but found this fully occupied by *péniches*. Péronne must be popular. We decided to try to find a quieter bank side mooring.

Encounters with *péniches* were now uppermost in our minds. On the Somme we had only met two during the whole trip. On the Canal du Nord we knew it would be different as this is a wide commercial thoroughfare. We had barely reached the junction when we heard the sound of one approaching. Looking north we saw it coming rapidly in our direction. Not wanting to be stuck behind it we put on a burst of speed and swept quickly out into the canal ahead of it.

The Canal du Nord was only completed in 1966, having been constructed to relieve the pressure on the parallel Canal de St. Quentin. It was originally started in 1908 and was three quarters built

56

in 1918 when war was declared. Sadly it suffered destruction during the war and wasn't continued until the economic boom of the 1950s, when the increase in commercial requirements for bulk transport made it necessary to construct another canal. It is 95 km long and cost 210 million FF.

We found this canal very impersonal after the softer, gentler river Somme. It is very straight, with banks reinforced by sloping concrete sides, making it characterless, and also difficult for pleasure boats to tie up.

It was full of litter in places; plastic bags, plastic bottles, tin cans and plastic wine boxes float on the surface. At one point there were so many floating plastic bottles we could scarcely see a metre of clear water between them. We were inclined to blame the fishermen until one night we saw a woman from a *péniche* empty a whole wheelie-bin of rubbish into the canal under cover of darkness.

Rubbish collection could definitely be improved on the French waterways. The number of bins at each mooring point seems to be the responsibility of the local *Department*. The small skips we saw at some of the locks are hardly adequate. At one mooring there might be re-cycling points for glass, plastic, cardboard and paper, whilst at another there wasn't even a bin. It is no wonder rubbish is tipped into the canals, and sewage likewise as there were no facilities for emptying chemical toilets or holding tanks as are found on the Norfolk Broads[3].

The construction of the canal for commercial traffic means that all the locks have the same dimensions, 91.60m by 6.00m, and they can accommodate push-tows made up of two 38.50 tonne barges, as well as the new class of barge loading 700 tonnes, designed specifically to operate on the route between the Seine basin and northern France. These locks are quite impersonal as the *éclusier* sits in a little cabin high above the lock, and operates the gates and sluices by pushing buttons. I missed the friendly *éclusiers* of the Somme, and passing the time of day with them. They would often take our lines which made using the

---

[3] All new mooring points are now required to have pump-out facilities.

lock much easier.

These bigger locks were quicker and more efficient, and we had no problems once we worked out a new method of tying up. They were very deep, probably about 10 - 12 metres, and the bollards are set into the lock wall at intervals, one below the other. The secret is to use short, fixed lines, fore and aft, and to transfer the lines to the bollards as the boat goes down (or up). The bollards are, of course, permanently wet which means that they were also covered in slime, and I generally emerged from a lock with mud on my T-shirt and hands. I eventually learned to keep my better clothes for going ashore.

The other thing I learned, from an encounter with a deck cleat, was to wear shoes which protected my toes. The shoes also needed to have a non-slip sole and to stay firmly on my feet when I jumped from the boat to the towpath or quay. Slip-ons were definitely out.

Before we found somewhere to tie up we negotiated our first tunnel. These have been constructed as an alternative to taking the canal over the summit of a hill via staircase locks. This first one was the *Souterraine de la Panneterie*, and it proved to be quite a tame affair compared with others we were to encounter later. The exit was clearly

We negotiate a tunnel

visible from the entrance. The inside was dank, and the lighting did little to dispel the gloom.

Rubbish reached its nadir in the tunnel, as the unhealthy smell at its heart seemed to indicate that, despite notices to the contrary, it had been used as a rubbish dump. We were glad to reach fresh air again.

Inside the tunnel it was a problem keeping sufficient way on the boat to ensure that we didn't bounce from side to side. Often we found ourselves scraping the sides, and were glad we had taken time to fix four large fenders horizontally, two on each side. This gave us a little taste of what was to come in the larger tunnels and we decided that a couple of wooden planks would be a useful addition to our fendering arrangements.

It was getting late in the day and we hadn't found anywhere to tie up. The locks were about to close so we were able to choose a mooring just outside the lock at Epénancourt.

Lynette and I went up to the lock to watch it in operation and were fortunate in getting a close view of a *péniche* as it negotiated the lock. The evening was warm, and snow-white lace curtains fluttered in the breeze, revealing a row of glass ornaments on the windowsill, and potted plants beyond. *Péniche* owners generally take great pride in their boats. These are, after all, their homes and their family travel with them. I was fascinated to see a rotary clothes drier on the foredeck with a basket of pegs close by. On other *péniches* we had seen plastic paddling pools on the cargo deck, and the family dog roaming the deck to keep strangers at bay when moored.

The flowers always delighted me. Most *péniches* carried window boxes crowded with geraniums and lobelia, and on one a wooden dinghy on the foredeck was turned into a flower garden. Tubs of herbs were usually close at hand, and many *péniches* carried the family car as well.

The women on board were often surprising too. Not for them the casual shorts or slacks of the *plaisanciers*. They were usually turned out immaculately in twin-sets and smart skirts, and their hair was beautifully styled. Some of them would not have looked out of place at a meeting of the local Townswomen's Guild. I felt very shabby in comparison. How did they manage not to get covered in mud when negotiating the locks?

Epénancourt was a large village with one church, one school and one auberge, and we were surprised to find the main street empty. Not a soul was to be seen. At the Auberge d'Etang, where we ate that evening we were the only customers in the restaurant. We had the personal attention of Chantal, a buxom Frenchwoman who was delighted that we spoke a little of her language. She urged us to take our time, and left dishes on a side table for us to help ourselves. The meal was *table d'hôte*, and we had pâté, followed by chicken, with ratatouille and pasta. Cheese and biscuits and plum tart completed the meal. All was accompanied by a bottle of very acceptable Muscadet.

The auberge was also the village shop as well as the bar, and when we left we were able to buy some groceries for the next day, under the amused eyes of two customers at the bar.

We planned to tie up next at Noyon, a large town, where we would be able to do some serious shopping and sightseeing. But again we wished we had obtained a *Navicarte*. Although we knew there was a town quay here we somehow managed to miss it. It must have been the quay by another silo where a *péniche* was loading grain, and which we thought was private.

It might also have helped to have known that the posts we had seen along the edge of the canal, marked PK16 or PK64 for example, were kilometre markers. Had we not been so slow to recognise this we would have been able to pinpoint the quay with greater accuracy.

We found a mooring close by a lock but John was unable to relax here as *péniches* had to come very close to *Chefren* as they lined up for their approach to the lock. At times it seemed they were merely inches away. The revving of their engines was quite terrifying at close quarters. At one point we timed them and discovered there was a *péniche* every five minutes.

We had anticipated problems with *péniches*, as we had been told they didn't like pleasure boats. But we didn't have any, and I think that was because they make a distinction between pleasure boaters who hire boats for a couple of weeks in the summer and who often disregard the rules of the waterway, perhaps because of ignorance, and boats which are privately owned, particularly those with their masts down who are obviously on their way to the sea. They recognise that we are aware of the regulations and observe them, and that we are used to boat handling. We understand about *péniches* being 'constrained by their draft' and respect this.

Many of the tales of rude *péniche* skippers have come from people who have used the Canal du Midi, where *éclusiers* are also reported to be surly, and fishermen bad tempered. The Canal du Midi probably has a higher concentration of pleasure boats. Need I say more?

John was keen to move on quickly but we did want to see Noyon, so we took it in turns to stay with the boat, and used our folding bikes for a trip into the town.

Noyon was founded in the 6th century by St. Médar, Charlemagne was crowned here in 768, and Calvin was born here. It is well worth a visit to see the fascinating ancient buildings and the 12th and 13th century Notre Dame cathedral. The guidebooks call it a 'forgotten city' as most tourists pass it by

Using the road on the right for the first time with our bikes was quite terrifying, as we had to carefully think out each manoeuvre, which in Britain would be automatic. I was so nervous at the first roundabout that I got off and walked, but managed the second more confidently. The roads into town were dual carriageways, lined with shops and houses and there was plenty of room but the traffic seemed to be travelling very fast.

Reaching the town centre we found it was pedestrianised and we were able to walk, admiring the fascinating old buildings which included a wooden library built in the 16th century, and dominated by the ancient cathedral, a remarkable example of Gothic style. But John had his mind on the safety of the boat and couldn't concentrate on old buildings. He had been reluctant to come at all. Dragging an unwilling spouse around even the most beautiful of cities is no fun, so I marked Noyon down for a visit at a later time and agreed to return to the boat.

On our return trip I almost lost John, twice. Once he was nearly mown down by a car when crossing a dual carriageway, forgetting that the traffic flow was from the opposite direction. On the second occasion we cycled off confidently enough, in single file, down a little side street, when the chain came off John's bike. I was blissfully unaware of his plight and the noise of the traffic drowned out his call. When I discovered he wasn't behind me I'd already turned off at a junction. Retracing my path I found a very worried John attempting to find someone who spoke English to direct him to the canal.

In towns we visited later we discovered that many have cycle paths laid out between the main road and the pedestrian way, and we could get around quite well on our bikes, but John was always a reluctant cyclist after this.

We were now both lost and decided to find the nearest route to the canal so that we could cycle back along the towpath. We found the canal but the towpath seemed at first sight to be inaccessible, being much lower than the road and fenced off. As we were trying to find a way down we were approached by a young family with a baby in a buggy. Isn't it always the way, in a strange place, the people you ask for directions are always visitors themselves? They asked John, in French, how to get down to the canal. John managed to understand their request and replied, in English: "I'm sorry I'm a stranger here myself!" They understood well enough and we all shared the joke.

We eventually found a rough footpath descending the steep slope of the canal bank down which we carried our bikes and the young family followed us.

Eventually reaching *Chefren* where John and Lynette had a welcome cup of tea waiting we made our plans to move the next day into the Canal Lateral à l'Oise and a quieter mooring.

CHAPTER 4 – Compiègne

Anacondas and Crocodiles

After a brief over night stop at Pont l'Eveque we set off again the next day, with Hobbs and Lynette cycling along the towpath to enjoy the countryside from a different perspective.

John and I followed with *Chefren*, but hadn't travelled more than 100 yards when black smoke began to belch from the engine compartment, and the engine began to make very strange noises. My heart leapt into my mouth, and my lassoing abilities were needed again as I threw a rope around a nearby kilometre marker to make us fast while we investigated.

Compiègne Town Hall

The problem was a broken fan belt. We had a spare so it was quickly fixed. What a relief. We would now need to look out for another spare, but were confident we could get this in Compiègne, the next big town, where we had been told there was a very good chandlery.

Before Compiègne we stayed overnight at Longueil-Annel, (or Janville – which is the name of the lock), which is a *péniche* rendezvous. On our approach the canal was lined with *péniches*, and in the town itself they were two and three abreast down a little used waterway behind an island. The waterway was loud with the cries and splashes of the children as they jumped from their floating homes into the cool, if somewhat murky, water of the canal.

We had made a brief lunch stop at Thourotte on the way, and enjoyed a glass of beer at a pavement café. The sight of a mouth-

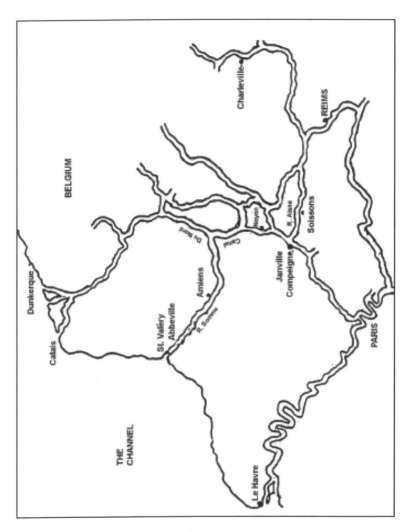

St Valéry to Reims

watering strawberry tart in the *patisserie* tempted me. The French have wonderful cake shops, very artistically laid out, displaying beautifully decorated cakes and tarts. Their cakes and pastries are different from ours, which I think is due to the French flour being lighter than its British equivalent. This is what makes baguettes and crêpes so wonderful and light. French flour is unsuited to making the scones and fruitcake we enjoy at home.

We were to get an opportunity to try some more French delicacies within the next few days as we found a homemade produce market in the town.

But first we had to go through another huge, double lock. This was our first descending, as opposed to ascending, lock and from a distance it looked like a quay, where a *péniche* was tied up. We moored behind it and imagine our surprise when we looked astern and saw lock gates appear from within the recess of the walls and close behind us. We had to quickly loosen our lines ready to pay them out as we went down. As we were doing so the *éclusier* beckoned urgently to us. Greenhorns that we were, we thought he wanted us to move away from the lock gates, and we moved further down, but he still beckoned. We eventually got the message, via sign language, that he wanted to see our ship's papers. This was a port of registration, our first since entering France.

Embarrassed, I hastily gathered up all our documents and made my way to his cabin above the lock. (Being the only French-speaker on board I get these jobs.) The *éclusier* searched through our papers, ignoring the insurance documents, the Certificate of Registry for British Ships, our passports, and our licence to use the French waterways, seizing instead our 'blue book'. This is the defunct Certificate of Registry which has now been replaced by a smart laminated certificate. But it was the 'blue book' he recognised and from which he proceeded to copy details into his ledger. Useless to protest that this was now out of date, I didn't have the language skills.

"Port of entry? Destination? How many persons?" he barked in

French. I supplied the information as best I could and was allowed to return to the boat.

This was the first time we had been asked to produce any documents. Occasionally *éclusiers* had asked the name of the boat but that seemed to be in order to notify the next lock we were on our way.

It was now that relationships on board became strained as John, at the wheel, was having difficulties holding the boat against the force of the sluice. It didn't help that the skipper of the *péniche* was holding his boat on engine. His propeller wash created further turbulence which was throwing us about.

Throughout the trip Hobbs had been suggesting we use the steerable leg to hold the boat against the side of a lock in these conditions, but John had other ideas. At this point I put forward the suggestion again, which produced a strong reaction in John, who was already under stress. "If you know so much about it, you take the wheel!" he barked. I hadn't been doing much helming so far as John and Hobbs had clearly enjoyed being 'in charge' of the boat, and my experience in Amiens had dented my confidence, but I wasn't going to say so.

"All right, I will," I said, grabbing the wheel and putting the engine leg into the position I believed it needed. (Hobbs at this point was 'on duty' on the forward line, and grinning all over his face at our contretemps but saying nothing.)

"You've put it over to starboard!"

"No, I haven't, that's port!"

"It's not, it's starboard!"

At this point Hobbs intervened in my support and a short but heated argument ensued. (It's very easy to confuse the positions of the steering handle, which are up and down instead of from side to side, and this is what John had done. I *had* put it over to port.)

I concentrated on what I was doing, waiting until the lock cleared for our departure. I prepared to relinquish the wheel to John, not resisting a small smile of triumph that my strategy had worked.

"Oh, no you don't! You're at the wheel; you can take us out of here," John insisted.

Trembling visibly and taking my courage in both hands I put the engine into gear and slowly edged us out of the lock. Immediately ahead of us was a *péniche*, approaching the lock, but imagine my horror when I realised he was on our side of the canal! He clearly had to disregard the rules of navigation in order to enter the lock. With my heart in my mouth I carefully manoeuvred past him, only to encounter another, this time on the right side of the canal. I had to take us between the two *péniches*.

I now hoped that John would take the helm, but instead he instructed me to tie up on the bank over on our starboard side. There were lots of boats already occupying this section of the river and only one small space where I could possibly moor, so I approached slowly and cautiously, nosed the bow into the bank and Hobbs jumped off with the forward line. John threw him the stern line and when the stern was close enough he also jumped ashore and helped make us fast. It was a bit like parking a car in a small space, but with a car you can reverse in. This is not so easy with a boat but I thought I had acquitted myself quite well.

When John returned to the boat he was grinning very shame-facedly, and apologised to us all. He had pulled his jacket over his head to shield himself from my wrath and he looked so funny we all burst into laughter. Tension defused, we ordered him to uncork a bottle of wine by way of punishment. Boating is often filled with such moments; things can get very tense in difficult situations. Good teamwork and a sense of humour are needed.

We found ourselves moored outside a hardware shop displaying a bottled gas sign. It was now about seven in the evening but they were still open and we needed some gas. It was run by a very helpful lady who called her husband from his workshop to discuss our needs. We wanted a bottle of propane gas to fit the gas installation which John had installed prior to leaving England, following advice in a leaflet issued to boat owners travelling abroad. He had installed what he believed to be continental fittings but no gas bottle in the shop would fit our attachments, and they had no adapters. From what was said we got the impression that gas fittings in France had all changed in response to recent regulations. They were very apologetic but unable to help.

Before we left I admired Madame's very unusual brown canary in a cage in the shop. I had always thought canaries were yellow.

Later that evening we noticed a barbecue taking place in a garden opposite; a crowd of young people were having a great time and getting very merry, but alcohol appeared to fuel their patriotism as, in the small hours, we were woken by the strains of the *Marseillaise* being played on a trumpet. I'm sure it was for our benefit but we all took it in good part. "It's all part of life's rich pattern," we said.

The following morning, Sunday, we had a pleasant stroll down the main street where a market was in progress. We bought a variety of locally grown vegetables, fresh eggs and several delicacies which aren't generally available, such as locally made liqueurs and jams. We tried a flan made from a local cheese known as Maroilles. It seemed rather similar in texture to the Reblochon of Savoie, very soft and ideal for cooking. Re-heated and served with salad the flan made an excellent lunch. I tried this cheese later in the trip to make cauliflower cheese. It worked quite well but I still prefer the harder cooking cheeses for this dish.

Everywhere in Longueil-Annel there were tubs of flowers such as geraniums and petunias, festooning lampposts, adorning front gardens, overhanging the canal and in the streets in novel arrangements, such as the shape of a barge. The French don't go in for gardens in the same way we do. Possibly the lighter rainfall makes it difficult. But they do love to grow flowers and will use all manner of containers to display them, usually in a most artistic and colourful way.

We were sad to leave this place, but the bigger cities were now calling and we headed for Compiègne, Soissons and Reims.

The first of these, Compiègne, was 6 kilometres away and to reach it we left the canal and briefly entered the river Oise, where a huge Colgate conglomerate dominates the countryside. When resuming our journey we would retrace our route and turn at this factory into the river Aisne.

We'd been told that Compiègne was a 'must' and as there is a town quay with free moorings that seemed like a good idea. There is also a yacht club where there are visitors' berths, but the entrance is rather difficult to find and the sign says 'complet' (full). What this really means is that there are no more berths to rent, but there is usually room for visitors, and the president of the yacht club is the head of the local police.

We gave the yacht club a miss and headed for the town quay where several Dutch boats were already moored, but there was room for us to squeeze in. This proved an ideal location. Although the quay itself was high and we needed the boat's ladder to get ashore, at water level there was a concrete walkway, which was just what we needed to do some emergency repairs to our gunwale. The epoxy which Hobbs had used to glue the pieces together back in England had melted in the extreme heat and the gunwale was coming apart, much to his disgust. He had taken great pride in fitting it, and had done a painstaking job. He felt betrayed by the failure of the epoxy and was keen to repair the gunwale before he and Lynette went home.

The heat had also melted the glue I had used to attach foam-backed headlining to the inside of the hull, and it was beginning to detach itself and droop down over Lynette's berth. I was really upset about this as I had spent hours re-lining the insides of the hull and had been proud of how it looked.

Before fixing the gunwale Hobbs and Lynette went off to discover times of trains back to Corbie to collect their car. While they were away John and I had a wander round the town. Compiègne itself was once a residence of kings and queens, and the magnificent royal chateau is only a short walk from the quay, surrounded by open parkland. The *Hotel de Ville* in the centre of the town was also an impressive sight. At the top of the central spire there is the oldest bell in France, which is struck by three figures in pantaloons known as *Picantins* painted in blue and gold. We joined the other fascinated tourists and watched it in operation.

The repairs to the gunwale got underway in the shadow of two large pantechnicons which dominated the quay. On the side of each, in letters 1 metre high was the legend *"Anacondas Vive, Alligators, Crocodiles"*. These creatures were to be on display to the public from 14h00 to 15h30 that day. There was little smell and no noise so we didn't pay much attention, but later all that was to change.

At five minutes to two, not only did they use a public address system to advertise their presence, but they began to play very loud music. Most of it was English pop music which we knew and liked, but at full blast, so close to our boat, in temperatures reaching 28 degrees C, it soon became intolerable. Fortunately the noise ended at 19h30 just before we got to the stage of doing damage to the amplifiers. Poor Lynette, first tractors then trumpets, now this.

The heat was sapping our energy. We did what we could to cool the boat down, but it was becoming obvious that for next year we would have to have at least one more opening hatch. This year we had fitted opening hatches to each of the small cabins, which had made the cabins lighter and airier. The hatches open onto the deck, and on passage the cabins could also be used as lockers for storage of sails and ropes.

Hobbs was sleeping in one of the rear cabins and found the hatch useful for climbing out onto deck in the early morning whilst John and I were still asleep. One morning there was a seagull standing on the deck just beside his hatch. He reached gingerly through and was able to gently place a finger on the bird's back before it gave a terrified squawk and flew away. There is now, somewhere in Compiègne, a seagull that has had a nervous breakdown.

I had made a wind scoop from a remnant of light material, sewing two pieces together down their length, at the centre. I hadn't finished it

70

off, being unsure how to attach it to the boat. It now became imperative that we fix it up to cool the interior. Two metal coat hangers became the stiffening for the top. As we had no mast we rigged a piece of wood rather like a clothes prop on the deck held by one of the safety lines. I sewed loops of cord to each corner and fixed hooks at corresponding corners of the hatch inside the boat, to hold it in place, and lo and behold we had a successful wind scoop. Being right over our bunk it gave us cooler nights.

Hobbs and Lynette now left to collect their car from Corbie and have a day sightseeing in Amiens, whilst John and I went on our bikes in search of the chandlery described by our guidebook as the best in France. We found it eventually on the right bank of the river, hiding behind a diesel station where the *péniches* re-fuelled. It was good, but we were to find better, and they couldn't supply us with a spare fan belt. They directed us to another supplier at the other end of town. Fortunately Compiègne is well endowed with cycle tracks and I felt quite confident in negotiating the traffic as we went in search of this supplier, a fifteen-minute ride away. John, however, was still a little apprehensive after his adventure in Noyon.

It was now reaching lunchtime and the heat was increasing, the movement of the bikes created a little breeze but we looked forward to returning to the boat for a cold shower and a siesta. We really appreciate the continental habit of the siesta and had fallen into this routine ourselves, coming alive again in the evening.

When we reached the supplier it was 12h00 and they were just shutting for the obligatory 2-hour lunch break. Hot, tired and disappointed we returned to the boat, not relishing the prospect of cycling back again. Fortunately Hobbs and Lynette would have their car the next day and we hoped they would give us a lift.

We were moored behind a huge barge which had been converted to a Chinese restaurant and to us its greatest attraction was its air-conditioning. We planned to eat there that evening. The crocodiles and anacondas were being packed up to go and we looked forward to a cool, quiet evening. But one job remained to be done – to fill the water tanks, not quite as easy as it sounds.

There was only one water tap on the quay, beside the Chinese restaurant. I visited them to get permission to use it, and in a mixture of Chinese, French and English, was given to understand that it didn't belong to them, that it was for the use of a trip boat moored forward of them. The trip boat was deserted, but, based on the premise that water is free; we felt justified in attempting to use the tap. Using the hose was another matter. This was attached to the tap with a jubilee clip, and wouldn't reach *Chefren*. In addition the tap did not have any visible means by which it could be turned on. It was obvious from its condition that several people had already attempted to obtain water by using pliers and spanners on it.

I now had further reason to be grateful for John's extensive understanding of all things mechanical and his problem-solving abilities. After a few moments grovelling around by the tap, surrounded by empty boxes and rubbish thrown out from the Chinese boat, he discovered that it was turned on by reaching into a small trap-door at its base. He then attached our own, longer hose and filled the water tanks. During this operation the staff from the restaurant peered interestedly from the windows, but made no attempt to either help or interfere.

When we turned up for a meal that evening they treated us with amused indulgence and enquired whether we had been successful.

We were served one of the best Chinese meals I have ever eaten. My own particular choice, Roast Duck Thai-style, was aromatic and spicy without being hot, and cooked to perfection.

At the end of the meal we were given a free liqueur, served in tiny pottery cups, rather like eggcups. In the base of each was a small glass sphere and when liquid was poured over it you could see pictures within – naked figures, the males displaying splendid sexual equipment and the ladies pleasuring themselves. I understand that in the Chinese culture these pictures symbolise good luck, and it was as such that we accepted our liqueur and thanked the staff of the restaurant before returning to our boat.

The following day was Hobbs' and Lynette's last. Having a car at our disposal we again tried to buy the fan belt – it was out of stock. The menfolk got on with the repairs to the gunwale and Lynette and I used the car to stock up with heavier goods, bottled water and diesel.

We decided to spend our last evening driving out of Compiègne for a barbecue and a game of boules. So we packed our picnic bags and a disposable barbecue. While Hobbs prepared a chicken, Lynette and I made up some salads and John packed the drinks.

We drove out into the Forest of Compiègne which is the largest of the great forests circling Paris, covering 15,380 hectares (38,000 acres). There are ponds and streams and the hunting trails of kings lead deep into the forest. The main roads through the forest are overshadowed by oak and beech trees.

Unpacking our gear at the start of one of these hunting trails we spread rugs onto some felled tree trunks, set up our barbecue and spent a pleasant evening perfecting our skills at boules, and enjoying Hobbs' mouth watering chicken.

The inevitable moment arrived the next day and John and I felt rather desolate as we waved Hobbs and Lynette off. It was the first time we had been on our own for nearly four weeks and it felt very strange. The moment had finally come when we had to handle the boat alone. Would we be able? What difficulties would we encounter?

Chefren in canal

I wanted to put off our departure to the following day, but John was keen to set off immediately. I suppose this was the sensible thing to do, otherwise we might still be there now, tied to the quay at Compiègne, worrying about whether we could successfully negotiate the locks and waterways on our own. We cast off, and I took the helm while John pushed us off the quay before climbing aboard. It's always an anxious moment for me when he does that. I have visions of him falling between the quay and the boat, or being left behind. But this became our regular routine and I haven't lost him yet!

CHAPTER 5 – River Aisne

Our Second Big City – Soissons

O nce beyond the industry of Compiègne, the river was pretty and tranquil, being overhung with trees and populated by herons and water birds.

I was looking forward to the highlight of this section - the city of Soissons.

We negotiated four locks without problems, the lock keepers were very friendly and efficient, and by the time we had negotiated the fourth lock, Couloisy, we were feeling more confident and ready for a lunch stop. I always prefer to pull in and have a good lunch, Continental style. Occasionally we had lunch on the move, particularly if we had a long distance to travel, but there seemed no point in hurrying. We had all summer, and I so enjoyed setting out a selection of bread, meat and cheeses, with a salad and wine, on our little cockpit table in the sunshine. Anyway the French baguette does not lend itself to the sandwich in the same way as the British sliced loaf.

We spotted a little pontoon with room for two boats at a place called Attichy. This was one of the pontoons put down by the VNF. They and the local Chambers of Commerce are gradually improving services for pleasure boat users but as yet the facilities at each of these mooring points is patchy. Here at Attichy we found only a drinking fountain, a small rubbish bin and the village information board.

As we approached we saw a smooth green reaching down to the river, dotted with rustic picnic tables. It looked very welcoming. A fair-haired boy and girl of about ten years of age were collecting 'conkers' from beneath a chestnut at the water's edge, their bicycles left carelessly by a small slipway. The only other person in sight was the driver of a motor caravan who came to fill his water carrier at the fountain. The only visible building was a farmhouse at the far side of the green where empty tables and chairs were set out in the shade.

We decided to explore the town where there were several small shops and were able to buy bread and groceries. Exploring the more modern outskirts we found a large campsite and a public swimming pool. Unsurprisingly in the extreme heat the pool was filled to overflowing with laughing, screaming children and their parents. Outside an ice cream van was doing a roaring trade, and we too gave it our custom. Licking our ices we made our way back to the boat and decided to stay the night.

We had tried to buy milk, but finding fresh milk is difficult in France. There are no house-to-house deliveries, and milk in the shops and *supermarchés* is usually 'long life' or even sterilised. Occasionally we found fresh milk but it sells out quickly, and never tastes quite the same as the milk at home. We learned to manage without milk and our consumption of English tea decreased noticeably as we travelled on.

We loved the old buildings of Attichy, huddled round an ancient church, but were surprised at the lack of curiosity of the inhabitants. They were not unfriendly and always polite but no one showed any inclination to chat or do anything other than take our money. It must have been obvious to them that we were foreign tourists. It was not that they were unfriendly, just disinterested. This was the only place in France where we found this. Perhaps they have had a bad experience of the British?

It was another very warm night, and I loved being able to stretch out, under the minimum of covers, beneath an open hatch through which the wind was filtered by our wind-scoop. We left all the hatches open and never felt there was a security problem. Our berth was very comfortable. Whilst at first I had thought that making our bed up each day would be a chore, we quickly developed a routine which took only a moment or two.

Waking in the mornings was a delight. The heat of the previous day had cooled and I learned to get the boat cleaning jobs done during the cool of the early morning.

Setting off the next day we wanted to reach Soissons by nightfall and it was still 24km and three locks away. The journey was likely to take us four to five hours. Leaving Attichy we passed through Vic-sur-Aisne and couldn't help wishing we had travelled a little further the previous day and tied up there. A beautifully kept green, decorated with vibrantly coloured flowers, ran down to the water's edge where there was a small quay. On the green were facilities for boats, including rubbish skips and best attraction of all, a toilet block. Its whole appearance seemed to say, "Please tie up here". Sadly we were now on our way and it was too late.

The lock at Vic was a *Bureau de Registration des Bateaux* where we had to present our papers again, but we were wise to this now and I only ever presented the new laminated certificate.

In the locks here the mushroom shaped bollards had been painted red, and dotted with white spots, like the mushrooms in an Enid Blyton illustration. The locks themselves were a joy to behold. Every form of container and decoration had been pressed into service to display flowers. Huge cartwheels, wheelbarrows, farm implements, tree trunks – all were garlanded with blooms.

We watched the ducks here play 'chicken' with a motorboat. Seven ducks set off across the canal, timing their departure to coincide with the passage of the boat. The result was that they had to take flight half way across to avoid being swept into the bow wave. The same game was played later by a mother and five tiny ducklings, and the ducklings shot out of the way at the last moment, like five tiny brown bullets.

Reaching Soissons, thoughts of all other places receded. The approach to the town was through well-kept parkland with mature trees, flowerbeds, and lawns sweeping down to the river. We found the public quay in the heart of the town, opposite a huge grain silo and not quite so picturesque. A main road runs alongside, making it rather noisy, but it was good to be close to the shops and restaurants. Mooring was free, but a sign told us we could not stay for more than one week. There were no facilities other than rubbish bins[4]; we would have to conserve our water until we could move on. Fortunately several trips to the drinking fountain in Attichy, with buckets and a large water container, had filled our tanks for the moment.

Soissons became the first capital of France after King Clovis defeated the Romans in 486 and still has sufficient interesting old buildings and towers to retain its charm in spite of the fighting and serious damage it sustained, particularly during the First World War.

It is full of war memorials; a very poignant one was a simple plaque to some American soldiers who died on a street corner during the liberation of Soissons at the end of the last war.

We enjoyed several forays into the city, and visited the Abbaye de St. Jean-des-Vignes, which is mainly a silhouette standing on the town's highest point. A few buildings, such as its armoury remain and the stonework is pockmarked with bullet and shell holes.

In the armoury we found, not a collection of old cannons and implements of war, but an exhibition of modern sculpture. The French seem to like to use the setting of historic buildings for displays of this kind. This one was a collection of sculptures made from scrap metal such as the drum of an old washing machine, a colander, and so on, welded

Abbaye de St. Jean-des-Vignes

---

[4] Water and electricity for pleasure boats were installed later.

together and decorated with coloured enamels. They were highly effective and very unusual. My favourite was a child standing on a chair, trying on a dress, her face raised, seeking approval.

Mentioning washing machines, a particular delight to me was the laundrette on the edge of the quay, with a huge 10 kg machine where I was able to wash our sleeping bags and all our laundry.

In the laundrette there were no instructions for use of the machines, or information about how much money was needed, either in French or English, so I was a little confused. The whole process was operated remotely, from a console on the wall into which you put your money, and from which you chose your machine. A Frenchman who was removing his own laundry from the drier was most helpful, and explained the system in impeccable English. He told us he had worked in London for two years.

On our second night we thought we would eat out at a café/bar close to the quay. It had tables laid out on the cobbled street and the advertised *plat du jour* was omelette and *frites*, something I had been looking forward to since we arrived in France.

However, returning from our sightseeing we discovered a rock band in occupation, under a little 'gazebo' erected amongst the tables. This might not have deterred us but for the fact that every single table was already occupied by the youth of the town, intent on listening to the group and drinking their beers and cokes.

Instead I made omelette with salad and French bread on the boat, and later had reason to be thankful that we were inside our snug cabin when we heard the distant crackle of thunder, and forks of lighting lit up the sky to the north. The thunder rolled ominously closer and was followed by rain, which fell in drops the size of pennies. The river was soon a-boil with the force of the raindrops, and the boat tugged impatiently at her mooring lines. The surface of the river turned brown with dead leaves washed from the culverts along the banks. We went to bed with the hatches closed for the first time in the trip.

Surprisingly by morning it had cleared and the townspeople were out again for their promenade along the quay, looking at the boats and exercising their dogs. We never ceased to be surprised by the sight of large, 'macho' Frenchmen, walking along the quay, with a tiny Pomeranian or Poodle trotting at the end of a lead.

The French don't have the obsession with pets that the British do, and their dogs are not so much companions, or faithful friends, as fashion accessories. They were often decked in little ribbons, or sporting coats which matched their owners' outfits.

An indication of the importance which the French people seem to give to their dogs was illustrated during a walk into the town. On one side of the street there was a male hairdresser, on the opposite side a ladies' hairdresser, and alongside this a poodle parlour. All members of the family catered for!

The owners' clothing interested us too, and one man in particular stood out, in more ways than one. He walked along the quay each day clad in a nylon bomber jacket and Lycra cycling shorts, which hugged his generous form so closely that absolutely nothing was left to the imagination.

Before leaving next day, I was dashing to my favourite *boulangerie* next door to the laundrette when I noticed an English flag. It was on a Westerly Centaur, a monohull, where breakfast was just being served in the cockpit. I stopped to say hello, although there wasn't time to have a longer chat. Being the first British yacht we had encountered I would have liked to exchange experiences, but we discovered that they were taking the same route as ourselves and promised to look out for them further down. The name of the boat was *Dolma*.

We now entered the Canal Lateral à l'Aisne, where evidence of the storm was all around us. Trees were down and others had shed their branches into the waterway, making navigation difficult in places. A Belgian boat left the quay at the same time as ourselves and travelled with us for most of the day.

Here we encountered our first radar-controlled locks. This was a learning experience and we had a few problems before we finally got it

80

worked out. This type of lock has a 'magic eye' which detects an approaching boat and prepares the lock. We had mounted our radar reflector on the pulpit in readiness.

A triangle of lights at the entrance gives signals to the boats. Until the approach of a boat the red light is showing. When the radar detects a boat, if the lock is empty an amber light indicates that it is preparing itself, and when it is ready the gates open. The green light then appears together with the amber which means 'approach with caution' and eventually the green light alone gives the all clear.

After the boat has passed into the lock another 'magic eye' detects this and the red light signals to other boats that the lock is occupied. The gates don't close until the boat in the lock has operated a lever to indicate that it is ready. The lock then fills (or empties) and the exit gates open automatically. When the radar detects that a boat has left the lock a bell rings warning that the gates are about to close, and one minute later they do so and the lock is now ready for another vessel from either direction.

We discovered that the locks are set to detect only one boat, assuming that this is a barge or a *péniche*, and the red light comes on after it has passed. If it is a small boat there is room for two or three in the locks, and you need to ignore the red light. When the Belgian boat, which was ahead of us, had entered the lock we saw the red light come on and assumed they had operated the lever. We therefore didn't approach the lock in case we were crushed in the gates, but had lots of nasty things to say about unhelpful boat owners who did not wait for other canal users! The Belgian boat in his turn must have wondered why we didn't share the lock with him and probably had equally nasty things to say about snobbish English people.

Further down the canal we found the Belgians attempting to enter another lock. The magic eye appeared not to have detected their approach and they were reversing up the canal in an attempt to trigger it again. Reluctant to cause further problems we decided the best course of action for us was to tie up to the bank, have our lunch, and wait until everything was clear.

We then watched developments while we had lunch. The Belgians were still circling in the middle of the canal when we heard the sound of an approaching *péniche*. Oh dear, now the Belgian would have to pull in and allow the commercial vessel right of way. The canal was quite narrow at this point and the poor Belgian must have had one or two anxious moments as he pulled out of the way. The name on this *péniche* was *Sebastien*.

But hang on a moment something else was happening! Yes, the lock was opening and there was yet another *péniche* getting ready to come out of the lock. That must have been why the Belgian was having no luck with the magic eye, the lock had already had a signal from the opposite direction!

We were glad we were well out of the way as they sorted themselves out and the two *péniches* inched past each other, whilst the Belgian boat cowered into the bank. In fact *Sebastien* allowed the Belgians to go into the lock first. Further on we ourselves caught up with *Sebastien*. He was fully loaded and making his ponderous way along the narrow and winding waterway. We had to fall in behind, with no hope of overtaking, or so we thought.

Never listen to everything you are told, or rather listen but make your own judgement. We had been informed that *péniches* travel very slowly, and if you get stuck behind one you may as well pack up for the day. This is only true in certain circumstances. A fully loaded *péniche* sometimes travels with the cargo decks almost awash, is very slow and has to keep in the centre of the waterway. But they can make good speed when empty, and often overtook us in the really wide rivers such as the Saône and the Rhône.

Sebastien proved our informants wrong. We had scarcely travelled three kilometres when, after negotiating a bend, the skipper slowed right down, pulled to one side, and indicated to us that we should overtake. We put on a burst of speed and shot past, waving our thanks as we did so.

Péniches themselves are quite characteristic and are different from the barges we were to encounter later, in that they are distinguished by two giant anchors protruding from their bows, like a bone in the teeth of a dog. They have a huge cargo capacity in the main hull and living quarters at the stern.

That night, we were heading for Berry-au-Bac, which translated would be Berry Ferry. Standing at the junction of three canals it was once a floating marshalling yard for commercial traffic and pleasure craft, with a fuel point, shop and restaurant. Nowadays there is little evidence of these except for a wide canal basin lined with *péniches*, and a rusted Esso sign dangling on one hinge, like a mirage in the desert, making empty promises to the weary traveller.

We chose not to pass through the lock into the basin that night as there was mooring on a grassy quay on the downstream side, where a post had been erected holding electrical points and water taps.

"Oh good we can fill up," we thought. Once moored our attempts to obtain water and electricity met with no response. Perhaps we needed to put in a token? I went to enquire of the lock keeper, who was sitting in his little cabin operating the lock via a console. His lock was very pretty, being an extension of the garden of his cottage, crowded with flowers in full bloom. Situated in the centre of the colourful display was a large, coiled hose together with a sign indicating that there was drinking water available.

I asked him about the electricity points. *"Non, non, il ne marche pas,"* he said. A familiar phrase, "It doesn't work." Apparently the points had been recently installed, but were not yet connected.

The old filling station with its rusting equipment led us to assume that there were no longer any facilities there. We completely missed the fact that there was a grocery store, a bread shop and a diesel point a short walk away. There is no doubt that we missed much of value and of interest on this first part of our journey because we didn't have more detailed guides. We probably were not as well prepared as we might have been, lacking specific information about each lock and mooring place which these guides would have given us.

We followed a *péniche* into the lock the next morning, bright and early. At this time of year the locks on this stretch operate from 06h30hrs. to 19h30hrs.

The *éclusier* wanted to know in which direction we were travelling. He would send a signal ahead of us to prepare the next lock, which was immediately round the corner and automatic.

We were now heading for Reims, after which we would approach the summit of navigation, the Mont de Billy tunnel, and then begin to descend. This next bit of the canal was going to be exciting, and probably quite hard work.

All twenty-four locks on this 58km stretch are equipped for automatic operation, with radar detection on some and poles to be manoeuvred on the approaches to the others. These poles are known as *batons*, and are suspended over the canal on a wire. Boats wishing to use the lock have to pass underneath and give them a quarter turn making a connection and sending a signal to the lock ahead.

We were approaching a series of locks which stretched for 12 kilometres and were automated in sequence. Immediately we passed out of the first lock the next one was visible, and we saw its *baton* suspended across the water. With the sun in our eyes we almost missed the first one. But John was able to manoeuvre the boat under it at the last moment, and I leapt nimbly to the foredeck and gave it a quick twist. I was apprehensive in case I hadn't done it correctly, but I was rewarded by a sharp click and the sight of an amber light as the lock prepared for our approach. After a short wait the gates opened and we moved into the lock.

Here, many of the lock keepers cottages were empty and derelict, in sharp contrast to the previous stretch. We had obviously entered another *departement*. Some of the locks were in need of repair with alarm systems out of action. At one lock there was a homemade notice, in French, telling us that in case of difficulty we would have to go to the next lock, 1km away. That would be a lot of help if your boat was stuck in the lock or worse if there was danger to life.

The only event of any note on this rather boring stretch was seeing a tiny motor boat bearing a Danish flag making its way in the opposite direction. It was scarcely more than 2m long, rather like an overgrown canoe, and a bearded chap seated at his tiller gave us a cheery wave as he passed. It was the smallest boat we had seen negotiating the waterways. There must have been just enough room for one berth inside (we presumed he was sleeping on board) but couldn't work out how he would have room for a cooker as well. His toilet arrangements didn't bear thinking about. But we admired his adventurous spirit and would have liked to meet him in a lock or on a mooring so we could have discovered more about his trip. As it was we were 'ships that passed' and we will never know.

At last we were approaching Reims. Our guidebook promised a well-equipped chandlery and fuel station after the last lock before the city, so we were on careful look out. But before sighting the chandlery we saw the unmistakable sign of a Leclerc *supermarché*. Leclerc are one of the biggest in France and it would be unthinkable to miss it. Fortunately there was a commercial quay close by. But the only way into the *supermarché* from the towpath was via a gap in the fence, which had obviously been used many times before. It was impossible to reach the correct entrance because of a very busy dual carriageway and a high bank.

This was not just a *supermarché*, but was a *hypermarché* with lots of smaller shops around the main section, selling everything from clothes and shoes to flowers and stationery. We were able to buy one or two things we needed, including a six-band radio on which we would be able to get the World Service, and some strong French glue for our headlining.

Back at the boat we had travelled less than 1km when we spotted a fuel sign, and the chandlery. Perhaps now we would be able to get our fan belt? No such luck. The chandlery was very run down and only sold fishing tackle. They had diesel, but only red diesel for barges. Unlike England, it is illegal for pleasure boats to burn the commercial red diesel and they have to use the white variety. It is more expensive

because it carries a higher rate of tax. Disappointed we moved on into
the city.

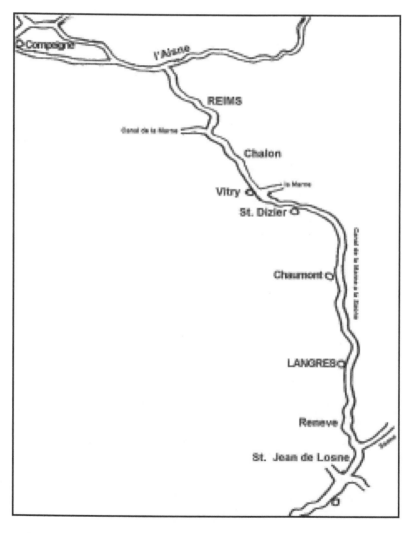

Reims to St Jean de Losne

CHAPTER 6 – Reims, City of Champagne and Coronations

The Total Eclipse

We were looking forward to spending the next few days in Reims and being able to view the total eclipse of the sun which would take place that year, as Reims was on the direct line. We were very excited that we had been able to do this, but we should not have been surprised to find that the port de plaisance was full. Of course lots of other people had the same idea.

Reims Cathedral

The city of Reims had been founded on the banks of the river and the marina had been constructed in the old port area where the river widened out. A long quay upriver of the marina was occupied by a dozen or so *péniches*, towering above us, but we were able to nudge into a tiny space where the water was too shallow for them.

The quay had been attractively laid out, newly gravelled and planted with rose arbours and a pitch. Rowing eights sped silently by on the river. It would have been idyllic but for the fact that on each bank of the river busy dual carriageways roared to each other across the water like hungry lions, making ordinary conversation difficult when outdoors. We were glad to be staying only a couple of nights.

On the other hand we were only a short walk from the heart of the city and all its facilities, including the famous cathedral – you can't have everything.

Many of the *péniches* that towered above us exemplified 'gracious living' as far as boat dwelling was concerned. These were not commercial barges, far from it. These boat owners were much more affluent and the *péniches* were probably holiday homes for their owners who could be seen on deck, basking in deck chairs and sipping the champagne for which the city is famous. Some had their own section of quay fenced off, and one had two fierce looking, and sounding, Alsatians to keep out the riff raff.

The sunshine which had been with us until Soissons now deserted us completely. Grey clouds threatened overhead and occasional showers attempted to dampen the spirits of the tourists. We pinned our hopes on having a fine day to-morrow and decided to spend the morning on some much-needed boat cleaning and maintenance. John set about checking batteries, oil and diesel levels, whilst I, with the use of several buckets of river water, proceeded to scrub the cockpit.

Throughout the morning there was a procession of tourists along the quay and we found ourselves the object of much interest. We nodded and smiled while carrying on with our tasks but paused in our labours when a family with two young boys who were greatly interested in *le bateau*, stopped to say 'good-morning'. They were an English family who were professional paragliders and had moved to the Haute Alpes region of France to be at the centre of the international paragliding community. The two boys, Andrew and George, were being educated in French, whilst speaking English at home. We invited them aboard for an English cup of tea. Andrew and George were greatly interested in our floating home.

As our guests were leaving, *Dolma*, the boat we had seen in Soissons, came by looking vainly for somewhere to moor. We invited them to tie alongside *Chefren*, which they were happy to do and were to do so many more times during our journey. We travelled in company with Steve and Maureen of *Dolma* for much of the remainder of our trip and they became firm friends.

The partnership of a shallow-draft catamaran, and a deeper draft monohull turned out to be ideal and we developed a good working arrangement. Whenever we reached a possible mooring place, if it seemed shallow, *Chefren* would go in first to test the depth. However, if the problem was one of limited space and manoeuvring might be difficult, the narrower boat, *Dolma*, would make the first assessment.

Steve and Maureen are from Surrey and in their late fifties. Steve had taken early retirement from his job as a telephone engineer, but Maureen would be returning to her part-time work with a well-known furniture retailer in the winter. Steve was of average height, with a wiry build and very proud of a full head of hair he had allowed to grow to below collar length, matched by a full flowing beard reaching to his chest. He looked like a lean and benevolent garden gnome and described himself as an ancient hippie. We loved his quirky sense of humour and his practicality. He and John got on very well, spending a lot of time together discussing various technical arrangements aboard the boats and lending each other tools.

Maureen in contrast was petite, with curly hair and long legs. She always looked as though she had just stepped out of a band box, putting me to shame with her range of smart tops and shorts, with skirts and heeled shoes for going ashore. Whilst I had brought some good clothes with me they had mostly remained in the lockers and I had lived in more practical T-shirt and shorts. I began to think I'd better dig out some smarter clothes.

The eclipse was scheduled to take place the following day, and John and I were planning a quiet contemplation, viewing it from the deck of the boat, away from the crowds and the possible intrusion of the street lights which would come on automatically, triggered by the darkness. It seemed a good idea to spend that afternoon having a look at the city and we threaded our way through a motley, good-tempered crowd which thronged the pavements and spilled onto the roads whilst traffic attempted to make its way through.

Walking up the main street, lined with department stores, we felt we could be in any European city – there was even a Marks and Spencer. Most of the historic buildings here were flattened in the world wars, but further into the city we saw buildings of regal magnitude towering above us. By the time we reached the cathedral square we were beginning to sense the history and character of the city.

As well as champagne, Reims is famous as the place where the coronations of the kings of France took place. The most famous of these was Charles III, crowned here by Joan of Arc, whose proud statue flanks the cathedral square and from where the inevitable *petit train* was picking up passengers for a tour of the city.

A network of scaffolding occupied the square, and on this were television cameras and a huge screen, where the crowds would be able to watch the progress of the eclipse. There was a platform above our heads where various personalities, including the cathedral and civic dignitaries, would stand and make speeches. Posters advertising singers and musical events were pasted to the fat, circular columns which are to be found in most continental towns, specifically for the display of advertisements. The atmosphere was palpable, with a feeling of anticipation everywhere.

The usual Job's comforters had warned of pickpockets and increased criminal activity whilst the police were busy dealing with the crowds, particularly at the moment of totality. We saw and heard no sign of this, and everyone, even the shopkeepers who were rushed off their feet, was good tempered.

The atmosphere continued the following day, despite grey skies and threatening rain. It rather looked as though we would all be disappointed.

As planned, we remained on *Chefren* whilst Maureen and Steve went into the city to enjoy the spectacle and the total experience. Several small groups of people had the same idea as ourselves and there were parties on the surrounding boats, and small groups gathered on the quayside with their special glasses to view the eclipse. A party atmosphere developed and some of the groups started a singsong. John and I sat on the boat, filming progress. The eclipse was due at 11h25 and by 11h00 we'd been rewarded by several breaks in the cloud. It was looking more hopeful. Maybe we'd be lucky and one of these breaks would coincide with the eclipse itself.

We waited with anticipation and as the time approached we had another gap in the clouds revealing the perfect circle of a pale sun, with the beginning of the eclipse like a small bite nibbled from it. Over the next half hour several similar gaps enabled us to chart progress,. The cloud cover proved to be an advantage, allowing us to view it with the naked eye. As the shadow moved across, the sun appeared like a sickle moon, whilst a lonely star was visible close by.

Then the moment arrived, and once it began it seemed to move exceedingly quickly. Daylight faded, and we moved from twilight to full darkness. The earth became eerily silent as though for a moment it had stopped turning. Even the birds stopped singing, although traffic continued to roar along the dual carriageways - there were obviously some people oblivious to this momentous event.

Situated, as we were, on the river, the streetlights did not spoil the atmosphere or the view of the eclipse. As if by magic, when the world was as dark as midnight, we were rewarded with a gap in the cloud and a great cheer arose from the people on the quay. Glasses were raised and there was more singing.

Steve and Maureen returned later to tell us what it had been like in the city. The square had been a sea of people, all jostling for a view of the screen, but continuing cheerful and well behaved. At the moment of totality, as the light left the sky and an awed silence fell upon the crowd, the powerful voice of Jessye Norman, the American singer, pierced the darkness and the strains of 'He's Got The Whole World in His Hands' floated above the crowd. The atmosphere was electric.

This day is probably something we will all remember for the rest of our lives and the re-telling will bore our grandchildren in our old age.

The following day it was 'business as usual'. We had decided to investigate the *Poste Restante* system in case we needed to receive mail from home. We had asked my daughter to send us a trial postcard to be collected here and that afternoon set off to find the post office and retrieve it.

We began at a tiny post office on the quay, where a very helpful assistant produced a map on which she marked the location of the *Bureau de Grande Poste* where we would need to go. The place she marked was just off the town hall square which we found without difficulty, but try as we might we couldn't find the post office. We walked round the square and the town hall three times before deciding to ask for further directions. Several people were very helpful, giving us detailed instructions but each seemed to send us in a different direction, and we still couldn't find the post office. I began to wonder if it was a situation like those I had read about, where people are so keen to help strangers and hate to be unhelpful that they give the wrong directions rather than admit that they don't know.

It enabled us to enjoy the varied architecture of the city. There were black and white timbered buildings mixed with the more modern ones, and one building I particularly enjoyed had a huge circular portal, probably for the passage of carriages in days gone by. At first floor level the walls were decorated with colourful murals depicting the process of wine making.

After walking round the town hall yet again - and it was a huge building, we finally obtained directions from a helpful official inside. It was then that we discovered that the lady in the sub post office had marked the wrong square. The *Bureau de Grande Poste* was in the next square by the market and the Mars Gate, and not the Town Hall Square.

The Mars Gate is one of the grandest triumphal arches of the Roman world, soaring high above us in one corner of the square which was now occupied by the remains of the modern market. It was awe-inspiring to contemplate how long ago the gate had been built. I expect this site had been a market place even then.

We found the post office and, sure enough, our postcard was ready for collection, and no charge. We now know the system works and were to use it to advantage later in the trip.

We had enjoyed seeing a little more of Reims on this sortie and laughed about it afterwards, but it was several days before I realised why I had had such difficulties following directions. It eventually dawned on me that our difficulties had been compounded because I hadn't appreciated the difference between *'tout droit'* (right on) and *'tournez droite'* (turn right). Apart from that I was becoming much more confident in my use of the language and my brain was translating much more quickly.

A tight fit in the lock.

Reims is the heart of the champagne producing area and it was here in the 17th century that Dom Perignon, the blind cellar master, turned tragedy into triumph after a particularly severe winter. Frozen bottles of wine, fermented twice, produced the delicious champagne we drink today. But we decided against a visit to the champagne caves, a must for most tourists, as we wanted to press on.

We were worrying about the locks on this next stretch because they are only 5 metres wide, 0.5 of a metre wider than *Chefren*. Poring over the map we realised that the nine locks before Reims had themselves been only 5m wide, and we had had no trouble. *Chefren* was always a neat fit in these locks, and on entering a cross wind, a violent sluice or contrary current were liable to threaten a collision with the lock gate. That happened only once and, generally speaking, it was like fitting a foot into a shoe. John became very expert and I took a position on the forward bow by our colourful fish marker to warn him of sluices and give hand signals to guide him.

Once the nose of *Chefren* was through the lock gates I would duck under the horizontal mast to reach the starboard side, take the forward line and leap to the cabin top, and from there do my Wyatt Earp act with the line and bollard. Passing the end of the line to John, I would then jump down into the cockpit and lasso another bollard with the stern line. All this had to be done in the space of time it took *Chefren* to station herself in the lock. If the reverse lock on the outdrive leg was playing up it had to be done quickly. I became very expert and also proud of my agility.

We had our first encounter with the peripatetic lock keeper system on this stretch. The *éclusier* (in this instance female) travelled with us through about six locks, put-putting along the towpath on a moped and waving as she passed. We were to encounter this system quite a lot during the central section of the trip.

We had developed a routine of keeping cans of beer and soft drinks in the fridge to hand out to the *éclusiers* as thanks for their assistance. It was hard, sweaty work in the sort of weather conditions we had been experiencing and most of them were very glad. Occasionally an *éclusier* would have a young assistant and these children were delighted to receive a can of soft drink, and sometimes to practise a little English.

Steve and Maureen had travelled this route before and we were glad of their company, especially as there would be two long tunnels to negotiate later.

The scenery on the outskirts of Reims was industrial again, with piles of glass for re-cycling much in evidence, but eventually green fields emerged, rising gently to distant hills where a windmill dominated the skyline. The countryside was reminiscent of England, but bathed in the famous light much beloved by artists.

We halted briefly at the *port de plaisance* at Sillery, a charming little marina in a basin, with a newly built *capitainerie* and where a few motorboats were tied up. We wanted to take on diesel and water, but it was lunchtime and there was no one in sight from whom we could get permission. We filled up with water but there were no diesel pumps which meant that on the next stretch (the sections between locks is called a *bief*) it was necessary to tie up close to a small town, Beaumont-sur-Vesle, and collect cans of diesel by bicycle.

It was now just 8 km to the Souterraine de Mont de Billy, to give it its full title. This tunnel is just over 2km long and controlled by lights. We tied up at the entrance where a low quay and rings were provided, and traffic lights controlled entry. We hoped we wouldn't have too long to wait. There were no other boats waiting, and soon a green light invited us to set off into the murky depths.

This was longer than the Panneterie, and several bats swooped overhead, enhancing the gloomy atmosphere, and we were glad of the friendly presence of Dolma ahead. But it was very narrow and *Chefren* scraped the sides several times. The tunnel was also cleaner than the Panneterie and we seemed to be through in no time, emerging into heavily wooded countryside. On the towpath in the tunnel there is a railway line as, before they had installed ventilation, it was necessary for boats to form a convoy and be towed through by a small railway engine. We saw one of these engines, literally put out to grass, on the side of the lock at Condé sur Marne our next halt.

The *port de plaisance* at Condé has a couple of pontoons for pleasure craft in a wide turning basin, and a flower bedecked picnic and barbecue area is laid out for boat users and motor caravans. There is water, rubbish disposal and an information board, all for a small charge. It is built onto the town quay by the inevitable silo, but harvest was over and our stay was quiet, and blessed by the return of the sunshine.

Living on board a boat one of the ever present hazards is of losing things overboard, a lesson which had been brought home to me at Noyon when I had consigned some cutlery to the watery depths when scraping plates overboard. We carry a very powerful magnet which has been useful in recovering the occasional tool, but on this occasion we had no success in the murky water of the canal. It helps if the water is clear enough for you to view what you are probing for.

Here at Condé I knocked overboard the cassette for our hose reel. It floated for a moment then disappeared below the surface before I could grab the boat hook. We poked around for ages but had no luck. From that point on my punishment was to be the one to coil up the hose, a job which had been made much easier by winding it onto the plastic cassette with a little handle.

Condé is a small town at the junction of three waterways, the Aisne, the Marne and the Canal Lateral á la Marne. The Marne is an alternative route for boats from Paris and we began to encounter many more of them making the journey to the Mediterranean, as well as the ubiquitous hire boats.

Walking into the small town the next day we found it deserted. It was well into August by now and presumably most people were taking their annual holiday. In the centre of the town, bathed in sunshine, we found an ancient wooden market place, with a vaulted roof supported by sturdy posts and decorated with colourful flowers. We learned that this market hall had been contrasted of Chestnut wood to deter the spiders who are discouraged by the smell of Chestnut. The *boulangerie* was open and we bought the most delicious bread we had eaten on the whole trip, and the memory of it is with me still, freshly baked, warm and crusty.

An ancient church dominated the town, and whilst the whole area had been badly damaged in the two wars, the ancient Roman belfry had escaped. Everything had been reconstructed in its former style, and the newly-built streets had been named after heroes of the Resistance. I liked this. It seemed a particularly fitting way to ensure that their sacrifice would never be forgotten.

By afternoon we were on our way again, turning into the Canal Lateral à la Marne. We planned to stop that night at Chalons-en-Champagne (or Chalons-sur-Marne). Eventually arriving at a lock just outside the town the *éclusier* provided us with a map, a guidebook and a book of regulations for use of the canal, a sure sign that we were now in an area used by pleasure craft.

Free moorings for boats are provided at a long quay, bordering a small park and overhung with chestnut trees. Several boats, mainly Dutch, and a huge *péniche*, Medea, were already in occupation. The quay is sheltered from the main waterway by an island known as the Isle des Rats for obvious reasons, although we didn't see any sign of these creatures.

Chalons is a busy town at the heart of the Champagne region, and proved well worth visiting. The 13th century cathedral with a 17th century façade, and the Notre Dame en Vaux church, are interesting architecturally, but it was the little side streets and squares which interested us most. Here we found traditional timber framed houses in ancient alleyways, some having external staircases. I tried to imagine what life must have been like when they were first built. Did the occupants descend in their nightclothes, I wondered?

Despite the ravages of the wars there were plenty of old buildings remaining. The centre of the town is bisected by two small rivers, the Mau and Nau, bordered by parkland and greenery, giving it a pleasant open aspect.

We were delighted to find a small *supermarché* in the covered market from where we could replenish our stores; and were also able to enjoy the delights of the outdoor produce market, returning to the boat weighed down with fresh fruit and vegetables, including two huge, sweet smelling, golden melons, after chilling in our fridge these made a delicious appetiser.

During our stay the skipper of *Medea* decided to turn his boat round. He pulled alongside and called to us to warn us that he was going to come very close. *Dolma*, as usual, was rafted alongside *Chefren* and protruding into the waterway. Steve offered to move but the skipper would have none of it. He told us that he had just had bow thrusters fitted, and we think he wanted to show off. He proceeded to turn his craft round in its own length (which must have been at least 30 m), his boat touching the bottom for most of the time, churning up mud and rotting 'conkers'. We watched with our hearts in our mouths. At one point I'm sure Steve could have climbed aboard.

We breathed a sigh of relief when he was finally on his way and reversing up the river. We saw him two days later taking on grain from the inevitable silo.

Maureen and Steve were leaving next day, but John and I were staying an extra night. On the evening before their departure we challenged them to a game of boules. There was no pitch as such, but the broad gravelled walk alongside seemed suitable, and so it was, except for the *crottins de chien*, which we had to avoid. The novices, much to our chagrin, beat the crew of *Chefren* but we hoped there would be other opportunities to regain our honour when we met again.

They left on another wet day, when rain dripped down our necks and misted our glasses. We were not sorry to be staying put, as there is nowhere to shelter from the rain in the cockpit of *Chefren*. We had had a spray hood fitted in Cornwall to keep the helmsman dry, but in the canals it restricted visibility and we had folded it down.

After waving *Dolma* on her way, John and I put the kettle on, got out our paperbacks, settling down for a cosy read in our snug, dry cabin. We were almost coming to the end of our small stock of books, and were looking forward to meeting up with other English-speaking boat owners so that we could swap them. The rain was disappointing but we counted our blessings after chatting to the owners of *Koala* which was moored across the river. They had travelled up from the South of France in an attempt to find good weather. They said it had rained every day.

There was an ex-hire boat moored astern of us. This was the type of boat generally nicknamed 'bumper boats' because the wide side-decks, protected by a thick (usually black) rubbing strake made them look rather like the dodgem cars you see on fairgrounds. This was named *Le Canard* (the duck), and was flying a French flag. I'm not in the habit of peering into people's boats but the interior of *Le Canard* was easily viewed from outside. It seemed very well appointed with the steering position in the saloon at the front of the boat, and what made me particularly envious was that there wasn't a thing out of place! I had waged a losing battle to keep the interior of *Chefren* tidy, and those who have experience of yachts will sympathise with me regarding the difficulties of finding a home for everything within the constraints of a sailing boat, even one with two hulls. I tried to insist on a 'place for everything and everything in its place', but this didn't always work, and we usually had lots of equipment out on the berth cushions and the table.

The following morning the occupants of *Le Canard* spoke to us as we were taking our rubbish ashore. They were not French, but American, and introduced themselves as Erica and Dick from

Maryland. They chose to use the French flag in order to blend into the scenery. They were a very sprightly couple, older than us, and we learned later that they come over to Europe every summer to travel the French waterways. Dick is a retired businessman and Erica does some travel and cookery writing.

They were travelling to Vitry le Francois, our next destination, and asked if they could travel with us. We were delighted as two boats in a lock is a lot easier than just one, particularly if the locks are automatic as these next ones would be.

By the end of our journey that day I'm not sure our American friends agreed with that last statement.

House with outside staircase, found in many old villages.

CHAPTER 7 – Vitry Le Francois

Locks, Weeds and Visitors

The weather was still dull and overcast as we set off, *Chefren* in the lead. Rain threatened but didn't fall, and I envied Dick sitting inside at the wheel of his 'bumper boat'. It looked rather like driving a car.

This canal is a straight stretch in the Marne valley, running alongside the river for much of its length, with green fields and woods on each side. It is a narrow canal with just room for two boats to pass in comfort.

Automatic lock mechanism

As usual we had several joggers running alongside us at various times. I think they were glad to have something against which to pace themselves, and usually outstripped us as we chugged along at a leisurely pace. Even if we had wanted to hurry, speeding is not allowed as the wash from the boats undermines the banks (6 kph is the usual speed and in some places signs limit speed further).

A lone Frenchman in a motorboat joined us at the second lock, St Germain, and asked if we would allow him to overtake once we were out of the lock. He forged ahead but when we reached the next lock (automatic) he was waiting for us, and this is when we got into difficulties.

When more than one boat uses a lock it is important that they all leave together as the automatic gate-closing mechanism is triggered immediately one boat has interrupted the radar beam. This was

101

something we had forgotten and in this lock we didn't follow the French boat out immediately as we were busy looking for a water hose. When it became obvious there wasn't one, we followed him out of the lock, but as we did so the alarm bell began to ring, warning that the gates were about to close. We put on a burst of speed and cleared the gates without problem but, horrors, *Le Canard* which was behind us, was still in the lock.

We watched in dismay as the gates began to close and saw Erica instinctively rush to pull the emergency lever. This was not the right thing to do as the gates now stopped, half closed and half open with *Le Canard* trapped in the lock, and nothing they could do until help arrived.

With hindsight the sensible thing would have been to allow the gates to close and to go through another operation of the lock.

They now had to wait for someone to come to override the automatic mechanism and let them out. That person had to come from elsewhere, by road. The whole operation delayed us about an hour. We felt responsible for their plight and tied up to the canal bank to wait for them.

The banks here were well maintained. They had recently been mown, which was evidenced by the matted rafts of grass and tangled brambles, a metre or more across, which had been allowed to fall into the canal. In time it would rot down and presumably not be a problem, but today, when it was freshly cut, it was difficult to avoid and coiled itself round our propeller, causing us to lose speed and steerage rather alarmingly. Reluctantly we pulled into the side to attempt to free it. *Le Canard* had to do the same.

First of all we tried reversing the propeller but it was too firmly attached. John had to clear it manually with his head and shoulders through a hatch in our rear platform, his legs waving in the air. At least he didn't have to go over the side to do it, as he might have done if we had been a monohull. He freed not only a mat of weed and brambles but a polythene bag as well. Landlubbers who allow these bags to get into the water do not realise what a hazard they are to boats.

The propeller fouled three times in the next half kilometre and we were getting very frustrated. On the third occasion we were near a small grassy quay and decided to tie up and have lunch. Here on the quay were little mounds of brambles and grass – other boats had done the same as us. Dick and Erica tied up too and went off into the village to find a restaurant which had been recommended, but returned a short while later having found it closed. The French realise there is more to life than commerce and close down their shops, banks and sometimes their restaurants on even the most obscure Saints' days. To the British on holiday in France it can seem as though this happens every week. We learned later that this day, August 15th, was the Feast of the Assumption, one of the biggest festivals in France, perhaps having the same importance as Easter in Britain.

Whilst the banks had been well maintained, the locks were not in a very good state of repair, and many lock-keepers' cottages were empty, the locks having been automated. The inhabited cottages usually had a patch of land where rows of vegetables thrust through the brown earth, and dogs barked ferociously at us. On one of these smallholdings there was a wooden barn which had been patched so many times with different coloured timbers that there were more patches than the original barn.

Occasionally we passed a village close to the canal, its cottages huddled around an ancient church, surrounded by outlying farms, and sometimes a small silo. At one of these, Couvrot, there was a small crowd of spectators at the bridge. They were French holidaymakers and one of them was filming our approach. I did my best to look suitably nautical, adjusting my baseball cap to a rakish angle. When we had passed they climbed into their car and drove to the next lock to watch us lock through, take more photographs and engage us in conversation. Dick and Erica chatted fluently to them. I exchanged a few words but my attention was needed elsewhere as this was a lock where, as we ascended, I had to re-attach the ropes to bollards which were set in the wall and I was trying to do this expertly. The lock was very ancient and particularly slimy and my hands and my clothes were soon covered with dark-green slime.

The holidaymakers were amazed and intrigued to discover we were going all the way to the sea, and that Dick and Erica were going to Strasbourg, in the opposite direction.

Vitry-le-François, our next stop, is an important junction. *Le Canard* would leave the Marne and head towards the Rhine, whilst we would travel south to the Saône. But both boats were planning to stay a couple of nights in the *port de plaisance*.

Approaching Vitry we found the canal had been diverted around the town, crossing an aqueduct to the east. All that remains of the old canal is a long *cul-de-sac* used as a permanent mooring for *péniches*, and on the other side of the town a smaller *cul-de-sac* which now houses a tiny *port de plaisance*.

Approaching the port we spotted a figure on the bank who seemed to be doing an Indian war dance. As we got closer we saw it was Steve, showing us where to turn for the port, and they had even chosen a berth for us. Unfortunately the port was so full there wasn't room for *Chefren* to make the turn into the berth and we had to moor up in the entrance cut. There would now be no room for the wider boats to get out of the port and we had to apologize and let them know we would move as soon as they wanted to leave.

The *Capitaine* lived in a typically French house with wooden shutters overlooking the port, and every day he opened a little hut from where he handed out leaflets describing the attractions of the town. On the outside of the hut was a street map which proved very useful later.

I tried out a little French on him, and he was soon chatting away to me as if I understood every word. In fact I only understood every other word, but it was from him I learned that today was the Feast of the Assumption.

There was water and electricity here, and rubbish skips which were emptied every day, a fact that greatly impressed us.

A sign told us we should not use the drinking water for washing down our boats and that we could stay free of charge for no longer than a week.

It was in the port here that we first met Dave and Beverley, owners of *Monica*, whose change of boat name was the talk of the waterways. Her original name was *Carefree Days*, which seemed to them to be pleasant enough. It wasn't until they went to Spain that they noticed people were laughing; well not exactly laughing, more a sort of sniggering behind their hands. Eventually someone explained that in Spain the supermarkets sell the brand of feminine hygiene products known as *Carefree*. They came home and changed the name – wouldn't you?

We also briefly glimpsed a small motorboat named *Orca*, flying a British flag and navigated by a single-handed sailor, whom we were to meet up with at Langres.

The following morning, before we were up, there was a loud knocking on our hull and we had to quickly don sweaters and jeans over our nightclothes and reverse *Chefren* into the canal to allow some of the boats, including *Dolma*, to leave. The space created allowed us to move onto a pontoon.

We planned to remain here for two or three nights, as we were about to have visitors. My daughter Carolyn and her husband John were driving over to France for a short camping holiday and would stay with us for a couple of nights. When they phoned to make the arrangements we thought this would be the ideal opportunity to get a fan belt from England. I rang our usual supplier to order it and he too was out of stock – there must have been a rush on them at home too. Not to worry, we now knew that the *Poste Restante* system worked well and asked him to post one to us. We had to give him the name of a town we would be passing through. I looked at the map and my eye alighted on Chalon-sur-Saône, further down, and this was the place I suggested. What I didn't realise was that Chalon was still two weeks travelling distance away, it looked so close on the map. It took me a long time to absorb the fact that we were only progressing at walking pace.

I was glad to be able to let Carolyn and John see our 'watery home'.

I'm sure Carolyn must have wondered what her mother was doing adventuring across France in a small boat, and be curious to know what it was like. She was also glad I was spending my retirement in such a fun way.

I spent the day shopping and cleaning the boat. There were two *supermarchés* within cycling distance, and the main shopping centre was only a short walk from the port. Vitry had all the shops and facilities one would expect of a bustling little town with a population of about 20,000. It had originally been built as a stronghold by King François I, hence the name. The streets all radiate from a central square in typical 16th century style, originally designed by an Italian architect, Geronimo Marini. Sadly Vitry was another casualty of the war, being destroyed in 1940 and 1944, when only the 17th century church escaped devastation. But the town has been rebuilt to the original plan.

Vitry is the capital of Perthois, and enjoys an unusual situation on a fertile plain between the right bank of the Marne and the forest of Trois Fontaines, at the foot of the cliffs of the Champagne district.

It has become an important little town for canal business because of its situation at the junction of three waterways forming the north-south (Lille-Marseille) and east-west (Paris-Strasbourg) routes, and a rail link. There are several ships' chandlers close to the canal, and two *bricolages* – the equivalent of our DIY supermarkets, as well as offices of the VNF. This proved a good place to buy, amongst other things, new fittings for our bottled gas.

Some time after our return to England, we saw Vitry-le-François featured in an old Burt Lancaster film about the last war, where he was attempting to sabotage a train carrying French art treasures into Germany. I think the film was called 'The Train'. I don't know whether it was shot on location but when we saw the name 'Vitry-le-François' on the station sign, it gave us quite a *frisson* to see somewhere we had visited featuring in a Hollywood film. It also solved a little mystery which had puzzled us for some time, and that was the function of clusters of what appeared to be loudspeakers on the top of high buildings in every town. They had them in the film too, and they

106

were air raid warnings. Their presence in modern France demonstrates the vulnerability its citizens still feel. They don't have the security of water surrounding them as we do.

We were hoping for good weather so that we could motor a little way down the canal with our visitors, demonstrating the workings of a lock and our life on board, but it was being very fickle. During the afternoon, when they were due to arrive, the sunshine disappeared completely and black clouds threatened overhead. Soon it began to rain, increasing in volume until it was coming straight down like stair rods. As twilight descended bright flashes of lightning rent the air followed by the rumble of approaching thunder.

We had given them instructions to the *port de plaisance,* describing its location in the *cul de sac* off the canal. Eventually the phone rang and Carolyn's voice said: "Well, we're here, but where are you?"

They had found the other *cul de sac* where the *péniches* were moored, and now needed instructions to find us. We gave them the details whilst standing outside the *Capitaine's* hut peering at his map, mobile phone in one hand, torch in the other, whilst John held an umbrella over us both. It was a very wet welcome for them.

Instead of the planned boat trip we went out the next day by car in search of the Lac der-Chantecoq. Our first stop was on an artificial embankment where bird watchers trained their binoculars on a vast expanse of water, reflecting the grey of the sky, and where choppy waves disturbed the surface. What we were looking at was the largest artificial lake in France, once a vast forest of oak (*der* comes from the Celtic for oak) and created in 1974 to regulate the flow of the rivers Seine and Marne. In the process of its creation three villages had been submerged, which seems a huge sacrifice.

Across the water we could see a modern building housing a water-sports centre and close by a picnic area which we set off to investigate.

We had a delicious picnic which included a range of cheeses and pâtés, a bottle of red wine and crusty bread collected from the *boulangerie* that morning. Afterwards we braved the wind for a short walk along the edge of the lake but were soon glad to retreat to the warmth of the car.

Our drive home was a meander through rustic villages of traditional timber-framed houses and churches. Only the addition of the metalled road and occasional level crossing reminded us that we were in the 20th century.

That evening we planned to introduce young John to more French food, and walked as far as the main street to a restaurant we had seen the previous day. We found the town almost deserted and the majority of the restaurants closed (August again!), including our intended eatery. Spotting another one down a side street we were about to cross the road to reach it when we were accosted by a middle-aged couple. *"Non, non. Il n'est pas bon,"* they said, shaking their heads and wagging their fingers in emphasis. They didn't think much of our restaurant choice, and directed us instead to the Market Square where we had the choice of two beautifully appointed restaurants and an opportunity to admire this attractive cobbled square, which still accommodates a weekly market.

So far on this trip we hadn't found the simple provincial cooking we would have preferred, not even at the auberge in Epénancourt.. I remembered with mouth-watering clarity a simple meal I had once had in a *Relais Routier* in Normandy. We were served with a huge pot of vegetable soup from which we helped ourselves, accompanied by a basket of French bread. This was followed by fish or meat (I can still remember that I had liver), cooked to perfection and accompanied by *frites* as only the French can cook them. All served without fuss by an ample French matron. I was hoping to repeat the experience.

Before John and Carolyn left the next day we had another wander round the town where we bought mouth-watering French pastries for our lunch, changed some money and, best of all, found a bookshop selling *Navicartes* - what joy. I was only able to get the one for this area, the Champagne-Ardenne, but now I knew they were obtainable from bookshops I vowed to haunt every decent-sized one in every town we came to until I had found the others we would need to complete the trip. This one covered our route as far as the River Saône.

We had an opportunity to lighten the boat of some of our unnecessary gear and send it home with Carolyn and John. We now loaded their boot with things we had brought from home which 'might be useful' plus an empty gas bottle we couldn't refill in France; and some heavy clothing which would have been necessary in Britain but not in France. I also sent my pressure cooker home, as I hadn't used it, finding a set of double frying pans just as effective and more versatile. I had two sets of these pans, and when I had first found them on the boat I was intrigued. Why would anyone want four frying pans? It wasn't until we were invited aboard another catamaran during our trip down to Cornwall that I discovered they were designed to fit together, in pairs. Barbara, the skipper's wife, was busy making a curry in her set of pans – and the penny dropped. They were known as double-skillets.

Chefren now floated an inch higher, I'd swear. It's too easy to accumulate things when you are living aboard, and the boat becomes heavier and more cluttered. In a small space the less gear you stow the easier it is to find what you want.

After waving our visitors off, John and I spent the evening studying our newly-acquired *Navicarte* and exclaiming over the information it contained which would have made the earlier part of our trip so much easier. As well as canal information, alongside the linear map was a tri-lingual description of the places we would pass through and the principal sights to see. We chuckled over the fractured English, we were told we would be assisted during our journey in certain areas 'for the manoeuvring of a series of locks' and warned that if we were not punctual we would 'disturb this assistance service for boats'.

It was now that we realised how long it would take us to reach Chalon-sur-Saône - two weeks, travelling every day, which meant we would have to get a move on if we were to get our fan belt. We understood that unclaimed post was often returned after two weeks. The *Navicarte* came in very useful to ensure we found moorings on the route and to speed us on our way.

CHAPTER 8 – Canal de La Marne á La Saône

The Spanish Cow

Having said good-bye to our visitors we left the following morning to begin our journey over the highest part of our route which provides a third of the main waterway across central France between Paris and Lyon. Within 225 km we would negotiate 114 locks. We would also pass through two tunnels and cross the Langres plateau before dropping down into the Vingeanne valley and the River Saône. The frequency of the locks would make it hard work, but we were looking forward to it. We had also got our system for using the locks worked out and were no longer apprehensive, time enough to worry about the bigger locks on the Saône and the Rhône when we got there.

The first day's travel brought home to us the snail-like progress we were making, taking all day to reach the tiny port de plaisance at St. Dizier, a stone's throw from the Lac der-Chantecoq where we had picnicked with Carolyn and John two days previously. On that occasion the journey had taken about an hour by car.

The port at St. Dizier is in what looked like a disused water sports area, where tiers of concrete steps for seating overlooked a small basin where water jousting would take place. There were toilets and water, and a small chandlery for the needs of the boating fraternity.

Several small boats were moored here, mostly laid up now and the only one with crew aboard was a Danish yacht we had seen in Vitry. I hate to think what they thought of our mooring procedure. It was that wretched reverse lock again. We were all prepared for a textbook mooring and I was poised on the foredeck with a rope. John had carefully negotiated us through the narrow entrance and chosen his spot alongside the concrete quay. We were approaching cautiously at a shallow angle when I heard an anguished cry from John. "It won't go into reverse! Get a rope on quickly!"

This meant getting off the boat as quickly as I could, but I had to wait for the gap between the boat and the quay to be narrow enough for me to jump, but not close enough for us to ram the quay. I perched myself outside the guardrail, leapt at the optimum moment and threw all my weight against Chefren as she continued towards the quay and was only partially successful. John was able to turn her away, but she still scraped the concrete and made a large scratch in the hull. Oh dear, what the *péniches* had failed to do, we had done for ourselves.

A visit to the chandlery proved fruitful. We were given permission to root around the yard for planks of wood from which to make rough 'fenders' in preparation for the tunnel which, after our experience in the Mont de Billy, we thought might be a good idea. They would also prevent mishaps like the one we had just had. We found a stout plank about 4m long, which John sawed into two lengths, drilling a hole at each end. We attached these outside the fenders at water level, to 'bridge the gaps' and give us a firmer protection in locks and tunnels where we might find ourselves scraping along the sides.

St. Dizier is the place where the word 'braggard' originated. It is a contraction of *brave gars*, the name given to the inhabitants by Francois I when advised of their resistance to the invading army of Charles V – 2,500 citizens against 100,000 soldiers.

Our éclusier the next day was another student, with shoulder length hair and brightly coloured shorts. At the second of two locks close by a road, where a modern sculpture of coloured vertical rods decorated the roundabout like a multi coloured porcupine, he was joined by two 'officials', a man and a woman. The woman, a large officious lady in a black dress and black dyed hair, wrote down our name in her notebook, and her companion plied us with leaflets about the town and surrounding countryside. We couldn't help thinking these would have been better given to us on our approach to the town yesterday, not on our way out today. They had a request for us. This was an automatic lock and in careful French they explained they needed us to operate the baton suspended over the canal as we left. A motorboat coming in the opposite direction had missed it, and the lock, which would close after us, needed re-opening for them. We were happy to oblige, and left with smiles and waves to continue our journey.

One of our guide books had told us that this part of the trip was boring, and that the usual practice was to stock up in Vitry and make all haste for the Saône and civilisation again, contradicting Stevenson when he said: "To travel hopefully is a better thing than to arrive".

We couldn't disagree more. It's true there are no large towns, and this did cause some problems with regard to provisioning, but for us this was part of the challenge of the trip. We were self-sufficient and didn't need large towns. We were passing through some of the most rural parts of France, and travelled very hopefully indeed, anticipating glimpses into local life.

Our first of these was the sight of charcoal burning in the traditional method. A huge pile of wood, covered with earth, and as big as a small bungalow, was burning slowly from the inside and emitting lazy curls of smoke from various parts of the circumference.

Close by on the canal bank, an elderly man in very shabby clothes sat beneath a makeshift shelter of tarpaulins ready to operate the swing bridge, a rusty can for financial contributions at his feet. I think he was a local entrepreneur.

There were two small towns on our route, Chaumont and Langres, both of which looked worth a visit. My greatest regret was that, because of our need to get to Chalons within two weeks, we were unable to spare the time to explore. But the canal itself provided us with entertainment enough, and the locks kept us busy. We had peripatetic *éclusiers* again, travelling alongside us on their mopeds, through several locks, which provided us with an opportunity for a little French conversation.

At Fontaines I disturbed one poor fellow at his lunch. As we approached we saw the lock gates were open, so we entered and tied up. Usually the *éclusier* would be there to greet us, and we would help him, or her, to close one set of gates and open the second after filling the lock. We waited five minutes or so and saw no sign of anyone, so I

113

scaled the lock-side ladder to investigate. The door of the cottage stood open and when I looked in I could see the family eating their lunch. I approached gingerly, and tapped on the door, feeling as though I was desecrating a church. In my best French I enquired when the lock would be open. Having had the experience earlier of being made to wait whilst the *éclusier* had lunch I expected to have to wait now. But there was consternation and a rapid conversation between father and son at the table. The son, a young man in his twenties with long hair, jumped up and followed me outside. He peered over the side of the lock, seeming surprised to see a boat there, and I felt guilty we had sneaked up on him. We would have been happy to wait and eat our own lunch, but he wouldn't hear of it.

We set about operating the lock together, and when the time came for *Chefren* to pass out of the lock, it was father on his moped who accompanied us through the next few locks and operated the two or three swing bridges in our path.

Father was a cheerful fellow, with a ruddy face, topped by a battered baseball cap - battered because he rammed his safety helmet on top of it whenever he hopped onto his moped to ride to the next lock.

At Autigny-le-Grand we had a new *éclusier*, an earnest little man in his late thirties, small and slightly bandy legged, with a pointed chin and protruding ears. We, somewhat unkindly, named him the monkey-man but he was very helpful and pleasant. I chatted to him a little about the traffic, or lack of it, on this stretch, and began to form the impression that he was possibly not very bright, and resolved to be particularly appreciative of his services as I imagined he would get a lot of teasing and leg-pulling.

As the afternoon wore on we began to think about tying up for the night and there was no *port de plaisance* on this stretch. We asked our *éclusier* if he knew of a suitable mooring place. He was delighted to have the opportunity of displaying his knowledge and, nodding his head vigorously, he burst into a torrent of French. I could just about make out that after his last lock with us he would go off along the towpath

114

and show us where we could moor. Unfortunately we didn't know which was his last lock and kept a wary eye out from that point. At Donjeux we came under a bridge and saw our *éclusier* dancing from foot to foot on the towpath, waving both arms and indicating the ground at his feet. Approaching with caution we saw a small quay which otherwise we might have missed, as the mooring rings were invisible in the grass. It was occupied by fishermen whom our *éclusier* harangued self-importantly until they made space for us. He helped us tie up and when we were secure I gave him, in addition to a cold beer, a small tip, which he took with a word of thanks, and put into a small black purse he produced from his pocket. He then reinforced the monkey impression by hunkering down beside the boat to drink his beer, keeping up a non-stop chat, and including the fishermen in shouted jokes to which they responded with hearty laughs. I had some difficulty understanding his accent but smiled politely whenever it seemed necessary.

He then did something I haven't seen since my grandmother died over 40 years ago. He reached into his pocket, took out a small circular aluminium tin, and shook a couple of pinches of a light brown powder onto his wrist. He then sniffed this up each nostril. I didn't think anyone took snuff these days, or that it was still being manufactured.

He then moved into the 20th century, took out his mobile phone and, after asking us what time we would like to set off tomorrow, made the necessary arrangements.

Later in the trip we met another English couple who had had this same *éclusier*, on the day of the eclipse. Someone must have told him about the possibility of going blind by staring at the sun, as when the eclipse began, he crouched down and pulled the hood of his anorak up over his head, shielding his eyes with it and one hand, even though he was operating the lock gates at the time.

That evening we were the only customers in a superb restaurant overlooking a tributary of the river, where an ancient quay hinted at times past. I amused myself by imagining Resistance workers hiding in the culverts as German patrols passed by.

Again it was a gourmet meal, even though the restaurant advertised itself as an auberge. I was becoming tired of rich sauces and unusual ingredients. My starter on this evening was a fan of melon with Parma ham served raw as the French like it, but it was not to my taste.

The canal and the river run side by side here, and on our way back we could see unmistakable signs of war damage to the bridges. All the bridge spans along this stretch were more recently built and of a different style of architecture to the piers. The Marne is where heavy fighting took place in both wars. We had a tough time in Britain, but I don't think we can conceive what it was like for the people of France, having the fighting literally in their gardens.

Early the next morning we left whilst the dew was still heavy on the grass and a white mist rose from the canal around us, heralding another hot day. As the mist lifted, the surface of the canal was like a mirror, untroubled by breezes as yet, and the ash trees along the bank, were perfectly reflected in its surface. Fields and woods stretched away on each side as we continued to climb towards another summit.

At Rouvroy, the 40th lock on this stretch, the lock keeper's cottage was No.1. Until 1907 the stretch of canal we had just travelled didn't exist. Rouvroy was the start of this section and a new canal was built to connect the Atlantic and Mediterranean sides of the system. Nowadays it is not much used. Less than 300 pleasure boats and 1,000 *péniches* per year travel this way. We had only seen one *péniche* and one pleasure boat since St. Dizier.

The date on the cottage was 1880, and a simple, country family were sitting outside finishing their 'petit dejeuner'. A pretty tortoiseshell cat detached itself from the group and came to survey us from the edge of the lock. The housewife helped the éclusier, and like so many people whom we had met along the way she was much taken with Roger, our fish windsock which had replaced the missing Dan buoy on the forward bow. She laughed, saying: "Poisson, eh?" revealing a mouth full of stained teeth with many gaps.

Since St. Dizier we had been aware of a very characteristic type of lock cottage on this stretch. They are tall and thin with a front door

116

opening onto the lock side, above which is the number and name of the lock on a blue plaque, and above this a single window under the gable end. Usually they are constructed of small stones set in concrete, similar to the flint buildings of East Anglia. Some of the occupants had extended their cottages by building a conservatory onto the front or side of the house. Most of the gardens were beautifully tended and the lock sides a riot of colour. One *éclusier* had adorned the

Lock cottage

lock side with figurines of Snow White and the seven dwarfs; perhaps this is the French equivalent of the garden gnome.

Because of the low volume of traffic on this stretch *Chefren* was something of a novelty. At the locks people would gather to stare and to chat, few of them spoke English. At Villiers, a lady cyclist commented on the width of the boat relative to the size of the lock, so I attempted a little joke in French. *"Oui, comme un pied dans une chaussure"* (like a foot in a shoe), she understood and laughed. I'm feeling quite proud of my prowess in French.

At Froncles, under a lean-to conservatory, a fat Frenchman in singlet and shorts was working on a window frame, laid on the dining table, smoothing down the wood with swift strokes of a hand plane. Two large Alsatian dogs were barking fiercely. "Don't get off that boat into our territory," they seemed to say, but one of them was also wagging his tail. Which end should we believe?

This area of the canal is ideal for walkers. The towpaths are well maintained and ramblers could travel faster than we could as we were held up by the locks.

By 11h00 it was very hot and we had reached Buxieres where a lady in her late fifties, appeared from the lock cottage in a flowing white flannel night-dress, her blonde, shoulder-length hair still tousled from sleep. Her nightdress was ankle length, with sleeves to the wrist, and a high neck, so you might say she was respectably dressed and she made her way to the lock gate without any embarrassment whatsoever and calmly assisted in the operation of the paddles, all the while engaging the *éclusier* in animated conversation.

Her garden was beautiful, being very English in its style with bushes and trees as well as colourful tubs of flowers and I wanted to photograph it, but was afraid I would embarrass *Madame* in her *deshabille*. So I took the camera and walked forward to assist with the gate, then pointed to the video camera, saying, *"S'il vous plaît?"* and indicated the garden. At this point she did show a little embarrassment at her attire but nodded her head with a smile.

This was the *éclusier's* last lock with us, but he travelled on to Granvaux to hand over to the most un-French *éclusier* I have seen so far, a cheerful fellow in his late thirties, with a round, rosy cheeked face and thinning blonde hair. He wore a red and black striped rugby shirt, black shorts and sturdy boots with thick socks. A pipe was clenched between his teeth.

"Bonjour!" I said.

"Good morning," he replied.

"Oh, you speak English!" I exclaimed.

"Yes, like a Spanish cow," he replied, and the laughter broke the ice between us. He spoke quite good English and we had a long conversation punctuated by the stretches between the locks.

On our way to Granvaux I had noticed that the *Navicarte* mentioned *rives (en beton) inclinées*. I translated this as 'concrete, sloping sides', which gave me some anxiety as I assumed it meant another sloping sided lock. Having made something of a dog's breakfast of the last one I was apprehensive, but I needn't have worried. The reference was to the canal banks outside the lock, which were reinforced with concrete for a couple of kilometres and fitted with chains for boats which might need to moor up, and ladders for access to the towpath.

At Vieville, whilst the lock was filling, our *éclusier* produced a key and let himself into the cottage. This looked like a masculine establishment, all very functional with no flowers, no toys, and no picnic furniture.

Emerging, he went to the fence at the side of the cottage and emitted a piercing whistle. We wondered whom he could possibly be calling, surely not his family; a dog maybe? The question was answered a few moments later when several goats appeared at the fence and put their heads forward for scratching. One pretty little black kid was so keen to be scratched, or perhaps to make sure he didn't miss any food, he nearly climbed over the wire fence.

Our *éclusier* told us that he made cheese with the goats' milk, and that one day he would like to get a farm in Galway. "Why Ireland?" we asked, and he explained that the young people there were deserting the land and farms could be bought or leased very cheaply.

He seemed a very intelligent young man to be doing an unskilled job such as lock keeping and he told us his story.

Originally he was a stonemason, travelling all over France, with his wife, working on churches and historic buildings and living in a motor caravan. This was fine until children came along and they needed a more settled existence so he gave it up. Sadly the marriage didn't last, and he told us: "My wife's lawyer, 'e want everything, even my 'ead."

So he had chosen to work at lock keeping, which he called 'a red-neck job' because it provided free accommodation but low pay. He remained in France in order to see his children, but planned to emigrate when they were grown.

He was a very unusual Frenchman in other ways. When we offered him a cold beer he refused, saying that he never drank alcohol, but would like a cup of tea, "Black with two sugars, please".

Handling the lock gates seemed quite effortless to this young man. He was well muscled and stocky, and whilst he may have been doing a 'red-neck' job he was doing it well, and with care and attention. Later in our trip we compared notes with other *plaisanciers* and several of them remembered the goatherd, as well as our little monkey-man from the previous day.

The goatherd had reprimanded one of the women for climbing the

119

ladder in the lock. "That is too dangerous for you," he had said. "You should let me 'elp you with your ropes"; a very responsible attitude. The ladders are often slippery and in a perilous condition, because many locks are kept full of water when not in use, to keep pressure of water on the lock sides and prevent cave-in.

The Condés tunnel, which was our next event, is so short at 308m it hardly deserves the name of tunnel. It is unique in that it is the only tunnel in the French waterways which allows passage of boats in both directions at once. It is 18 m. wide. No problem there, but there was to be another tunnel soon, Balèsmes. Our goatherd *éclusier* told us that during the last war the church at Balèsmes was bombed and fell into the tunnel. Now, particularly on Sundays in winter, when the air is clear and cold, he said it is possible to hear the church bells ringing.

It was with some sadness that we said 'good-bye' to him. Before leaving us he performed one more service, disappearing into the VNF office at the lock at Chaumont, and reappearing carrying a handful of rubbish disposal bags for our use, and a guidebook for this part of the waterway system. The last we saw of him was as he rode away on his moped, his pipe still firmly clenched between his teeth. I hope he gets his farm and is able to rear his goats in contentment.

CHAPTER 9 – We Reach The Summit

Two More Locks

The *port de plaisance* at Chaumont is quite the finest we had encountered since St. Valéry. Landscaped gardens and a gravelled path edged a quay big enough for six or seven boats, whilst a building at the rear of manicured lawns housed the reception, a sitting area with magazines, toilet block, showers and laundry. In the gardens was a concrete table tennis table, and at the edge of the quay were water and electricity points for each boat. Rubbish collection was at the rear of the toilets. The cost per night was 40FF and for that we had free use of all the facilities. There were lots of boats here and we met up again with Beverley and Dave, of *Monica*.

Chaumont is a historical town in the centre of the Haute Marne region of France and noted for a viaduct 600m long and 52m high, taking the railway from Paris to Basle. It is also famous for its culinary traditions. Grey truffles are cultivated here and still picked in the wild in the traditional manner. *Foie gras* production and snail breeding are also local specialities. I have never tasted a truffle, nor been able to bring myself to eat a snail. But other specialities such as charcuterie meats, poultry and rabbits are more to my taste.. The local cheese is soft and orange coloured with a smooth, edible crust and a strong taste which I enjoyed. John prefers mild cheeses such as St. Aubin and St. Nectaire.

We had been asked by the *éclusier* about our departure time next day. Being Sunday we arranged for 10h00 to give him a lie in. The first lock was just round the corner from the *port de plaisance* and at 09h58 a new *éclusier* was waiting. He was a dark-bearded fellow with a very surly manner, and had difficulty meeting my eye, even though I greeted him, as usual, with a cheery *"Bonjour!"* To date the *éclusiers* had been very friendly and when they pass us on the towpath they toot their horn or wave. This man did neither and I regarded this as a challenge.

At the first lock he made no attempt to take a rope from me, and didn't even tell me that there were no bollards on the side of the lock where I was preparing to tie up. Bollards are often missing in older locks where wear and tear over 120 years has caused them to break off. I had to do a limbo-dance under the mast with my coil of rope and tie up at the other side.

I continued to give him a smile and a greeting at every lock and at about the third one he began to thaw out, smiled and even took my rope. Success!

We were still climbing but once through the Balèsmes tunnel the next day we would start to descend and feel that we were truly on our way to the Mediterranean.

The canal here girdles the shoulder of a hill, and has required quite complex engineering work in its construction There were quays and ramparts made of granite blocks, and on the approach to several locks we found narrow, walled in 'cuts', known as 'goose-feet'. It needed a lot of skill to manoeuvre *Chefren* into this narrow approach, especially as there was usually a sluice just outside, and the force of the water would throw the bows off course.

The lock gardens were pretty, but many of the cottages empty and neglected. At Vesaignes the cottage had become a small-holding and there was an orchard shared by turkeys, geese, hens and ducks, and a battery of hutches housing rabbits and pigeons – obviously some of the local specialities I had learned about. On the towpath close by we discovered fruit trees, bearing plums and apples, and were told that these were for the use of the boats. I wonder if that was to ensure that the families on the *péniches* had fresh fruit in the days before handy shops and *supermarchés*? Most of the lock keepers would have sold honey, vegetables, eggs and even cheese in those days too.

A lift bridge between Verbiesles and Luzy was something of a surprise. Usually the lifting bridges tilt at one side, or split in the middle, counterbalanced with a huge weight, like the famous one painted by Van Gogh at Arles.

This one lifted horizontally like a guillotine and passing underneath it I half expected it to descend and cut the boat in half.

We passed through three more locks which should have been automated, but which were all *'en panne'*. Nettles and weeds growing round the operating mechanisms showed how long they had been out of action. In pantomime the *éclusier*, a cheerful older man, demonstrated that he would push the buttons manually to operate the lock.

At Thivet, two students took over and wanted to know how far we were travelling in order to make the necessary arrangements for lock opening. Our planned stopping point was Moulin Rouge, just north of Langres, and the closest mooring point to the tunnel. We were not sure whether we could make it, as there was still 13km to go, including eight locks and another swing bridge. It was already mid-afternoon and we estimated this would take us six hours.

In this respect having peripatetic *éclusiers* is a disadvantage. We can't always tell them when we will be stopping, and we have little opportunity to change our minds if we spot an attractive mooring. However, the advantages were that we travelled more quickly, the locks were usually open and we could motor straight in. They don't seem to be as worried about wasting water in the French waterways as we are in Britain; except in very dry seasons, and often they pass a boat through the lock even though another one is close behind.

However, with the help of our two students we were greatly relieved to make it all the way to Langres by 19h.30 which is when the locks closed.

In the final lock we caught up with *Orca* again. *Orca* is a tiny motorboat, about 6m (20ft) long, belching smoke from its exhaust. The skipper, a well-built, muscular Englishman, with a tanned complexion and hairy chest, was nonchalantly stepping ashore with his lines, clad only in bright yellow shorts. His tiny boat bobbed and swayed as he transferred his weight from boat to lock ladder. His name is Colin and he was making his way alone through the canals. He lives in Spain, but originally came from Southport, very close to our home on the Wirral. He wandered ashore and collected some yellow plums from one of the trees by the towpath, and we ate them, still warm from the afternoon sun. It reminded me of the Kenneth More and Suzannah Yorke film, 'Greengage Summer', which was set in France.

Colin moored behind us at Moulin Rouge close to the town of Langres which could be seen a few kilometres away, perched high on a rocky promontory, surrounded by ancient walls.

I enjoyed reading the fractured English in the guidebook, which describes the town. "The forLirled *(sic)* town of Langres dominates the Marne valley from its rocky spur, 130 m. high. Gallic city ("Lee Lingons"), Gallo-Roman fonress *(sic)*, whose triumphal area is still embedded in the ramparts, fortiried *(sic)* town and bishoprie *(sic)*, Langres relains *(sic)* many buildings from its glorious past."

It also mentioned "a foresled *(sic)* plateau, the commereial *(sic)* quarter, Renaissanee *(sic)* houses", and I am eager to experience a "Glided *(sic)* Lour *(sic)*", especially if it also happens to be a "bank elosing *(sic)* day."

As we approached the mooring we were delighted to see *Dolma* tied up at the quay with several other boats. On noticing our approach Steve leapt out and took our lines and when we were all secured we introduced Colin.

Whilst I had hoped to persuade John to stay another night in order to explore Langres he was keen to keep on going, especially as we could have the company of *Dolma* through the tunnel. I had to content myself with learning about the town from Steve and Maureen who had already had a wander round. The fortifications, which are a masterpiece of military architecture, date back to the 3rd century and the ramparts stretch for 4 km around the town making a very pleasant walk. There are seven towers and seven gateways and a multitude of small alleys and covered passages. I have added Langres to my list of places to visit when I return to France.

Moored close to us were several large barges, which had been either specially built or converted for living aboard. One called *Vive La Vie* belonged to a French family who spoke good English. We learned that this was their farewell trip, as the boat was proving too expensive and they had put it up for sale. I cast longing eyes at it, as I was so enjoying life on the French canals I could be persuaded to forget about going to Greece and spend my retirement pottering about here. But John is a sailing man and wouldn't entertain the idea.

Another barge here was *Redquest* owned by another English couple, Gwen and Gordon from York. Gordon had built her himself on the lines of an old Barnsley coal barge, when he found he couldn't buy one that he liked. They are a sprightly, white haired couple in their seventies, living permanently on the French canals. They winter on the river Loire at Roanne, where there are lots of other permanent boat dwellers enjoying an International community. We were to get to know Gwen and Gordon better over the next few days, as we all travelled in convoy to the Saône with *Redquest* and *Dolma* taking the first lock, and *Orca* and *Chefren* following behind.

Now we were approaching the Balèsmes tunnel and were 340 metres (1041 feet) above sea level. At the lock, Batailles, a display informed us that we were in the Côte d'Or region, and this was depicted on a map about 2m high made of coloured seeds and grains. The lady *éclusier* said *"toute de suite"* which I translated as "quickly". What she was actually saying was "immediately". At this stage we didn't realise that she had any connection with the tunnel, being under the misapprehension, led by the guide book, that it was controlled by lights, and that there were specified times for travelling in each direction. Imagine our surprise when we reached the tunnel and found the entry lights covered with a black plastic bag. Puzzled, we tried using the telephone provided, but there was no reply. We had a discussion with Colin over the radio, and concluded that, although this was not the time for traffic from our direction, *Redquest* and *Dolma* must have already gone through and in fact be still in the tunnel so there shouldn't be any traffic coming in the opposite direction. We decided to go for it.

At the tunnel mouth we saw a small figure in yellow. Aha, I

125

thought, they now have a manual system, and this person will tell us whether it is OK. The figure hailed us as we approached and spoke to us in rapid French. I asked her to repeat more slowly and in English she replied: "Could you give us a lift through the tunnel?" At the same time a male figure emerged from the tunnel behind her, wheeling two bikes. "We wish to go through and the towpath is blocked." They were a young German couple on a cycling holiday, and we were only too happy to oblige. Their bikes were hoisted aboard and laid on the capacious fore-deck of *Chefren* and we set off again.

The tunnel was dark and dank. Automatic lighting came on as we approached, but it only served to accentuate the darkness. The water was inky black and the towpath to our right wet and muddy, and littered with huge sections of trees, which had obviously been hauled out of the water at some time. Bats swooped eerily overhead.

John was at the wheel and I was stationed on the foredeck with a searchlight. My job was to scan the surface of the water for floating debris. It was a boring journey and I needed to concentrate on what I was doing, but I did manage to converse a little with our passengers and discovered that they were from Trier, one of the most beautiful and historic German cities I have ever visited.

If they had managed to cycle through the tunnel I think it would have been a very depressing ride.

Our nightmare was that we might see the lights of an approaching *péniche* and be forced to reverse the whole 5 km. to the entrance. Fortunately nothing appeared, but imagine our horror to find one waiting as we emerged. We had a little panic in case it started to move before Colin was out, but we heard the *péniche* skipper talking on the radio to a tunnel official, and mentioning '*deux petits bateaux*'. It became clear that the lady *éclusier* had radioed to let them know we were on our way, and the *péniche* was waiting. The Germans disembarked at the next lock.

Now the locks were descending, which made it much easier to tie up as the bollards were at the level of the boat, instead of overhead.

A series of eight locks followed forming a staircase over 4 km. The countryside was spread at our feet, the sun shone on an eiderdown of fields and trees but we had little time to admire it, as we were too busy working the locks. We had no sooner cleared one lock than we had to prepare the ropes for the next one. We had short breather at the sixth lock when the automatic mechanism failed while we were still in the lock and we found ourselves stuck. Whilst we were still wondering what to do someone came from a nearby cottage and freed us.

We had made plans to meet up with *Dolma* and *Redquest*, at Villegusien, but when we arrived there was no sign of them and we could not see anywhere to tie up. There was no pontoon and no quay suitable for boats of our size. This was very frustrating as there was a bread shop, a grocery and a butcher here, and we at least needed some fresh bread. On one of the locks earlier we had seen a sign advertising a *boulangerie* but on closer inspection it said it was closed on Mondays. Guess what day it was?

We carried on, through six more locks, and there was still no sign of *Dolma* and *Redquest*, and no place to tie up, until at Croix Rouge, just above Dommarien, as we entered the lock we saw them below us moored at the bank. We soon emerged onto their level and joined them.

The mooring place was in a turning basin with a tiny quay and room for only one boat, but we hammered ronds into the bank and made ourselves fast, using our plank to get ashore. Alongside the canal was a large vegetable garden, (a *potager*) probably the village allotment, where several people were working. No one took any notice of our arrival, or greeted us. We watched them tending their cabbages and sprouts and were amused to see one of them watering his huge plot with a tiny watering can. Water is precious in France as a whole, and they are lucky here to have the canal from which to draw water for their vegetables.

We still needed to buy bread, so Colin and I walked into the village in search of a *boulangerie*. We passed one or two well tended farms, and a *gîte* festooned with colourful flowers. We explored a couple of the village streets, admiring the traditional French cottages and farmhouses

127

bathed in the evening sunlight. There was no sign of a shop, and the only people we saw were chatting at a cottage gate.

We approached them, and asked if there was a *boulangerie* in the village. They told us that there were no shops at all. Discovering that we were here by boat they shared our dismay at being without bread and the woman from the cottage asked if a *morceau* would do? Disappearing into the cottage she re-appeared a few moments later with a *baguette* from which one end had already been cut. She pressed it onto us, and when we offered payment she refused. "*Non, non, un cadeau,*" she said. We thanked her profusely and set off back reflecting upon the generosity and helpfulness of the French people. Colin, like John, had begun his journey with the assumption that all French people hated the British, and that we would encounter rudeness or, at best, indifference. This could not be further from the truth. The people had been friendly, helpful and always courteous, even the young.

Colin too had been very generous, the night before he had insisted on giving John and I two small *baguettes,* when he learned we had run out of bread. I suspected they were his last. He now told me why.

Many years previously, when he had been on an assignment for the Special Investigation Unit of the Army, he had to go to Carlisle in the middle of a particularly cold winter. The journey took 24 hours in an unheated train with no restaurant car, and they arrived at their destination cold, tired and very hungry.

Imagine their dismay to discover that no meal had been prepared for them and there were no shops or restaurants within reach. Consoling themselves with thoughts of a warm bed they made their way to their allotted Nissen hut. But, yet another blow - it had no windows or doors, and the wind was whistling through. The prospect was bleak, but at one end of the hut six Scousers were already installed. They had found an old oil drum, filled it with all the scrap timber they could find, and had a cheery blaze going. They were seated at a trestle table eating their 'sarnies'.

"Where's your food?" they asked. "Food?" said Colin, "we thought there'd be a hot meal for us when we got here."

"'Ey-up lads," said one of the party, looking at his mates, and without a further word, a piece of wrapping paper was placed in the middle of the table and every one of the Scousers put sandwiches from his own pack onto it. In the end Colin and his mates had more sandwiches than the chaps from Liverpool.

"I vowed then," Colin told me, "that no Scouser would ever go hungry when I could help, and this is the third time I've been able to repay the debt."

I was touched by the story, but felt honour-bound to point out that we weren't exactly Scousers, being from the Wirral, but to Colin it didn't make any difference. He just saw it as an opportunity to keep his vow.

Surprisingly it rained in the night, but by morning it was dry and when the sun came out it was much warmer than it had been for several days. Perhaps it was because we were at a lower altitude.

We became aware of an unusual phenomenon here. The water was a vivid dark green, which was marbled with a brilliant lighter green pattern in whorls and swirls that changed as the boats passed. There was a bright green 'tide-mark' on the sides of the locks, and the rocks at the water's edge, rather as if someone had been round with a brush and a pot of paint to mark the water level. It seemed to be algae. It was like the marbling patterns we used to make at school, dropping oil paint onto the surface of a bowl of water for decorating sheets of paper, and was quite beautiful.

The countryside was pastoral. We saw fields of hay, maize and sunflowers, and white Charolais cattle, as well as flight after flight of heron. Dragon flies (or were they damsel flies?) of navy blue, bottle green, blue-green and amber were all around us, and often hitched a ride on our guard-rails before flying off.

The descent continued to be steep and the locks were still less than 1 km. apart, keeping us busy. At the first of two manned (or should it be womanned?) locks the *éclusier* was a toothless, elderly woman, dressed in leggings and a T-shirt. She had two plump female 'assistants' of the same age. She was thin and wiry and showed surprising strength as she operated the lock mechanism. They chatted volubly amongst themselves as we passed through, almost as though we didn't exist, but acknowledged my wave, and wished us, "*Bon voyage*".

At the next lock it was a man, bewhiskered and elderly in a baseball cap. I tried some conversation saying, "*Il fait chaud*" but this produced nothing but a nod. Maybe he was deaf.

We noted that in places along the bank old tyres had been used to shore it up where it has been undermined by the wash of boats - an interesting form of re-cycling.

The locks on this stretch were never ready and there was always a flurry of activity when they saw us coming.

Most of the *éclusiers* were middle-aged, overweight women who seemed to find it a great effort, unlike the sprightly older lady earlier. One poor lady was manning more than one lock and left us to let ourselves out, as she rushed off in her car to prepare another lock for a *péniche* going the opposite way.

We had passed this *péniche* earlier and he was having great difficulty negotiating the shallow canal. In order to let us past he kindly stopped completely whilst we edged by. The skipper came out of his cabin to

Laden *péniche*

wave us on and indicate to us not to get too close to the bank where it was very shallow.

As we approached the next lock, St. Seine, which was automatic, the expected light didn't turn green. The gates were open and the lock ready so we took *Chefren* in. But before Colin could follow the gates closed and *Orca* was left outside. We should have learned from our experience with *Le Canard* and just gone through to wait for Colin on the other side. Instead John pulled the red alarm lever. Nothing happened and Colin reversed and triggered the radar again. This opened the gates and he joined us in the lock. We operated the lever and closed the gates, but then nothing further happened. The *éclusier's* cottage was uninhabited and there were no buildings around, other than the little hut which housed the emergency telephone. We used this to call for assistance. I had enough French to explain our predicament but found it difficult to understand the reply. One bit I did understand was, "*J'envois*". He sent someone quite quickly to operate the mechanism and release us. We thanked him and were on our way again.

Whilst we were waiting to be rescued Colin spotted an apple tree growing by the lock and collected cooking apples for us all.

At the next lock we had an accident, or rather John did. A passing boat had bent the automatic operating mechanism, and as John leant against it to get a good purchase he caught the skin on his chest between the upright rod and the ring holding it in place. He developed a huge bruise to which, thanks to our fridge, I was able to apply ice.

This provided us with one of the best jokes of the trip, when Steve later asked him if he had a ½"nipple for some job or other. John replied: "No, but I'm working on it!"

I asked the lady *éclusier* at the next lock where the nearest *boulangerie* was to be found. She told us it was at Fontaine-le-Francois, 3 km away but asked if it was just bread we needed. When I said, yes, she went to the boot of her car and returned with a freshly baked *baguette*, still in its wrapping from the shop, which she sold to us - such helpfulness.

There should have been mooring points at the various little villages along this stretch, but we couldn't find the places indicated, even with the *Navicartes*. The bank sides were shallow and there were no bollards to be seen. *Dolma* and *Redquest* were ahead of us again so we were relying on them to find a suitable stopping place.

We also wanted to fill up with water and fuel, and as a whole range of facilities were listed at the lock, Blagny sur Vingeanne, I asked the *éclusier* where the water and fuel points were. He told us to carry on to

Reneve - two more locks.

A call on the radio from *Dolma* told us that they had found a mooring place just beyond the lock at Reneve and we looked forward to stopping for the night and filling up too, so we asked again about water when we reached Reneve. The reply was the same: "Two more locks." I think water probably was available but it was now 19h.15, the *éclusier* finished at 19h.30 and wanted to get home. He started the lock mechanism (it was part automatic), jumped on his scooter, and buzzed off, pausing only to enquire what time we wanted the lock opening on the following day.

This is a very pretty stretch of the canal with little villages, lakes, and chateaux to delight the eye, but the facilities are limited and boats need to travel with sufficient food, water and fuel, or be prepared to get on their bikes to go in search of it. *Redquest* and *Dolma* had found a turning basin where it was possible to moor all four boats, but there was no water or electricity, and not even a rubbish bin.

That night we were invited aboard *Dolma* for drinks. This was the first time we had had an opportunity to chat to Gordon and Gwen from *Redquest* for any length of time and we discovered that Gordon had had his own leisure narrow boat company before he built *Redquest* and retired.

We had a very merry evening, but a shadow was cast over it when Steve upset a mosquito candle, which fell from the coach roof into the cabin, spilling candle wax all over the headlining and cushions. He wasn't Maureen's favourite person that night, especially as he had only just re-done the headlining, and she had just recovered the cushions.

Redquest left early to be sure of getting a good mooring on the town quay at our next stop, Pontailler, on the river Saône. There is a *port de plaisance* there but *Redquest* is too big to make use of it. *Dolma*, *Orca* and *Chefren* left later and all managed to fit in one lock. It was the same lock keeper as last night, and guess what he said to us when we asked him about the promised fuel and water. "Two more locks". Perhaps it is the only English he knows.

A short while after leaving our mooring at Reneve we spotted a pretty little pontoon mooring just 2 km further on, which was obviously too new to be in the book. There was a grassy picnic area and a small quay with bollards. It looked so well appointed that I was sure there would be water there, but we were on our way now. *"C'est la vie!"*

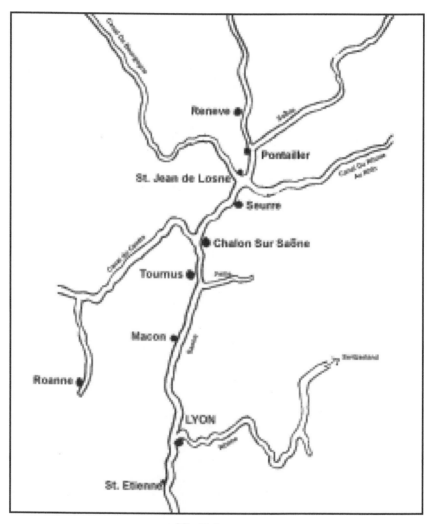

The Saône

CHAPTER 10 – The Saône

Gare d'eau

It was very exciting to be reaching the end of the canal system and approaching the River Saône, which would be wider than any river or canal we had used so far, and we would begin to travel faster, assisted by a swift flowing current. The locks would be bigger but they would be fewer and this also would contribute to swifter progress.

We could see a procession of small boats passing the end of the canal. It looked quite busy, and we anticipated that we would have to stop at the end of the canal and give way to them, choosing our moment to move out into the river. As it turned out the river was free of traffic when we reached it and the boats we had seen passing were waiting outside the gates of a huge lock. We joined them and played ring o'roses, circling with the other boats until the lock gates opened.

This lock was not as deep as those we were to encounter on the Rhône, but was certainly wider and longer than any we had used so far, including the ones on the Canal du Nord. It was 38.5m long, 5.2m wide and 1.98m deep, which would have accommodated eight single-decker buses, two abreast.

Chefren and *Dolma* in Saône lock

We knew we could get water at this lock, but weren't brave enough to try as we thought we would hold up the other boats who were now jostling for space and tying alongside each other to fit in, all eager to be on their way again. They were all shapes and sizes and many of them were hire boats returning to Pontailler and St. Jean-de-Losne With hindsight I don't think getting water would have been a problem, the *éclusier* had honey for sale and people were leaving their boats to make purchases whilst the lock was filling, and we could probably have used this time to fill up with water. But we were faint-hearted and decided to wait until we reached Pontailler-sur-Saône, only 4 km away.

When we entered the lock I used the technique which had served us well in the canals, attaching the stern line only and holding the boat on the engine. It was fortunate that I had coiled another line on the forward deck, just in case, because the *éclusier* leaned forward with a long boat-hook and helped himself to this, passing it round a bollard and handing the end back to me. I felt reprimanded, but consoled myself that he maybe thought I had prepared the line ready for him. From that point on in the Saône locks we used two lines – message understood.

There was plenty of room to manoeuvre in the river, and we could overtake, and be overtaken without problem. Its fast flowing current made a difference to our speed immediately. I'm sure if I'd stood on the bank and looked at this river I would have been apprehensive about using it because of its sheer size, but we had built up to it gradually and I was now feeling very confident. John was showing no sign of concern and I have a lot of faith in his boat handling skills.

The Saône is one of the great rivers of France and much of its length has been canalised, making it the backbone of the French waterway network. In spite of much dredging there are still banks and shoals to be avoided. All navigational features are marked and the buoyage system is excellent. There are huge stakes marking the channel, red to port and black and white stripes to starboard. There is no danger, providing boats keep to the main channel and always approach the banks with caution when mooring. At times of flood the Saône spreads over the nearby fields and these stakes are then vital to navigation. We found the *Navicarte* particularly helpful in warning us of the hazards, such as the submerged dykes that are used to encourage the river to form a natural channel. A new feature was that occasionally the direction of traffic flow would change, for example when going under a bridge. We had to cross to the opposite side of the river and upstream traffic would be on our right. On the French waterways you drive on the right as you do on the roads.

There were no more locks before Pontailler, and in fact there would now only be another eight before we reached Lyon and its junction with the Rhône, 250 km. away. This was roughly one lock every 31km. After having had one every ½ km as we came over the summit, this was luxury.

For the first time in many days I could get out the deckchair and relax, soaking up the sun and taking an interest in the passing scenery.

The river was mainly tree-lined at first with small creeks and islands providing shelter for a lunch stop or overnight anchoring. Green fields stretched into the distance. On most of the bends sandbars had formed, and some of these had been roped off to form bathing areas. We had been told by the occupants of *Maja* that French people used the rivers and often the canals for swimming but the colour of the water in the canals had never encouraged me to try it. The water was cleaner here, but still quite murky.

I would have preferred to use one of the little swimming pools we saw being towed by some of the hire boats. These were about 2m square, and coupled onto the rear of the boat. Each pool had a hard cover, presumably to keep out leaves and flies, and the water would be warmed by the heat of the sun. It was a nice idea for a family holiday. The kids would love it, but I wondered if it might interfere with the manoeuvrability of the boat.

There were hire boats in abundance here and I began to see why fishermen and bargees hated them. Many were driven far too fast with disregard for other river users. Their wash made us bounce up and down uncomfortably, and caused further erosion to the banks of the river.

Reaching Pontailler we found *Redquest* already tied up alongside a very steep, stepped quay. We decided to join them and keep our little party together, rather than go into the *port de plaisance*. There was only one disadvantage – there was no water tap here, other than that in the public toilets on the quay above, where a group of teenage boys were sitting holding hands and being generally affectionate with each other. Occasionally one or other would roar off on his moped, and return a few minutes later with a squeal of brakes and a scattering of gravel, to resume the hand holding. They were a little noisy, but otherwise well behaved, and ignored us.

Investigation of the toilet block revealed taps of the kind which had to be held down to obtain a continuous flow of water, and it would need a long hose to reach the boats. Undaunted, Colin and John set about linking two hoses together. Whilst Colin held the tap down, John opened the boats' water tanks and filled up. In Britain this activity would probably have produced a petty official telling us it was forbidden, but no one bothered us here. It might not have been drinking water, but we use bottled mineral water for drinking anyway. This was for all the other important activities such as washing and washing-up.

If we had gone into the *port de plaisance* there would have been a charge of around 50FF just for filling water tanks.

I did go into the port on foot. It had good facilities and was well laid out, with two basins shaded by mature trees, but its main attraction for me was that they had *Navicartes* on sale. I was very excited and was able to buy one for the Saône which would last us as far as Lyon.

On the quay, the four boats in our convoy had taken up most of the remaining space and shortly after we tied up, a German motor boat of the type with a flying bridge deck wanted to moor also.

Steve untied his lines and moved *Dolma* closer to us, so that the newcomer could squeeze in and then he helped them to tie up. Later he regretted being so helpful as the German boat was now overlooking their cockpit and one of the crew spent the rest of the afternoon on the bridge deck, robbing them of privacy. Not only that, but there had been no word of thanks to Steve for moving his boat and helping them moor.

A very disgruntled Steve and Maureen decided to brave the river water and go for a swim. They returned somewhat abashed. When they were swimming past the German boat, the skipper leaned overboard and presented them with a bottle of wine. International relations were now restored.

Pontailler is a market town constructed on a natural island of the Saône at the foot of a small mountain, Mount Ardoux, and at the end of the main street an ancient bridge connects the town to the mountain. The shops are strung out along this street, and a tiny greengrocer cum supermarket supplied most of our needs. The owner was most polite and helpful, but didn't like his customers helping themselves from his fruit and vegetable displays. He indicated his displeasure with much 'tut-tutting' and head shaking. I felt that he would have liked to rap my knuckles as I tried, as if I was a naughty schoolgirl.

There was a good restaurant and a couple of pavement café/bars here. Having become hot and sticky during our shopping we chose one with tree-shaded tables and over a cold beer we contemplated the buildings around us.

We were opposite the *Hotel de Ville* and it was at this point I discovered that neither John nor Colin had realised that the *Hotel de Ville* is actually the Town Hall. They both thought that the French were rather unimaginative in their choice of hotel names.

We got to know Colin a little better as we sat sipping our beers. He told us about life in Fuengirola, where he had lived for seven years since his divorce and where he had a house and a circle of friends of all nationalities. He had children living in England whom he had just been visiting, and where he bought *Orca*.

When he first moved to Spain he owned a bar and some holiday apartments. After a series of break-ins he had a re-think, he really didn't need the hassle and wasn't in very great need of the money. He called a family conference during which his children assured him they had no need of his money, and so he sold up and retired. He had enough for his needs, so why work just to put money in the bank? We couldn't agree more.

He had retired from the army after an accident during combat training that damaged his hip and spine. He now walks well and seems quite active, climbing up and down lock ladders and on and off his boat. He attributed this to the use of an alternative medicine, Glucosamine Sulphate, which had been prescribed by a doctor in Spain.

After buying *Orca* on the east coast she was given a brief overhaul and he had set off to cross to France from Boston, Lincolnshire. We thought he was either very brave or foolhardy as he told us about his adventures. *Orca* is not a sea-going boat, as she has no keel to stabilise her in rough weather and is only 6m long. Colin had never sailed his own boat before and was learning as he went along. A short way out from Boston he became aware of thick black smoke coming from the engine compartment. By this time he was too far offshore to turn back, but fortunately there were some mooring dolphins close by and he tied up to them. There was a fire in the engine compartment caused by overheating, and the polystyrene soundproofing was in flames. Fortunately he was able to douse the fire, strip out the lining, and set off once more, but it must have been quite frightening.

His next adventure was when crossing the English Channel. This would be a hazardous experience in a boat such as *Orca*. A successful trip would need very calm conditions. Having seen the way *Orca* swayed from side to side in the locks I could understand what had happened.

He told us he had been dozing at the helm when a huge ferry appeared from nowhere doing a tremendous speed. (I guess it was the Superseacat out from Newhaven.) It passed very close to *Orca* and caught her in its wash. She was tossed up and down and from side to side and Colin had difficulty keeping her upright. The Seacat seemed to have a huge wash made of multiple waves.

Colin was very scared. *Orca* seemed in danger of turning over.

Water was coming into the cockpit with each bounce and when he switched on the bilge pumps nothing happened. The darned things were blocked. He was really worried then and getting ready to call the lifeboat and abandon ship when he found a portable electric pump in one of the lockers. Just in the nick of time, and when *Orca* had stopped bouncing he was able to bail her out. He thought his last moments had come.

We were relieved to hear that when Colin took *Orca* from Southern France to his home in Spain he would be taking some extra crew with him. He'd probably be wise to hire a life raft for the journey as well.

He told us that he would like to travel in company with us for as long as he could, but if we stopped or diverted he would need to push on as he had a deadline to meet. We felt concerned for him. His boat was so tiny, and we wished him well. We envisaged he might have difficulties on the Rhône.

We were all thinking about where we were going to lay up the boats at the end of the season. John and I are members of the Cruising Association and had sent for a copy of their Mediterranean lay-up directory, compiled by members with experience of the marinas listed.

One we had been considering is called Port Napoleon and is close to Port St-Louis-du-Rhône, where the river meets the sea. It is said to be very big, not expensive, and is miles from anywhere, which, although there is good security on site, gives extra protection. Dick and Erica in *Le Canard* had used this marina one year and endorsed the recommendation.

Steve and Maureen had also had a good report of it, so we planned to check it out when we got near enough. Gwen and Gordon would be wintering at Roanne as usual

We had an opportunity to see inside *Redquest* that evening. She is such a smart looking boat and I had been longing to do so.

We were invited aboard for drinks and began the evening sitting outside on the upper deck under a striped awning in folding wooden deck chairs like the ones they use on film sets.

Before we had finished our first glass a cool breeze sprang up and rain threatened so Gwen invited us inboard. Descending to the main saloon via the wheelhouse we found a small cabin, approximately 4m x 4m where a gas, living flame stove in a tiled alcove, provided warmth in winter. Gwen told us that this had recently replaced a wood-burning stove, which they mainly fuelled on driftwood.

The cabin was furnished with cottage-style furniture and I found myself sitting on a convertible settee, the twin of the one I use at home for extra guests.

They had decorated the inside of the barge in traditional manner with lace curtains and delicate glass and china ornaments. On the walls were photographs of their family and one or two pictures of their favourite places. A row of ornamental plates on the shelf behind me completed the décor.

I would have liked to see the main bedroom and shower room (they don't call it the Heads on a barge), but I was too polite to ask. We did get a good look at the wheelhouse though, and at the magnificent ship's wheel that was a retirement present from Gordon's work colleagues.

Whilst Gordon was showing us the workings of the wheelhouse we discovered that he and John share a passion for re-cycling. The portholes of the barge were wheel trims from an old Mercedes.

Also like John, he served his time as an electrician and moved on to other things after being made redundant. In Gordon's case he ended up working on narrow boats, and later formed his own company running trips on the Leeds-Liverpool canal.

The *Marchioness* disaster on the River Thames in 1989, when a pleasure boat was struck by a dredger with heavy loss of life, spawned a rash of reactive legislation, much of which didn't apply to canal boats but was nevertheless applied rigorously. It was tedious to comply with and expensive, so they eventually sold up.

They were the only people we met who had been told, by the river police, to remove tyres which they had been using as fenders. Tyres are forbidden unless inflated with inner tubes, as they tend to fall off and jam the lock gates, get trapped in lock mechanisms and foul propellers.

Gordon told us of one occasion when a tyre had attached itself to their propeller in such a way that all three blades were encased in it. Another time a wire-sprung bedstead became entangled in the prop, and took two days to cut away. Perhaps our brambles and polythene bags weren't so bad after all.

The following day our little flotilla headed for St. Jean-de-Losne, stopping on the way for lunch at the old fortified town of Auxonne, where pontoons have been put down for pleasure boats.

Auxonne's claim to fame is that a certain Lieutenant Bonaparte arrived there in 1788 when he was 18 years old. He had come to the attention of his superiors because of his tremendous ambition, and his desire to instruct at the royal artillery school there. In 1791 he moved on to Valence, where he joined the Grenoble regiment. The Revolution greatly assisted his career and marked the beginning of his rise to glory.

There was just time for a quick look around the town and to find his statue in Armes square, in front of the 15th century brick-built town hall, across from the restored 13th century church of Notre Dame.

I found the centre of the town criss-crossed with narrow streets where half-timbered houses, some with courtyard stairs, jostled each other for space. On the outskirts were the remains of ramparts, with a couple of ancient gates and some towers by the river.

On our way again we passed through fairly flat countryside, edged with patches of water lilies and fringed with trees. These water lilies often marked the position of an underwater dyke.

In order to turn the Saône into a navigable river *derivation* canals have been built at intervals to by-pass some of the longer meanders, which in many cases have formed ox-bow lakes. These *derivations* are straight pieces of man-made canal with a gate at the upstream end, and a lock at the other. The gates close off the canal at times of flooding.

Downstream of Auxonne the river widens again and begins to lose some of its pastoral charm having been transformed into a high capacity waterway, navigable by barges and huge push-tows, usually at least two barges long.

Two important routes from the Seine basin join the Saône close by here. These are the Canal de Bourgogne which enters at St. Jean-de-Losne, and the Canal du Centre, which enters at Chalon-sur-Saône. A third waterway, the Canal du Rhône au Rhine also joins the Saône just north of St. Jean.

Because the river is so wide the huge push-tows that we encountered were not a problem, although Maureen, who was in front, usually radioed a warning when there was a particularly big one. On one occasion she told us we might recognise the name. The barge in question was a giant, towering over us as it passed. Not only was it one barge, pushing another, but it also had a third alongside, all of them dwarfing *Chefren* as it passed. On its stern we saw the name *Orca* and watched in amusement as it passed its diminutive namesake. I wonder if the skipper of the barge noticed the name. We tried to hail him on the radio but got not response.

Some of these push-tows were so heavily laden that they were almost submerged and difficult to see from a distance. We learned to look for the bow wave which often appeared on a bend, long before the pushing boat came into view.

At St. Jean-de-Losne there is a public quay, and three separate *ports de plaisance*. As well as being an important junction, St Jean is one of the smallest French communes but has become the regional capital of inland navigation and every year in June or July there is an Inland Navigation Feast. There are actually two towns St. Jean, and Losne, which face each other on opposite banks of the river, joined by a bridge.

As we approached we could see *Redquest*, in company with many other boats filling the entire quay. We had no option but to find somewhere else to moor and this was a time when it proved useful to be travelling in company with a monohull. *Dolma* went ahead to investigate the *ports de plaisance* housed in a huge basin known as the Gare d'Eau at the mouth of the Bourgogne canal. This basin houses a number of establishments; a collection of moorings known as the Port

144

Fluvial, a *port de plaisance* named H$_2$O, and the depot of the Crown Blue Line hire boats.

The Port Fluvial is run by an ex-barge skipper, Joel Blanqart, who has a chandlery and offices aboard a large barge. It was very busy and crowded with *péniches* in various states of repair. Maureen and Steve found space in H$_2$O where *Orca, Dolma* and *Chefren* could moor fairly close together. Receiving their signal we entered the basin and the sight that met our eyes was wall-to-wall boats - if canal basins can be said to have walls. We tied up in the midst of hundreds of boats, of all shapes and sizes, *péniches*, barges, motorboats and yachts of all nationalities, many of which were live-aboards. Some of the boats bore signs indicating they were for sale as there was a large brokerage here, and Colin showed interest in a Colvic Watson motorboat moored opposite.

The marina offered a range of other services, but we formed the opinion that they had either expanded beyond their ability to cope, or had become complacent, as the whole site was beginning to look rather run down, a fact that was not enhanced by the rows of British, red phone boxes rusting away in a weed-overgrown yard at the side of the *Capitainerie*. Apparently they were bought with a view to selling them on, but hadn't attracted any buyers. Maybe this is where the one at Cappy had come from?

Some overgrown trees had been allowed to droop into the basin from an island where an abandoned barge lay half-submerged, completing the air of neglect.

There was an excellent chandlery here, where fluent English was spoken and, my favourite, a book exchange where the charming lady who ran it was so overwhelmed that she begged people to take as many books as they liked. I was now able to stock up our library.

There was no laundrette or shower block. These amenities were provided by the *Syndicate d'Initiative* just around the corner, where there was also a large *supermarché*. The tumble dryer was *en panne* and, as it began to rain that evening, just as we were all queuing to do our laundry, we had wet washing hanging around in the spare cabin all evening reminding us of our days of sailing in Britain.

But all that was forgotten when the sun shone the next day, and washing was festooned over the guard rails to blow in the light breeze. Best of all, I was able to buy our final *Navicarte*, for the Rhône, in the chandlery.

We had been travelling hard for the past two days and decided to stay here an extra night, allowing us to explore the old town of St. Jean-de-Losne which, as well as a river frontage, consisted of one street of shops and lots of smaller streets running away from it into little squares and courtyards.

Outside the church on the main street was a memorial to commemorate a key historical event in 1636, when several hundred men stood fast against the 60,000 soldiers of the invading Austrian army.

The ancient church had been burned in the 14th century and rebuilt in the 15th and 16th. It was unusual in that its apse faced west, contrary to tradition.

Also in the main street we found the oldest house in St. Jean, which accommodates an art exhibition downstairs, and a *péniche* museum upstairs, plus photographs of the old town, the bridge and the damage done during the wars.

The art exhibition featured extremely garish paintings of women in the flounced skirts of *Can-Can* dancers, in various poses revealing intimate parts of their anatomy. They were very striking, painted in bold primary colours. In Britain these might have caused many raised eyebrows, as we seem to have a different attitude to the body from the French. I believe we still struggle with the legacy of Victorian prudery, whilst the French take these things very much for granted

The house itself was constructed of wattle and daub with wooden floors and timber beams. We mounted the stairs to discover ancient panelling and a life-sized Madonna and Child on the staircase carved in wood. The Madonna had been very badly mutilated – the war or the Revolution?

Upstairs, the *péniche* exhibition fascinated us and filled in some gaps in our knowledge. It made me glad I wasn't making this journey in the days before engines. There was a picture of an elderly woman towing a laden barge against the river current by means of a leather yoke fixed across her chest. I thought her expression was rather pained.

Model *péniches* showed details of their construction, and I was delighted to find a picture of a convoy of boats being pulled through a tunnel by a little engine like the one we saw at Condé.

On a trailer, similar to a golf trolley, was one of the earliest outboard motors, dated around 1920. It had shiny brass propellers and petrol tank and looked very different to our modern ones, but nevertheless heralding a new age in boating.

The invention of the engine has certainly transformed life on the waterways. In future when I feel tempted to moan about life aboard, and find myself longing for my automatic washing machine, or my car, I will be grateful that I don't have to physically haul the boat with a leather yoke.

CHAPTER 11 – The Lower Saône

Poste Restante

The small town of Seurre, was our next overnight stop. A tiny port had been created at the end of a *derivation*, making use of the shelter of a natural peninsula. The pontoons here are managed by H$_2$O from St. Jean, and a charming white-haired lady came round for our fees in the late afternoon, a bus conductor's moneybag slung on her hip.

There was water and electricity here, as well as shops and restaurants, and a *boules* court on the quay. Across the river there was a public swimming pool and campground.

Seurre dates back to the 5th century and today has about 2,800 inhabitants. Like St. Jean it was once besieged, but in this case by Louis XIV. It has also been burned down several times in its history, but in the town there are still some interesting old stone and timber buildings, and a town hall that was once a convent.

Later in the day I was taking a siesta in our deck chair under the sun canopy (which was draped as usual over the mast and supported by the boat hook pushed through one of the eyelet holes) when several hire boats, newly out from St. Jean, began to fill up the pontoons. They were obviously newcomers to boating and there was much revving of engines and shouting of instructions. We pretended not to notice so as not to embarrass them. But when one of them decided to tie up alongside *Chefren*, and came perilously close to ramming us. John grabbed the boat hook to fend them off, forgetting in his haste that it was attached to the sun canopy. There was an ominous ripping sound. I'll have to make that white one now.

An English boat tied up alongside *Orca*, and Colin discovered that the skipper was a friend of his former commanding officer. He was making his way back from the Mediterranean in the reverse direction to us and gave Colin lots of information about new pontoons, and recommended some stopping places he had used. This proved extremely useful over the next few days, particularly on the Rhône where stopping places are hard to find. I never knew his name, but as his information figured quite a bit in the latter half of our trip I shall call him Charles.

That evening we invited everyone aboard *Chefren*. It was still pleasantly warm and we sat in the cockpit, laughing and swapping tales. Our hilarity was echoed from the river where the ducks were settling down for the night along the shore, their quacks sounding incredibly like human laughter. We put our searchlight on to have a closer look and to our amazement millions of tiny white moths were immediately attracted to the beam. Ducks forgotten, we switched on the navigation lights and watched them as they danced in the light, moving so fast that each one looked like a tiny illuminated caterpillar. Spiders had been busy weaving webs along the end of the mast where it overhung the stern, and in the space of seconds these webs were filled with the flies which also flew around our heads and threatened to get caught in our hair. We retreated inside the cabin and dimmed the light to prevent a flying invasion. In the morning there were hundreds of corpses in our dinghy, on the deck, and caught in spiders' webs on the pontoon fittings. It was like a late snowfall.

The next day we left early, but a little way down the river at the only lock on this leg, the *éclusier* made us wait for all the hire boats to catch up before locking us through. We might just as well have had a lie-in. As they were motorboats they pulled ahead of us once they were out of the lock and we didn't see them again.

Motoring more slowly along we saw, against the bank in several places, tiny open rowing boats rocking at their moorings, with huge fishing nets attached to their sterns, suspended from a long arched pole. The nets were stretched over a rigid, four sided, curved framework attached from the centre to the pole which arched over the river. They reminded me of the four-sided, domed food covers my grandmother used to use to keep flies off our food. John thought they might be for catching small fish.

Approaching Chalon we saw a group of yachts moored in the centre of the river, perhaps for lunch, but what interested us most was that these yachts had their masts in place. They were the first boats with masts we had seen since leaving St. Valéry. The Saône is a wide river and the bridges are very high, there are no locks, and yachts are able to sail for several kilometres on the river. Chalon has a yacht club too, in a 'blind' arm of the river that was planned as a *derivation* canal, to by-pass a bend, but was never completed. Charles had told us of a new pontoon here, which was just big enough for two boats. A peninsula had been formed between the river and the canal, where there was access to a speedboat and water skiing area. The afternoon was sultry and a few cars were parked under the shade of nearby trees, and anglers were fishing in the river, but no one troubled us apart from the occasional water skier who seemed compelled to buzz around our boats. There were no facilities on the pontoon, and Chalon was 2 km. away, across the canal arm, but it made a good overnight stop, and Maureen and Steve had another swim.

The only buildings were those of the yacht club. If we'd walked up there and introduced ourselves we thought we might have been given temporary membership, but a very prominent sign bore the legend *YCC PRIVÉ*. Derek Bowskill in 'The Channel to the Med' writes that he hadn't found anyone who had been made welcome, so we didn't bother. One or two returning yachts waved, but none approached us. Most of them had their masts up and were sailing in, but others had their masts on the deck, like us. I assumed they had been further afield, perhaps even down to the Med and were returning at the end of the season – it was already August 29th.

We now needed to make plans to retrieve our parcel from the post office in Chalon. It was exactly two weeks from when we estimated it would have arrived and hoped it would still be waiting. We decided to move into the *port de plaisance* in Chalon from where we would be able to walk into the town.

Steve and Maureen were contemplating joining *Redquest* on a detour up the pretty River Seille, just beyond Chalon, although Steve was unsure whether the river would be deep enough for *Dolma*. Colin decided he needed to press on so our little flotilla was breaking up. Once again, we said good-bye, I took the helm and we cast off, waving until their boats had become specks in the distance.

Reaching the port we found plenty of room, together with water and electricity, showers and laundry, and a pleasant welcome. The cost was 120FF, for us comparatively expensive, but as most of our moorings so far had been free, this wouldn't ruin our budget.

The marina is situated across the river from the town, separated from it by the Isle St-Laurent, which was first settled many centuries ago. The old hospital and gaol are still here, surrounded by narrow streets of ancient shops and restaurants. The hospital is still in use, with some modern building attached so, I presume, is the gaol although we didn't see any faces at the barred windows as we passed.

We crossed a footbridge onto the island, and a road bridge from there into the city and into the oldest part of the main town, which has been largely pedestrianised. Hurrying to collect our parcel before the post office closed at 12h00 we promised ourselves a more thorough exploration on our return.

We found the *Bureau de Grande Poste* without difficulty, in the Place de l'Obelisque, where lines of traffic waited impatiently at the lights. Close by was a large grassy square, shaded by plane trees, making an island of calm in the frenetic rush of the city.

At the post office we were attended by a pleasant female assistant, who searched for our mail in a large filing cabinet, but without success! Oh dear, had the system failed, I wondered? She checked with us as to how it might have been addressed and suggested that it might have gone to another post office, some distance away. She gave us this information in French and I translated for John. When she discovered we were on foot, and hoping to depart the next day, she offered to telephone and arrange for them to send our parcel to this office. The package was indeed there and she asked us to return by 17h00 that afternoon. I can tell the time in French by the 12hr clock, which is how I had been taught in school, but I had a little trouble with translating the 24hr clock as I still hadn't fully grasped this in English. A charming French lady in the queue behind us, who spoke excellent English, volunteered her services as translator. Yet another example of the general friendliness and helpfulness we were encountering, and now coupled with the efficiency of the post office.

In the old town we found many interesting buildings: former residences of the *bourgeoisie* with traditional timber upper floors. Sandwiched between two other buildings we discovered an old clock tower, which used to be part of the old town hall and seemed straight out of the pages of Victor Hugo.

We poked around the mediaeval streets, finding narrow alleyways and squares, pausing in the warm sunshine to listen to a South American band busking on a street corner. Their evocative music filled the air around the shops and lightened the steps of the passers by.

Exhausted by our tour of the old town, and the heat, we retreated to the Place de l'Obelisque where we eased our tired feet on a bench under the trees. We had bought an English paper to catch up on the news. It is reasonably easy to buy English papers in the larger towns, but they cost twice the cover price, and can be up to two days old.

At 17h00 we returned to the post office and, to our surprise and delight, our package was waiting. They say the British postal system is wonderful, but this takes some beating.

On our return we stopped in the Cathedral Square, to enjoy a beer at a pavement café, and watch the world go by. Children and dogs were playing in the water of an aggressively modern fountain. To my mind

Cathedral Square, Chalon

this fountain didn't 'fit' with the architecture of the old buildings and ancient cathedral in the square. It was a huge sphere, about 2 metres high, like an orange with a segment removed and was positioned off-centre in the square, as though it had been temporarily abandoned until they could think of somewhere better to place it.

Many of the customers of the cafés were young people, probably on their way home from school. It was delightful to watch them greet each other, going round their circle of friends, shaking their hands before sitting down, and the girls kissed each other on both cheeks. I wonder what effect this has on the social development of the young people. I feel it must help them to be more civilised. You can't shake someone's hand and the next moment offer violence to them.

We left the next day in the cool of the morning, passing a beautiful floral display on the downstream headland of the Isle St-Laurent which is annually planted and dated, and has become a signature of the town.

After we had cleared the suburbs of this former capital of Burgundy and once important steel town, our attention was caught by the strange behaviour of some ducks close inshore. They didn't seem to be moving and as we drew closer we saw they had no eyes - they were decoys. On the bank a few yards away we could see a hide - a rough hut covered in reeds. We saw several more further down, but no more ducks. It seemed very unsporting to lure the ducks with decoys in this way.

The scenery was changing again, and the flat countryside of Burgundy began to give way to a few low hills beyond the tree-lined banks.

The old Saône locks, now replaced by bigger ones, have been converted into *ports de plaisance*. The first of these was at Gigny, which also seemed to be a popular camping spot. As well as the characterful cottages and farmhouses straggling along the water's edge there were several frame tents pitched along the river.

Another catamaran flying a British flag was in the lock at Ormes when we reached it but we were so busy attaching our ropes we had little time to do more than wave and make a note of their name, which

154

was *Gee Bee*. Once out of the lock we pulled alongside. They were heading for the same place as ourselves, Tournus, and we arranged to meet.

The mooring arrangements at Tournus have undergone some changes. Originally there were two semi-public quays, and few facilities. The upstream quay was partly reserved for trip boats and hotel barges, and pleasure boats would have to jostle for places on the downstream quay. Mooring was often difficult, particularly when the water level in the river was high, because of the low pitch of the stone quay. But now a new, long pontoon has been erected on the downstream side of the bridge, adjoining the old quay, where free water and electricity are available. The pontoons rise and fall with the level of the river, and are reached from the quay by means of a walkway guarded by a wicket gate where a notice announces that only boat people may use them.

Imagine our surprise to see *Redquest* on the pontoon, and the tall figure of Gordon waiting to take our lines. It was a lovely surprise, as we hadn't expected to see them again. They were planning their trip up the Seille for the next day.

Gee Bee arrived later and introduced themselves as Lesley and (another) Steve who were Australians, living in Malta. They were a couple in their fifties but looked much younger and had a very youthful approach to life.

Lesley bounced along to our boat with a huge bundle of laundry clutched in one hand. They were off to find a laundrette and as our laundry bag was bursting at the seams we decided to accompany them. First we found the tourist office where we obtained a map of the town, details of what to see, and directions to the laundrette. We then spent the rest of the afternoon, watching our laundry go round, sitting on the window seat in the deserted laundrette, and getting to know some new friends. During the course of the afternoon I took a short walk up the street to get some change for the machines, and formed an impression of an interesting little town, with narrow streets where ancient buildings leaned against each other, and decided to return for a closer inspection later.

Back at the laundrette we learned that Steve's work was based in Australia but he did most of it over the Internet, with only occasional trips back to Oz. He is a computer programmer and - wait for it - writes programmes for condom vending machines. His partner in Australia markets the programmes. Having a computer on board he was able to continue to work throughout the trip, usually for two to three hours, and then use the telephone in the *port de plaisance* to download his work. Surely only an Australian would have worked out such an unusual lifestyle?

Lesley taught English as a foreign language in Malta, and her students mostly come from North Africa.

They weren't travelling as fast as us, because of Steve's need to work. While he worked Lesley read or went sightseeing.

Lesley was someone I would describe as a typical Australian, forthright and very natural, with a great sense of humour. Occasionally she was overcome with remorse in case she had said something that offended us, but her candour was very refreshing. Of average height and slim build her usual outfit was a T-shirt, topping a pair of baggy jogging pants. Her brown hair flopped over her face occasionally and she told me that before leaving England she had had it cut to ½ length so that she could just let it grow during the trip.

Steve was a quieter personality, equally laid back but having more of the British reticence in his character. (He was born and brought up in Britain before emigrating with his family to Oz.)

We arranged to join them for a meal that evening, and I told Lesley I was looking for a simple restaurant, serving *frites* if possible, and we thought that the one on the quay looked a likely place. But the best laid plans...

When the time came for us to go ashore there was great excitement on the pontoon amongst a group of fishermen, who shouldn't have been there anyway. Steve thought one had snagged his line and invited him aboard *Gee Bee* to free it, only to discover that he was trying to land a huge carp, and the Frenchman and three of his friends all boarded *Gee Bee*. There was much Gallic shouting and waving of hands, and giving of advice, even from townspeople on the quay. Other people came onto the pontoon to offer encouragement.

It was taking him a very long time to land his catch and we wanted to go for our meal, but we were concerned about the safety of *Gee Bee*. Fortunately Gwen and Gordon offered to keep an eye on things. On our return they reported that the fish was successfully landed, and all the fishermen had departed except for one small boy of about nine who had taken advantage of the excitement to wander amongst the boats. He had tried to go aboard *Redquest* but was dissuaded.

Gwen told us they had been advised not to allow children aboard the boats because there had been instances of them falling in the water, and even one or two drownings. It made sense for insurance purposes too.

Before the excitement had begun one of the fishermen had told Steve about his brother's restaurant which was called the *Hotel aux Terrasses*, set back from the quay on the outskirts of town. Persuaded by his description we strolled up there and found it was actually a pleasant and popular hotel, a little dearer than we had anticipated, and no *frites*, but we agreed to try it.

We had a lovely meal for about 100FF per head, three-courses, lots of extras such as sweetmeats, and some little cheesy pancakes, which were served whilst we waited for our starter; and of course wine.

Before leaving the following morning, I made my promised visit into town to visit the old abbey while John prepared the boat for off. The shops were just beginning to open and the town was coming to life. I strolled through streets of ancient houses and shops to eventually reach a walled abbey, founded in the 6th century on the site where St. Valerien, the first evangelist in Gaul, was beheaded in 179, turning the town into a place of pilgrimage. It was so picturesque I became completely absorbed in taking photographs and was nearly knocked down by a car coming though the old gate which straddles the street as I attempted to get a shot of the two round gate towers, topped by pointed roofs. As I wandered amongst the abbey buildings

157

within the walled area I could have been back in time but for the incongruous sight of large wheelie-bins placed on the street ready for collection by the very twentieth century refuse collection vehicle.

The monastery was granted to the monks of St. Philibert in 975 by the king (Charles the Bald!) when many of the present buildings were erected. The Abbots Lodging behind the abbey was a charming ivy covered building.

Like many towns in France Tournus has had a chequered history. The Hungarians burned it in 937 and in 1562 the Huguenots sacked it. In 1815 Napoleon, back from exile, awarded the town the Legion of Honour for its courage in chasing away the Austrians the previous year.

I left the abbey and turned down a tiny street where the morning sun was warming the cobbles and the only sign of life was a black cat languorously crossing the road. Reaching the Quai du Nord, I found a plaque on one of the cottages announcing that this was the birthplace of the wife of Marat, a French Revolutionary leader, murdered in 1793.

I could see *Chefren* on the other side of the bridge, and John was preparing her lines for departure. I quickened my steps. It was time to go.

Travelling south the pointed roofs of Burgundy began to give way to red roofs, furrowed with concave tiles. Small hills fringed the river to the west, and we passed occasional campsites and waterside restaurants with their own quays.

Reaching Mâcon, *Gee Bee* chose to go into the *port de plaisance* to have use of their telephone, but we chose a free pontoon, of which Charles had told us, just by the bridge into town, which would make shopping and sightseeing easier. We had scarcely finished tying up when we were hailed by another boat approaching from downstream. It was *Dolma,* and she joined us on the pontoon.

They had gone a little way up the Seille with *Redquest,* but approaching the second lock the keel of their boat hit an underwater obstruction. This confirmed their fears that the river would be too shallow and they gave up whilst they were still afloat.

Later the four of us went on a sightseeing trip. The old town is a warren of narrow cobbled streets where cafés sprawled out into ancient squares, and where traffic is banned. We began at the tourist office to obtain a map, and our next stop was the Soufflot Residence, now an old people's home but once a charity hospital where foundlings were cared for. St. Vincent de Paul, its founder, was a local parish priest. The tourists come to wonder at the *tour* by the main door. This *tour* is a revolving barrel (upright), with a section removed, into which abandoned children were placed. It was then rotated and the child was passed into the hospital, whilst the mother remained anonymous. There has been talk of reviving this practice in Germany recently. They say that 'what goes around comes around'.

We wandered through streets thronged with tourists like ourselves, past the Ursuline Convent used as a prison during the Revolution, and on to the 16th century *Maison du Bois*, the oldest house in Mâcon, now a café. Its façade is constructed entirely of wood, and decorated with saucy statuettes of grimacing men, and monkey's masks, which after the Soufflot residence is the most popular spot in Mâcon. We ended our walk at the ruins of the 7th century cathedral of St. Vincent. All that remains now are two towers and an arch, from one of which there is a breathtaking panorama of Mâcon, and the Saône can be see glinting in the sunlight below.

Making our way back we found we were getting the hang of crossing the road, French-style. In the north motorists don't stop for pedestrians unless they are actually on a crossing. If you stand on the edge of the pavement, as in Britain, they ignore you. In the larger towns the crossings are controlled by lights, but we learned not to take the 'green man' too seriously, as there could still be traffic turning from a side road. Although you have precedence you can't rely on them seeing you. However, in Reims, we had been amazed to find that traffic did stop when we were waiting on the edge of the pavement but, here in Mâcon no such luck. The crossings seemed to be ignored unless controlled by lights, and the technique was to find one with a pedestrian refuge in the middle. What you did then was to wait for a gap in the traffic on your side of the road, and run like mad for the safety of the refuge where you could draw breath and repeat the procedure. It was increasingly hazardous as we had to remember to look left, instead of right.

A Dutch catamaran, named *Panta Rhei*, joined us on our pontoon in the late afternoon, and the following day *Gee Bee* and *Panta Rhei* joined our little flotilla of three catamarans and one monohull. I learned that *Panta Rhei* is an ancient Roman philosophy of acceptance that life is constantly changing.

The river continued to be well marked with green or black channel markers, (the black ones are being changed gradually to red), and as we left Mâcon I saw a heron perched on top of one of them, reminding me of the hermit who lived on a pillar. We also saw a cormorant balancing on a float marker, spreading his wings to dry in the sun and later a fish eagle in a tree near the water's edge.

Looking back we saw carvings on the town bridge, one of which was a representation of the *tour* outside the Soufflot residence.

Islands were more numerous now but the channel was clearly marked, unlike the smaller rivers and canals, and we always knew which side to go.

Sand is extracted in the countryside round here, and *étangs* have been formed alongside the river by its removal. Sand barges take on their cargoes here, emerging fully laden into the river. At the entrance to each *étang* were signs warning us to sound our horn but the rivers had been so quiet on the earlier part of the trip we had got out of the habit of obeying these signs, feeling rather foolish sounding our horn on a deserted river. We ignored them here too but regretted this when a ponderous barge emerged slowly into our path, causing us to take avoiding action. Fortunately there was plenty of room and no problem, but after that I made sure we had our horn handy, and used it.

We had got into the habit of calling ahead to the locks to let them know we were on our way, and that job fell to me, as the French speaker. I had shied away from it until now, as I couldn't always understand the reply, unaccompanied by body language and eye

160

contact. But we realised that not only would it speed our progress to have the lock prepared for us, but that it was also courtesy. I took my courage in both hands and called up the next lock at Drace and was informed that it would be ready in five minutes. I wondered what I had been worrying about.

We all passed through in company with a Belgian boat, and the *éclusier* took our lines, which was unusual for a large lock. I think he wanted to hurry us on as there was a *péniche* waiting on the other side of the lock gates when we got out.

The countryside began to take on the flavour of Provence, with little towns and villages perched on top of each hill and poplar trees peeping above the buildings.

We had been travelling all day and were now searching for a mooring. The *ports de plaisance* were full of small boats laid up for the winter and we couldn't find any quays. Passing through Trevoux I searched in vain with the binoculars for a place, because it looked such an interesting old town, with many old buildings cascading downhill in a blaze of sunlight. It had a distinct Roman appearance. It must surely have had a quay but I couldn't see it, and none was marked on the map. We motored on to Neuville-sur-Saône where we eventually found a good quay where all four boats could tie up, and which displayed a drinking water sign. The quay and the nearby buildings were a dazzling white. The town itself was built on a level stretch of the riverbank approached from the quay by a set of concrete steps.

The heat was still intense and Maureen and Steve were preparing for their usual swim. We were all persuaded to join them as the river water was just a little cleaner here. All except Lesley who said that after the clear, blue waters of home she couldn't be tempted. We were now able to have a look at the underside of the boats and John had a quick look at our steering leg. It was then that we discovered that Ed, on *Panta Rhei,* was having the same problem and John went aboard to discuss it with him and to see whether he could help. But, although the boats had the same problem, *Panta Rhei* had a different system.

What had happened on our boat was that the pin, over which the mechanism for the leg hooks when it is in the locked position, had bent following years of wear and tear. Very often it didn't connect, or if it did it unhooked at inopportune moments. There was nothing we could do until the boat was lifted out of the water, as the pin must be straightened.

The couple on *Panta Rhei* were Ed and Riet. They were in their seventies, but very lean and fit, and full of *joie de vivre*. We got to know them better that evening as Lesley arranged for us all to have a meal together, and we sat opposite them. Ed was a very talkative individual, and had an excellent command of English and French. Riet was quieter and only began to chat when she had had a few drinks. She had been a model in her younger days – they called them mannequins then – and she still had the statuesque carriage.

Ed wanted to smoke, and the others were quite surprised that John was brave enough to say Yes when asked if we objected. I think the general feeling was that we might have offended Ed by our refusal, but in this situation I believe we had the right to express our preferences, which we did very politely. Ed went outside to smoke, and was able to assert his own rights later when we went aboard *Panta Rhei* for drinks. We assured him it would then be up to us to move away if we found the smoke objectionable.

Ed offered us some ancient slivovitch (plum brandy) which he had bought from a lock keeper. It was very strong, and none of us liked it. John accepted a second glass to be polite but later I saw him surreptitiously pour it over the side.

Panta Rhei had an interesting feature, a hatch in the floor of the cabin. Dutch regulations require all catamarans to have these in case of capsize. This hatch can be opened to give a circulation of cool air in warmer climates and we were very grateful for this now, even late in the evening.

The belief that catamarans capsize is something of an 'urban myth'. It is usually small racing cats which do, as they are very light and often over-canvassed - sailing dinghies, whether monohull or catamaran, regularly capsize, that's part of the fun. These regulations for cats are usually made by monohull sailors without any catamaran experience.

I had gone into the stability factor of cats at some depth with owners in Cornwall. I won't go into technical detail but as long as the boat is not over-canvassed it is no more likely to capsize than any other boat. Someone also gave me an interesting quote from Jim Brown, an American boat designer. He said, "Cats might turn over but they don't sink, and I'd rather be sitting warm and dry in an upside down, floating catamaran feeling embarrassed, than right way up in a monohull at the bottom of the ocean."

Neuville is a very small town, built around a square, in the centre of which is the church of *Notre Dame d'Assomption*, with beautiful stained glass. Narrow streets of small shops radiate from this square, and the main road out of town is lined with more modern shops.

It is not called Neuville because it is or was a new town, but because one of the 17th century archbishops from Lyon, Camille de Neuville, used to take his holidays here.

The four boats were quite an attraction and people came down to the quay to have a look. One old lady engaged us in conversation. We were shocked when she commiserated with us on the death of 'the son of our queen' in an aeroplane crash. When we questioned her she could not remember his name but it wasn't Charles. By process of elimination we decided it could only be Andrew. However, there had been nothing on the World Service news or in any of the papers about what was surely a tragic event. We eventually concluded that she must have been referring to the son of ex-President Kennedy who had been killed in an aeroplane accident some months previously. However, we scanned the newspapers anxiously for the next few days, just in case. I suppose to some of the ordinary French people one English speaking nation is much like another, and our heads of state get confused. How many English people could name the French president for example and if his son was involved in an accident might not some of them confuse him with the president of Germany?

The next day a street market was set up on the quay and we were able to get fresh vegetables and local produce before we left, but it wasn't the Provencal flea market for which we had hoped, but sold furniture and bric-a-brac..

Before departing we investigated the drinking water tap, which turned out to be another one of those to which it was well nigh impossible to attach a hose. Most of us decided to wait until we could get water at another stop, but Lesley and Steve were very low and Lesley spent a good half hour walking between their boat and the tap with gallon water containers. She was exhausted before they set off.

Travelling along we found the weather was much cooler, and we wondered whether this might be a sign that autumn was approaching, which seemed appropriate as we only had one more stop before reaching the Rhône, and that would be Lyon, arguably France's second largest city.

CHAPTER 12 – Lyon

The Mighty Rhône at Last

We swept quickly down the Saône and soon were in the suburbs of Lyon. As we approached the city itself our first impression was of a big, dirty, noisy city. Traffic raced by on both banks, where tall buildings towered above the river. The water was full of

Notre Dame de Fouvière

rubbish and was now a muddy brown colour. The walls lining the quay/walkway were covered with interesting French graffiti. There was quite a lot of river traffic, all going far too fast, causing a strong wash which bounced us about as if we were at sea in a mild storm. The atmosphere was frenetic.

Lyon competes with Marseilles for the title of second city in France, having a population of over 1,200,000 who all seemed to be on the move that day, by water or by road.

To our right the old city, a jumble of buildings, clung to the side of a steep hill, where the Basilica of Notre Dame de Fourvière dominated the skyline. This glistening white building looks as though it is made of icing sugar. It has an ornamental tower at each corner, and another topped by a gilded statue. It looked like the palace of Snow White and Steve christened it the Disney cathedral.

We moored up at St. Just quay in the heart of the city, which is below street level, and where the wash from passing boats sent water splashing onto the walkway, I would guess it is covered with water during the spring floods.

Flooding is an ever-present hazard on the rivers, and even here in the heart of France's second city there are logs and tree branches passing down the river from the higher reaches. John and Steve fished out a small tree trunk and one or two of the larger logs to prevent damage to the boat propellers.

John also spent some time with his head through the hatch in *Chefren's* rear platform, removing a blue plastic shopping bag, which had become entangled in the propeller.

The quay is used by dog walkers, joggers, lovers and bag ladies alike, and we became concerned about security. Whenever we left the boats we pretended there was someone still on board and called out "See you later, John," as we climbed ashore.

The town council had thoughtfully provided dog toilets on the quay, carefully marked. These are circular patches of earth, surrounded by low concrete walls but I never saw a dog use one during the time we were moored there. We always had to check our shoes when we came aboard.

Similar efforts had been made in Mâcon where the pavements had been marked with a picture of a dog, and arrows indicating that they should use the gutters. But of course the dogs can't read these signs, and their owners don't seem to bother.

There is supposed to be drinking water for the boats here and there is a sign on the opposite bank, but no evidence of a tap. We saw several boats attempt to find it without success and we suspected that it might be hidden beneath a steel cover. Fortunately we weren't low on water so we didn't join the search.

There might not be water, but there was a diesel barge just down the quay. John went off with *Dolma* taking our spare can, whilst I stretched out in the sunshine and did some mending. Yes, I occasionally have to sew on buttons, and mend tears so I carry a small sewing kit. A problem I had in Britain was trying to stop my needles from going rusty in the sea air. But this didn't seem to be happening in the drier climate of France.

When *Dolma* returned Maureen was waving a bottle of *rosé*, given to them by the friendly bargee. Steve was keen that we should sample it immediately and his suggestion met with general approval. Glasses were produced and we enjoyed the wine in the sunshine of *Chefren's* cockpit.

Darkness was heralded that evening by another glorious sunset. The sky over the Fourvière hill looked as though it had been delicately streaked by an artist's brush in shades of rose and pale blue, and when the light finally faded we saw why Lyon is called the city of light. Carefully arranged coloured lights and spotlights picked out the important buildings and lit up the steps to the old city across the river. Rows of lights like jewelled necklaces outlined the bridge. Street and traffic lights added to the colour, together with the moving lights from cars and lorries which hurtled over the bridge downstream, well into the night. Restaurant barges plied up and down the river, adding to the display with fluorescent lights in vivid green, orange and electric blue. Throughout Lyon 150 sites are illuminated, bringing the whole city to life.

We stayed here for two nights and spent our time exploring the city, old and new. It is far more beautiful than it seemed when we approached along the river. St. Just quay is on a peninsula formed between the Saône, and the Rhône which joins it south of the city. This peninsula is the modern centre of Lyon and contains shops, museums and restaurants, built around open spaces containing fountains and greenery. The Place Bellecour (once the Place Royale) in the centre of the peninsula houses the Office du Tourism and is one of the largest squares in Europe. A statue of Louis XIV still stands at its centre and it is fringed with open-air cafes.

Above the river on the right bank the Fourvière hill is where the early Roman settlers built the old city of Lugdunum (the hill of the crow) in 43BC. The next day we crossed the river by a footbridge, took the funicular railway to the top and walked through Hauteurs Park to the Roman amphitheatre (which is actually two theatres) and the museum. Walking down the steps between the tiered seats was quite an effort as the day had become very hot. The theatre is still used for open-air performances and stage equipment, and floodlights were carefully concealed amongst the ancient stones.

Behind the stage we found Roman gravestones, and stone coffins, laid out in the brilliant Provençal sunshine. This had once been the Roman cemetery and some of the stones still had clearly decipherable inscriptions. I was particularly taken with one bearing the name Cordelia. I wondered who she was and what her life had been like in this city so far from her native Rome? Had she been happy? I gather the Romans generally liked it here and stayed for 600 years until the fall of Rome in 476AD.

The splendid Musée de la Civilisation Gallo-Romaine has been built on several levels overlooking the theatres and was disgorging various parties of foreign tourists as it was now lunchtime. We walked on to the pompous, mock-Byzantine basilica of Notre Dame de Fourvière, which we had seen from the river. It was built in the late 19th century to demonstrate the wealth of the Roman Catholic Church and compensate for the fact that the political clout of the church had waned. It was difficult to realise that it had stood through two world wars, as the dazzling white stonework had an air of having been built only last year.

Standing on the esplanade beside the basilica we could see the whole city of Lyon laid out before us in the shimmering heat and beyond it a vista of the countryside. Snaking into the city were the two rivers, the Saône, which had brought us here, and the Rhône which we would be travelling down the next day.

Back at river level we found the ancient cathedral of St. Jean Primatiale, which looked much more solid and welcoming than the pretentious basilica above. It has stood on this spot since the 15th century withstanding the sieges of time, revolution and war, and is a perfect illustration of transition from Roman to Gothic architecture.

We planned next to visit old Lyon (*le vieux Lyon*) and decided to fortify ourselves with lunch first. I finally got my *frites*, at a pavement café in the Place St. Jean. They were cooked to golden brown perfection, and were every bit as good as I remembered, especially when eaten with a classic French omelette, accompanied by red wine and French bread. The French cut their *frites* much thinner than we cut our chips, with a crispier result.

I had been looking forward to visiting the old city, which consists of the Saint-Georges, Saint-Jean and Saint-Paul quarters, and in particular I wanted to see the *Traboules Lyonnaises*, vaulted passage-ways cut through the heart of the buildings. This whole area is a living community as well as being Europe's largest Renaissance area and France's leading restored area, reflecting the splendour of Lyon in the 15th and 16th centuries. The tenements are built round courtyards, reached from the street through *traboules*. They were once the homes of silk workers (*canuts*). They were part of the army of 3,000 such workers who, prior to the industrial revolution, worked at looms on the upper floors of their houses. The *traboules* were used for transporting bolts of silk across the city, quickly and under cover, as silk spoils if it gets wet.

Traboules can also be found in the districts of Croix Rousse and Merciere St Antoine in another part of the city where the silk workers also lived.

During the last war, when Lyon was the centre of the Resistance movement the *traboules* were used by Resistance workers avoiding German street patrols. Nowadays they're a tourist attraction and a sign on the door of our first one told us that these ancient passage ways give access to residences within the buildings and an agreement had been reached between the city council and the residents to the effect that the residents would be responsible for opening the door during daylight hours to allow access to tourists, and the council responsible for keeping them free of rubbish and emptying the dust bins. That seemed a fair arrangement.

Passing through the *traboules* you reach open courtyards where you can see the balconies of the apartments above. I felt like an intruder, seeing people's washing, children's toys and evidence of their personal

169

lives opened out for the prying eyes of tourists. In some cases access to the apartments was via a spiral, stone staircase, although occasionally a lift had been installed.

That day the old city was thronged with tourists of all nationalities, admiring the mediaeval and Renaissance buildings which were once the residences of Italian merchants and bankers. Street musicians and entertainers, as well as street traders, added to the atmosphere of festivity and colour.

At the end of one *traboule* we found a mediaeval boutique selling replica dresses from the Middle Ages: hooded cloaks, pointed shoes, tabards and velvet dresses, even a suit of armour. The lighting was dim and ancient music added to the atmosphere. I almost expected the French equivalent of Merlin to materialise out of the stonework. It seemed entirely in keeping.

Another old courtyard amongst the merchant's houses was an architectural gem, with an old well in one corner, filled with red and white geraniums, and decorative overhangs supporting the spiral staircases, which were delicately fluted and formed into a fan.

John was intrigued with the way the old buildings were repaired. Often a crack in a stone block would be held together with an iron rivet. There must be lots of problems in maintaining these old buildings.

Sightseeing over, it was not without some apprehension that we viewed the final leg of our journey down the mighty Rhône, which begins in Switzerland and carries the melt-water from the glaciers to a delta formed above Arles by two rivers, the Small Rhône, which ends at the town of Saintes Maries-de-la-Mare where the gypsy festival is held every year, and the Big Rhône which joins the sea at Port St-Louis-du-Rhône, our final destination, but still several days away. We had been told to expect a mighty flowing river with plenty of hazards, and were glad to have Steve and Maureen with us; they had done it before and were able to reassure us.

The stories I had heard about the Rhône had been very worrying. We were about to discover the reality – the Rhône is a big wide river,

170

used as a trading route since ancient times and with a reputation for violent currents, shoals, rocks and cliffs, making it quite hazardous. This reputation was well deserved until the late 19th century when it was tamed by the use of dams, locks and groynes to slow down the current and create a good channel. Going down used to be not too bad, but coming up was a struggle, and the early navigators, without engines, had to resort to a variety of methods of travelling against the fast-flowing current such as we had seen in the museum at St. Jean-de-Losne. As well as towing the boats manually or with animals, they also used grappling irons.

Since the last war the old locks have been abandoned and diversion canals have been built with huge new locks at the downstream end. At each lock there is a hydroelectric scheme, enabling the generation of 16,000 million KWh of electricity per year – about a third of France's total consumption.

In the *Navicarte* I found the following notes:

"The hydro-electric harnessing of the river by the C.N.R. (Compagnie Nationale du Rhône), transformed its initially strong fall into some sort of stairs whose steps are the locks, the little fall between them allowing navigation without major difficulties. However by periods (sic) of strong flow the overflow weirs are opened and the current can locally reach up to 7 - 11km per hour. Then the river carries driftwood and other floating objects which are dangerous for the screws (propellers). Your engine will have to be powerful enough to stem the current. If you are going downriver your speed is even higher than that of the river and a collision with a fixed obstacle will most certainly mean shipwreck. Navigation without danger can no langer (sic) be assured when the flow of the Rhône exceeds the P.H.E.N level (highest navigable water-level)."

Scary stuff but we had few problems, although after we reached Port Napoleon we came across a boat whose crew had had a moment's inattention and were swept onto a groyne, piercing their hull. Of course the boat sank, but the water was quite shallow. Apart from the damage to the boat they got off quite lightly.

The current wasn't too fierce and assisted our passage. We soon got the hang of the locks, and any problems we did have were due to the boat and that confounded steerable leg, and the weather.

When we left Lyon a strong breeze was blowing, which freshened as the morning advanced. Blowing, as it was, against the current it whipped the tops off the waves and threw spray high in the air and over the foredecks of the boats. We needed light wet weather gear to prevent us getting soaked whenever a particularly big one caught us on the nose. It got very choppy and we wished we had our masts up so that we could use the sails to steady the boats. We were glad we were used to sailing in rough weather at sea, and had keelboats, rather than flat-bottomed riverboats as our keels helped to steady us. Riverboats would find it very rough in these conditions and I wondered how *Orca* had got on.

The first of the huge locks was just outside Lyon and then we were in the Rhône proper. The industrial suburbs were left behind, and the countryside of Provence began to reveal itself. The hills were bathed in sunshine, and covered with vineyards, whilst red-roofed villages and ancient churches clung to their sides. We hadn't expected the Rhône to be so beautiful – I thought it would be all industrial.

We travelled at about 8 km per hour but this didn't seem very fast. The main channel was clearly marked by red and black stakes, and all the diversion canals were also easily identifiable.

On this first day we had three locks to negotiate, and their size was awesome, dwarfing all other locks we had encountered so far. Generally they were about 12 metres wide, 195 metres long and almost 12 metres deep. I reckoned this would accommodate 216 double-decker buses in three layers, with four rows of 18 buses in each layer – quite a size.

Our procedure was to call the *éclusier* and request permission for 'two little English boats' to use the lock. He (they were all male on this river, usually being ex-barge skippers) would reply telling us how long we could expect to wait. Small pleasure boats could expect to wait up to 45 minutes, and were passed through in groups whenever possible. On this first day the longest we waited was 20 minutes.

Commercial traffic had priority and we gave way to a huge tourist boat at our second lock. He gave us quite a fright by sounding a loud long blast on his horn demanding his right of way. We pulled over hastily and allowed him into the lock.

The bollards to which we attached our ropes were set into the wall of these locks on huge posts, and slid up and down with the boat so that there was no need to adjust the length of the rope, or re-attach it. This made using them very easy. Beside each bollard was a ladder, for access to the lock side. Occasionally bollards would be broken and ladders missing and these were marked with a red flag.

Chefren in Rhone lock

At each lock there were notices telling us that life jackets must be worn in the locks, but we had never seen anyone wearing one, and this is France after all. We ourselves hadn't felt the need. If anything happened I wouldn't want to depend on a life jacket, I would grab the ladder and be up there as fast as my legs would take me. I got into the habit of always choosing a bollard where the ladder was intact.

The action of the locks was so smooth we almost weren't aware that we were moving, except that we gradually descended into a concrete lined hole. I expected to feel claustrophobic but they were so big this didn't happen.

By the time we reached the lock at Vaugris, which was completed in 1980, we were feeling quite *blasé*, but pride always comes before a fall. We had problems with the reverse lock – again. John couldn't use the engine to stop the boat and I had to get a line on a bollard very fast. I managed to get the forward line on without problems, but the stern line caught under a deck cleat – Murphy's Law. I managed to untangle it and get it on the bollard just in time to prevent the stern swinging out into the lock, but I was left shaking at the knees. I'm

173

learning how to have the lines prepared for these locks and what to look out for.

The final lock of the day was Sablons at the end of an 8 km. diversion. Leaving the lock we found the surface of the river was a sea of floating logs. Both Maureen and I mounted watch on our respective foredecks as our skippers steered a careful route between them. Fortunately the logs had collected in one part of the river only, and we were through them after about 1 km

By lunchtime we were in the shelter of the hills and the wind seemed less strong, but it continued very hot and I was steaming in my waterproof. It was too early in the day to stop for the night so we passed on through les Roches-de-Condrieu where there is a *port de plaisance*. It was a very attractive town spread over both banks of the river and I was so busy filming the scenery that I quite missed the fact that Lesley, from *Gee Bee,* was waving frantically from the port, where Steve was laid up with a twisted back. They stayed there a few days and she communicated with me by e-mail.

We were now in the heart of the Côte Rotie (red wine) district. The wine here is very expensive because harvesting the grapes must be done by hand as the hillsides are so steep that mechanical equipment cannot be used. I'm not sure that this makes the wine any better.

At the town of Ampuis there were water sports in progress and two large rowing boats, accompanied by several smaller boats, were preparing for a water tournament, encouraged by an excited crowd on the riverbank. It was a kind of water-borne joust. A man was standing up at the end of each boat on a platform, holding a long pole (like a lance), and wearing a padded breastplate indented in the centre to hold the lance. As we passed I could see figures being pushed into the water from the boats.

Water sports are, or have been, very popular on the French rivers and canals. We came across several places where specially created areas led off the main river, and where there were tiers of concrete seats for the spectators, as there had been at St. Dizier. We understand that the jousting began on the rafts of wood which were being floated down

174

the rivers to Paris (the *flottage*).

Further downriver we lost the shelter of the hills and were into the wind again, which seemed to be strengthening. The weather worsened and we regretted not stopping at Condrieu but it was too late. The boat was hobby horsing over the waves and the sensation became very unpleasant. If we'd been sailing at sea we would have taken shelter in a harbour, but here there was nowhere. The first possible mooring was a set of dolphins, huge mooring posts, several metres apart, designed for the big barges. We didn't even contemplate tying up there because of the distance between them.

We'd closed all the windows and hatches on board to keep out the spray and as the day progressed the temperature inside rose to 30 degrees C. It was wet and windy outside and unbearably hot inside. By late afternoon we had had enough and I was stationed permanently on deck with binoculars, scanning the banks anxiously for somewhere to tie up.

At Andancette, the next town, there was a pontoon but it was occupied by a large motorboat, and across the river the town quay at Andance was in the teeth of the wind, the boats would have been blown against it and damaged. We were forced to press on, exploring every possible creek and had barely time to notice the three Calvaries on a jagged rock above the town, built to commemorate three young girls who had thrown themselves into the river in despair when their fiancés did not return from the crusades.

Just below the town we found a tiny river, marked as the Bancel. At its mouth there should have been a small quay, marked on the map as *bateau dancing*. We took this to mean some kind of disco boat, but there was nothing to be seen and the river was much too shallow for our boats anyway. We were growing even more desperate.

The river widened by the town of Laveyron where a *quai nautic loisirs* (quay for leisure boats) was marked. Steve called us to ask if we would go in first and assess the depth. Our echo sounder showed 0.6m, which was much too shallow for either boat.

Approaching the quay had been a tricky operation against the current and into the wind. *Chefren* has a large area above the water compared to the amount below and catches the wind easily. It didn't help that we had trouble with the steerable leg again and discovered a new problem. The leg kept changing from port to starboard of its own accord. Just when we thought we were headed away from the quay, the boat would begin to approach again. I had to stand at the helm and hold the lever into position whilst John turned the boat round and got back into the channel again. We assumed this was linked to the problems with the steerable leg.

Once out in the river Steve called us again. This time he had spotted what appeared to be a small quay on the left bank, almost hidden by bushes. We took *Chefren* in very gingerly. I prepared ropes ready to lasso the mooring bollards if it proved suitable, and it did, being just long enough for *Chefren*. There were rocks under the water against the quay and we needed to use the ladder *Dolma* carried to hold us off and prevent the hull hitting the rocks. But we were just able to clear them and moor up with *Dolma* rafted alongside. What a relief. By now it was 17h30; we were all exhausted, and a little wet, and it was time for that panacea of all ills, a cup of tea. We subsided into our respective cockpits, side by side, and enjoyed the sunshine, sheltered from the wind.

This place is called La Ronseraie, with a chateau close by. It was Sunday evening and we could hear distant hymn singing. We were close to a footpath where families passed on their evening stroll, their younger offspring in the inevitable buggies.

Steve regaled us with tales of their experiences on the early part of their trip, down the Seine. At one point they had had some crew with them, and in one of the locks an enthusiastic crew member had thrown a rope to another boat, but forgot to tie it onto their own boat first, much to everyone's embarrassment. Steve's comment was: "One of the first rules of boating is that when you throw a rope you always make sure it's tied on." We reminded him of this later in the trip!

176

CHAPTER 13 – Provence

Camels and Llamas, and Wine 'en vrac'

That night was very disturbed. The water was still restless and *Dolma*'s ladder was gently hitting the quay all night, its metallic clang serving as counterpoint to the cicadas and the frogs, underscored by the sound of the water slapping against the hull.

Morning brought cloud and an attempt at rain but this eventually cleared giving us weak sunlight and an uncomfortable temperature of 20 degrees C by 10h00. The wind was still with us but had died down somewhat.

As the journey progressed the scenery became quite spectacular. The low hills gave way to rocky crags, each one topped by its own ruined castle. There were lots of trees, especially the characteristic Lombardy poplar lifting its dark spikes to the sky.

We were now in the Côte du Rhone district, and vineyards occupied every inch of the hills on each side of the river, surrounding the little towns and villages, conjuring up vistas similar to the Rhine. Each vineyard was proudly marked with the owner's name.

But a pervading smell which had been with us since the previous day was polluting the atmosphere. It was a strong smell, as if there were a gas leak, and which spoiled this otherwise beautiful area. I understand that this was only temporary as it quite put me off the idea of drinking wine from this region.

On this day there were only two locks. At the first we had to wait for a commercial barge, *Hiroshimo*, to catch us up and he had precedence into the lock. We took the opportunity for a break, with real French coffee and croissants. This was becoming a mid-morning ritual, which I counted as a small success because John refuses to eat croissants at home. The *confiture des groseilles*, which we had bought at the street market in Longueil-Annel, complemented them well, and of course you can't eat croissants without real butter. We were just finishing when we were given the green light to enter the lock.

We put on a burst of speed after the lock to keep up with *Hiroshimo*, and saved time by going through the next lock with her.

We were now within reach of Valence where we hoped to spend the night in the *port de plaisance*. Having learned our lesson from the previous day we kept to our decision to stay there, even though it was only 12h30 when we arrived. We didn't want to find ourselves without a mooring again.

The entry into the marina was quite difficult due to a submerged dyke, but the channel was clearly marked by buoys. Having negotiated the entrance we found a very well maintained marina, with water and electricity, toilets, showers and a laundry, with a chandlery and a crane close by; a *supermarché* within walking distance; and a swimming pool at the nearby campsite.

Beyond the visitors' pontoon at the entrance, several finger pontoons extended from the grassy shore, each one with its own little gate. In all there was accommodation for 300 boats.

It was lunchtime and the *Capitainerie* was closed. Being British and obeying instructions we tied up at the visitors' pontoon, had our lunch and filled up with water. A German motorboat, arriving later, made his way straight into the marina to tie up alongside a compatriot, who seemed to be waiting for him. When we went to book in later he was in the *Capitainerie* and for the first time we saw French officialdom in action. The German wanted to stay where he was on the pontoon with his friend, but *Le Capitaine* was having none of it. There was quite an altercation but *Le Capitaine* was adamant despite the German's *fait accompli*. *"Non, non, Pontoon D,"* *Le Capitaine* insisted, and the German had to move his boat to another pontoon – he was not pleased. *Dolma* and *Chefren* were split up too, which seemed to be something to do with the relative sizes of the boats. *Dolma* was two pontoons away from *Chefren*. It was a big marina so we had a long walk to socialise. We solved the problem by using our ship's radio.

Later in the day we all walked to the *supermarché* about 1 km across the motorway. We were happily gazing at the delicatessen counter, deciding what to eat that night, when we became aware of an unusual sound. We were in the midst of a cloudburst and torrential rain was drumming on the roof of the *supermarché*. We were totally unprepared for this, being still dressed in shorts and open sandals. Lightning flashed overhead, rain came down vertically and the car park was soon awash. We waited until it had eased a little before setting off back, laden with plastic bags containing our purchases, but not only did we get rather wet, so did *Chefren*. We had left the main overhead hatch in our cabin wide open and the whole cabin was soaked. The cushions on which we were to sleep that night had taken the full force of the rain, and there was a major mopping up operation to be done. Fortunately we had lots of newspaper on board, which is very absorbent, and also an efficient heater, which helped the drying out process, and our night wasn't too damp.

Everything was still wet by morning and a heavy mist hung around obscuring the beauty of the surrounding hills – and the river still smelled.

We were told we would need to wait at our first lock, Beauchastel, but this had its compensations; the mist had lifted and we had a superb view down the Val d'Isere to the distant Alps.

After 30 minutes a huge barge emerged from the lock, shadowed by a small German yacht, like a buffalo with its attendant ox-pecker. The lock was very slow in operation and it was 1½ hrs before we were on our way again. We are never frustrated by these delays as we might be in other circumstances. It is all part of the experience, and we are in no hurry.

At La Voulte sur Rhône, the next town, there was a low quay. We weren't planning to tie up here, which was just as well because as we approached the town quay we saw it was occupied by some animals, cropping the short grass. Closer inspection revealed they were camels – yes camels – together with a llama and some horses. A large yellow van with open doors stood close by. The circus must have been in town.

We had another wait at Baix-Logis-Neuf while a *péniche* cleared the lock. When he emerged we prepared to approach but a red light appeared alongside the green. I radioed the *éclusier* to ask if we could enter and the reply came back, "*Non*". He then said something about *sauvetage*, which I didn't understand but thought that perhaps he was saying that there was some danger and we should tie up again, which we did.

After a long period of waiting the green light eventually appeared and we entered the lock. As we were tying up the *éclusier*, a man of about 40, with a friendly smile and pleasant manner, came to greet us (or so we thought). He said: "*Vous ne comprenez pas - les gilets de sauvetage?*"

Suddenly I got it! He wanted us to put on our life jackets. I relayed the message to *Dolma*, and Steve and Maureen looked faintly ridiculous in bathing suits and life jackets.

We knew why he was enforcing the rule. Gwen and Gordon had told us there had been a bad accident at one of the Rhône locks recently. It had involved a *péniche*, and the wife of the skipper had drowned. From what we could gather the wrong sluices had been opened, and the *péniche* had been trapped under the sill of the lock gates and filled with water. The woman was in the cabin of the boat but I couldn't see how a life jacket would have helped her, but perhaps I had got the story wrong. From this point onwards we always put on our life jackets before entering a lock.

We now waited in this lock for a very long time. The gates opened, but the light remained red. There was no sign of any boats waiting to enter and John was all for casting off and going but his crew rebelled. Instead I called the *éclusier*, who told us that there was a '*petite probleme*', which turned out to be dredging outside the gate. If we had tried to leave we would have encountered a line of floating booms blocking our exit. On our way out I took some film of the dredgers, and waved to a young man at the edge of the dredging platform. He nodded in return and I realised that he couldn't wave, he was having a pee in the river, but like all Frenchmen he was quite unconcerned.

At Cruas we passed our first nuclear power station, one of the cooling towers was decorated with a huge mural of a child pouring water from a shell in its hand. We were obviously being given some kind of a message by the picture. The water is safe for children to play with, perhaps?

There is a small *port de plaisance* at Viviers where we planned to stay that night. It is managed jointly by a yacht club and a motorboat club. As we approached it looked very full and there was no one about to welcome us. It was reported to be very shallow so we decided to moor on the quay outside, but the top of this quay was a good metre above our heads and I was unsure how I was going to get ashore with a rope, especially as the bollards were set back from the edge. I didn't think I could lasso that far.

The problem was solved when the boat came to a sudden halt. We had gone aground. The depth here was reported to be 3m and we were approaching gingerly, only to find the actual depth was 1.2m close in and there was something under the water which the *Navicarte* referred to as a berm. In the French translation this is given as *banquette*, which we assumed was a flat rock under water. It was a long time later before we learned that a berm is a protruding area of reinforcement at the bottom of a wall.

Whilst we were aground we took advantage of the situation and grabbed one of our planks, which we leaned against the quay wall at an angle of 45 degrees. There was no time to argue as John placed one hand firmly on my rear end and pushed me up the plank to the quay with the rope in my hand. I then tied our lines to the bollards and we poled ourselves off the obstruction. *Dolma* tied alongside and fixed their ladder between *Chefren* and the quay for access to the shore.

This part of France was once part of the Roman empire. The town of Viviers is midway between Lyon and Port St- Louis-du-Rhone, our final stop, and commands a good strategic position at the confluence of two rivers where cliffs give a good view in all directions.

In the 14th century this region was embroiled in the Albigensian Crusade, which many believe was a simple conflict of Rome against the

Protestants. In fact it was not Protestants who were persecuted but Cathar heretics. These were dissident, pacifist Christians who believed that an evil deity had created the material world and a good god all the invisible rest. The crusade began in 1209 under the most powerful of the medieval popes, Innocent III, who instigated a reign of terror which lasted 20 bloody years. The crusade was followed by the birth of the Inquisition, expressly formed to hunt down and burn the remaining Cathars. As a result there was permanent conflict between the bishop and the count of the area which was only resolved when France became a kingdom.

Cesar Borgia, son of Pope Alexander VI, was the first duke here. The dukedom later passed on to the notorious Diane de Poitiers, mistress of Henry II, and was later inherited by the Grimaldi family of Monaco who kept it until the French Revolution.

Another famous historical figure associated with the town was Bonaparte who seems, like Queen Elizabeth I of England, to have stopped everywhere. He was here in 1785 as an adolescent second lieutenant with the town's garrison.

An all-too-brief tour revealed winding alleyways and narrow streets in an old part of town on a hill above the modern centre. A hot and dusty climb led us to a terrace on the north side of the cathedral, where we had a spectacular view of the route we would travel next, including the Montelimar plain and the Chateauneuf power station. A sign on the cathedral informed us that we were now entering the 'midi' proper. We could expect it to get much hotter from here on.

When we were finally on our way we saw the cathedral standing proudly above the entrance to the gorge.

We were now in that part of Provence settled by the Romans as a province around 123 BC. In letters home they talked about 'going to the province' and thus the name of the area was born. Evidence of the Roman Empire, including amphitheatres like the one in Lyon, is found all over Provence.

Leaving Viviers we quickly entered the Defilé de Donzère where we were swept rapidly between steep cliffs on the one hand and tree-clad hills on the other. It was spectacular rather than scary. At the end of the gorge we turned into a 28km deviation canal where we passed the nuclear power stations of Pierrelatte and Tricastin, which processes the enriched uranium France uses for its nuclear armaments and atomic submarines. There was also a crocodile farm. There could be the makings of a blockbuster film in this – "Lyon overrun by mutant crocodiles affected by nuclear fall-out" – that sort of thing.

We eventually reached the Bollène lock, the most recent and the biggest on the Lower Rhône and probably the biggest in France at 23m rise and fall (five double-decker buses), and also, at the time of its construction, the highest in the world. It was begun after the liberation of France and in a period of five years 600,000 cubic metres of concrete were used in its construction and 50 million cubic metres of earth were moved. It came into service in 1952 as part of the hydro-electric scheme, and provided another 2 billion KWh of energy per year for the grid system, more than 10% of production at that time.

We waited for a German motorboat to catch up and as we circled outside the lock we had problems with the reverse lock again. John thought he had fixed it but as we entered the lock it jumped out again. "Quick, quick, get a rope on," shouted John, "the stern's swinging out!"

I secured the forward line over the bollard and as the stern began to swing John threw me a line, cunningly disguised as a tangle of rope. I couldn't sort it out quickly enough to get it over the bollard. Instead I grabbed the boat hook and took a purchase with that until I could untangle the line. I try very hard to coil ropes in such a way as to remove the tangles, but it's Murphy's Law that whenever you need to throw one in a hurry it will take perverse revenge and twist itself into a Gorgon's head.

The *éclusier* came down to take the names of the boats, as this was a port of registration. We were all dutifully wearing our lifejackets, but no one on the German boat was wearing one and nothing was said to them. There is no consistency in the rules.

Considering this was the biggest lock on the Rhone it was badly

183

maintained. Most of the ladders had either been taken away or rusted away and there were holes in the sides of the lock, only tiny ones but as we went down spouts of water showered onto us. Sheer concrete walls towered above us as we descended and there was time to admire the feat of engineering which had designed and built this awesome edifice. As we descended I waited in anticipation for the gate to appear, like a giant guillotine rising ominously over the boat and dripping water onto our heads.

Our stopping place for that night was to be St-Etienne-des-Sorts, a great contrast to the mighty, modern lock, being an ancient village with few facilities but lots of character and charm. We spotted its small, new pontoon just before lunch. It looked big enough to hold our two boats and was empty. Then we became aware of a motorboat coming fast from the opposite direction, looking as though it had every intention of mooring on the pontoon. We put on a burst of speed and attempted to beat him to it, but he was much too fast for us. Ruefully we exchanged smiles and Gallic shrugs, saying '*C'est la vie*' as he tied up and we squeezed on the end with *Dolma* rafted alongside. The motorboat was a workboat belonging to the Rhône navigation and we realised later that he had only pulled in for lunch. *Dolma* was able to take his place later and it was soon their turn to have another boat rafted alongside. This was a small Danish boat named *Joker* who requested permission to tie up. The skipper, Torben, was a thin, grey-haired elderly man, who had left his wife at home to make this journey. He was glad to have someone to talk to and spoke good English, telling us he got very lonely at times. He travelled with us the next day as far as Avignon, and then went on ahead to finish the trip quickly. We met him again in Port-St- Louis where he was leaving *Joker* for the winter.

St. Etienne is a delightful village, a mixture of old and not so old buildings, with new bungalows on the outskirts. We wandered down narrow streets of old stone houses and discovered the 'commercial heart of the village', a narrow street which widened out at one end, where the local bar/restaurant, Le Platane, had placed tables in the

184

shade. At the narrow end of the road was a bread shop bearing a hand-made sign boasting that it sold butter and drinks, and a grocery that also sold Butagaz. Both shops were closed. We saw a lunch menu on a blackboard outside Le Platane and went in to inquire about an evening meal. We found an all-male clientele, seated at scrupulously clean tables applying themselves seriously to their meal. They were seated at one end of a long, low ceilinged room, with a flagged floor and stone walls decorated with amateur murals of rustic scenes, and a bar by the doorway. We approached the lady behind the bar and were told the evening meal would be served between 19h00 and 21h00 and that the price would be 65FF. We booked a table and left to continue our exploration of the village.

The Mairie was also the post office where one could buy stamps and telephone cards. It was located in a modern building on the outskirts, but was closed for lunch. Making our way back to the boat along the river we discovered the local co-operative wine *cave*. Earlier in the day we had seen tractors pulling trailers filled with grapes along the main street. This then was their destination, and a notice told us that they were allowed to use the title Côte du Rhône Villages and sold wine *en vrac*. There was no smell here so we returned later with some of our own bottles to have them filled from a barrel using a pump rather like the ones used at petrol stations. It was dispensed in a huge barn-like building with concrete floor and walls. Around the walls were big cylindrical vats of wine, turned on their sides like a series of gypsy caravans. It was all very informal and the price of the wine was less than £1 per litre.

Almost every day Maureen and Steve had been swimming in the river. I had never liked the look of the water, but today it seemed a little clearer, and it was so hot that after lunch John and I decided to join them. I lowered my steaming body into water which had come from the glaciers of Switzerland and listened for a sizzling sound. The water had warmed up slightly and after the first shock I was able to enjoy the pleasant sensation of the cool water on my over-heated body and had a pleasant swim.

185

In the evening we returned to the bar/restaurant for our meal. We were intrigued because again all the customers in the restaurant were male. There were about seven of them grouped round the television set by the door. We concluded that they must be workers, perhaps here for the *vendange*, the grape harvest, and their wives and families must have been left at home.

I had hoped this would turn out to be the country meal I had been longing for, but again it was quite elaborate. *Tarte au Poireaux* was followed by mouth-watering *Boeuf Bourguignon* served with pasta, a platter of local cheeses, and generous babas which dripped rum down our chins and hands, together with fresh coffee. We also sampled a couple of pitchers of the local wine, which was very acceptable, and which I would buy as an alternative to the Côtes du Rhone.

During the meal there was great excitement from the football spectators round the television. Whenever a goal was scored there was a loud, long drawn out shout of *"Oui!"* (Wheeeee!) Not until the match was over did they turn to their tables and apply themselves to the meal. Not for them TV watching whilst eating. This is France.

Afterwards walking back through the town in the warm summer evening we were struck again by the mixture of old and new. An ancient church dominated the village, where old buildings had been modernised and tiny modern apartments constructed over ancient stables, accessed via decrepit courtyards. Built on to the church was an apartment, perhaps for the *curé*, where a parrot in a cage overhung the street.

This had been a pleasant interlude in a rural setting; things would be different tomorrow as we were heading for the bright lights and the tourist areas.

Lyon to the Mediterranean

CHAPTER 14 – Arles and Avignon

The Bridge and The Bulls

S teve knocked us up early the next morning to report that Torben (in *Joker*) had untied and was already on his way. We hastily cast off ourselves in order to catch him up and use the locks together. This would save a lot of time. A

Bridge at Avignon

German motorboat which had been anchored on the other side the river also followed us, obviously with the same idea.

The towns and villages here were beginning to look very Mediterranean, built of pale yellow stone, their roofs constructed of typical red curving tiles looking very picturesque and providing a perfect nesting site for house martins under the eaves.

After 4 km, shortly before the deviation canal, we saw another atomic energy centre but were quickly past it and into the countryside again.

Soon we were passing Chateauneuf du Pape, which has given its name to one of the most prestigious vintages of the Côtes du Rhône. The chateau has had a very chequered history since it was built by Pope John XXII in the 14th century. It was plundered and burnt in 1562, later re-built by the bishop of Avignon, only to be demolished again in 1944 by bombs. All that can be seen now is a piece of wall and a tall tower.

We found *Joker* waiting at the first lock, Caderousse, tied to a small pontoon. Torben was ostentatiously wearing a bright orange safety harness of the type used for securing oneself to the boat at night. He explained that he did not have a life jacket, so he put that on and no one had challenged him. It probably looked like a life jacket from a distance.

This lock was just a baby at a mere 9.50 metres, and there would only be one more before Avignon.

Once through this lock the German boat which had hung back since St. Étienne put on a burst of speed. I suspected he was heading for the *port de plaisance* and wanted to get there before us to be sure of a place. As he raced past us I contemplated waving a symbolic towel, but thought better of it. Sure enough when we reached Avignon he was already installed. Fortunately for international relations there was plenty of space.

Approaching Avignon the river divides and re-joins below the city, forming an island. The city itself with its *port de plaisance* is on the smaller branch, just outside the walls of the old city by the famous bridge, and we had to travel down the main stream and turn back into the smaller branch to reach the port. When we turned we were motoring against a very strong current, which caused some problems in mooring.

Dolma went ahead to find spaces for us, but the only one that seemed wide enough for *Chefren* was one we would have to reverse into, and the current would be with us. It is much easier to manoeuvre a boat in a small space if the current, the tide or the wind is against the boat. This gives better steerage. In this situation we had more fun and games. Whenever we started to reverse, the current took us sideways. John was getting quite steamed up and shouting to me to get a line on but he wasn't able to bring her close enough for me to do so. In any case I couldn't work out which side of the boat he was going to bring alongside the pontoon.

By now Steve and Maureen had tied up and they, together with a small crowd, were waving frantically from the edge of the pontoon. They had found another berth which we could approach up-current. Once we understood what they were telling us we made an approach into the new berth where we found willing helpers to take our lines. These were some of the permanent residents of a small international community based in the port who made us very welcome.

It felt good to be tied up in Avignon with its world famous Pont St-Bénézet. Our first sight of the *port de plaisance* had been as in a photograph, framed by one of the arches, the boats bathed in sunlight, which dappled the water around them.

There was drinking water and electricity by every boat here, and reporting later to the *Capitainerie* we found all the facilities one could need – telephone, shower, laundry, guide books and maps. The marina had been purpose-built by the local Chamber of Commerce, and could take boats up to 13m long. Bigger boats could tie up to a quay a little further upstream.

The temperature reached a searing 32 degrees C by noon, sapping all our energy. I now know why people who live in hot countries are thought to be lazy. A siesta followed by a dip in the river was the best way to spend the afternoon. We found the current extremely strong but the water clearer.

It was dusk before I could bestir myself to do some housekeeping, and I got out the washing machine to take advantage of the water and electricity on tap. Washing in that heat was a steamy process and I lifted the machine into the cockpit under the sun canopy, where the atmosphere soon resembled an old-time Chinese laundry. John and I worked together. I washed everything in the machine in sudsy hot water, whilst John rinsed in a bucket of cold and we pegged the clothes on the guardrail. Very soon we were bathed in perspiration with our hair hanging in damp tendrils around our faces.

In the midst of this the couple from the motorboat alongside came round, eager to swap some English books. The woman was English but I think her partner was French. It was difficult to tell as he spoke excellent English with scarcely any accent. They told us they were leaving the next day to attend the christening of his nephew in Paris so I might have been right. They had lived in this marina for seven years and worked locally. I asked them what the weather was like in winter. They told us it was cold but at least dry, with blue skies and sunshine every day. It was hard to imagine it ever being cold here.

That evening as the sun set beyond the rooftops of Villeneuve-lès-Avignon on the opposite bank, the sky was a blaze of rose and gold, lighting up the stonework of the famous bridge. Later it was illuminated by floodlights picking out the symmetry of the ancient arches and throwing them into shadow. The traffic became quieter and an air of stillness fell on the river, allowing us to relax on deck, enjoying the beauty of the bridge and the town walls beyond.

Built during the 12th century this bridge once spanned both arms of the river and the island between them. It was the only crossing point on the Rhône, the natural boundary between the Kingdom of France and Empire of Rome. The banks of the river are still known today as Kingdom and Empire. Legend has it that the bridge was inspired by a young shepherd boy, Bénézet, who heard divine voices instructing him to build the bridge (shades of Joan of Arc). It was destroyed by Louis VIII during the Albigensian Crusade, and rebuilt in the late 13th century, but the locks and barrages had not been built then, and raging floodwaters damaged it again. It was finally abandoned in the 17th century. All that remains today are four of the original arches, and a chapel dedicated to the bridge's patron saint. But it is a great tourist attraction.

The song about the bridge is known the world over, and whilst we all sing *sur le pont* (on the bridge), it should really be *sous le pont* (under), as the dancing used to take place on the island, under the bridge.

The next morning dawned clear, dry and warm, perfect for sightseeing. There was no dew so the washing was almost dry.

On our way into town we paid a visit to a boat on another pontoon. It was the twin sister of our own, a Prout Snowgoose named *Wild Goose*. The owner was underneath the stern of his boat, in his dinghy. Guess what? He was having problems with his steerable leg. He and John compared notes and he asked if we knew of a boat repair yard. We told him about the one at Valence. He was making his way back to Britain single-handed, having been delayed by the problems with the leg, and his crew had gone home to return to work. A single-handed journey would be very difficult with a faulty reverse as he wouldn't be able to rely on crew to lasso bollards. He was rather preoccupied so didn't invite us aboard, but promised to call on us before we left. However, we didn't see him again, and at intervals during the rest of the trip my thoughts returned to his problem and I wondered whether he made it.

We began our tour of Avignon from the famous bridge and were able to look down at our boats riding peacefully at their moorings whilst the Rhône flowed swiftly beneath the arches. Looking towards Avignon rising on its hill, we could see a jumble of ancient golden buildings with the Palace of the Popes and the Cathedral of Notre Dame des Doms dominating the lower roofs. At the side of the cathedral were trees and high rocks, which we planned to climb for another view.

We left the bridge by way of a little house built into the city wall and climbed the steps of the Rue Pente Rapide, to the Place du Palais, where the mighty Pope's Palace forms one side of a wide cobbled square. It looks like a sumptuous fortress, which it once was, having been the residence of the Popes in exile in the 14th century, and the biggest Gothic palace in the world. The Popes only stayed for 100 years or so but their legacy dominates the town. Avignon once rivalled Rome as the centre of the Catholic world.

In the square tourists were queuing for the ubiquitous *petite train*, whilst others were leisurely sipping coffee at pavement cafes, shaded by plane trees.

It was almost too hot to climb the exposed steps leading to the gardens above but the view was worth it. We could see over the Rhône and the bridge towards Villeneuve-lès-Avignon on a hill. crowned by a great golden fort, and below it the tawny roofs of the old town bathed in sunlight. Villeneuve is sometimes mistaken for Avignon itself, or thought to be a suburb, but it is a completely separate town. It was built in what was the kingdom of France, so that the king's servants could keep an eye on the potentially hostile empire just across the river. The crafty cardinals of Avignon, in the Holy Roman Empire, built sumptuous palaces here from which they used to commute across the bridge, because prices were cheaper in France, and the politics less turbulent.

In English we might translate the name of Villeneuve-lès-Avignon as Avignon New Town, but in fact the *lès* means near (as opposed to *les* meaning 'the' plural). So it is New Town Near Avignon.

Oddly enough the kingdom of France 'owned' the Rhône, and when it flooded, as it often did in spring, the French exchequer taxed those residents of Avignon whose houses had been flooded, and therefore 'used' the water.

We recovered on a seat under a tree before retracing our steps and taking the Rue Peyrollerie (the street of the coppersmiths), which hugs the walls of the palace. We passed beneath a huge buttress supporting its Grande Chapelle and I took a moment in this narrow, twisting street with its ancient stone walls and pavement to absorb the atmosphere of mediaeval Avignon. Little seems to have changed.

Emerging into the Place de l'Horloge, we found the Banque de France on the corner, protected by huge iron gates. We fondly imagined we might be able to change some money here, but were stopped at the gates by a disembodied voice from the intercom telling us they were *ferme*.

In fact we found it incredibly difficult to get change for travellers cheques in Avignon. We tried several banks until finally we were directed to the Credit Agricole where not only did they change the cheques but didn't charge commission. Pity we had to get this far on our journey before finding this out. We also discovered later that we could have used the post office.

The banks in France are quite awesome. In even the smallest towns the entry is usually via a locked door, with an intercom system. In others there is a double set of doors, often accommodating only one person at a time, which is rather like entering into the Star Ship Enterprise. You pass through one set of doors, which close after you and find yourself in what feels like a glass escape hatch. You then wait for a second set of doors to open. I felt like saying, "Beam me up, Scottie!"

Larger banks have an armed security guard at the door, and there are always armed guards around when the money is being delivered. The citizens of France are allowed to carry guns, and we had seen guns on sale in specialist shops. Armed robberies must be quite a reality.

The Place de l'Horloge is a vast open space, the centre of Avignon's street life and it was thronged with tourists. Once it was the forum of the Roman city and the clock of its name is all that remains of a mediaeval tower, adapted to become a bell tower in the 15th century.

Nowadays pavement cafés line one side of the long square, facing the *Hotel de Ville*, and we pushed our way through the leisurely crowd to where a huge carousel of galloping horses dominated one corner. I always think that carousels look better at night when the noise of the traffic is stilled and the organ music and bright lights can come into their own. But even in the heat of the day the carousel had attracted customers and the supercilious-looking, gilded horses were rising and falling to the strains of a fairground organ, their nostrils flaring and their bright harnesses flashing in the sun. The faces of the children were like those the world over, a mixture of apprehension and delight – as they clung to their wooden steeds. For a moment I was seized with a childish desire to join them, and relive again one of the pleasures of childhood, but my inhibitions got in the way and I turned instead to enjoy the spectacle of a couple of smaller carousels where diminutive fire engines and motorcars offered alternative transport for the very young. Close by a caricature artist had found a small space in which to work and a line of street traders faced the cafés, poised to attract customers, and were selling the usual tawdry souvenirs.

After a little wander through the crowded streets we returned to the port, via a gate in the wall and through the car parks outside the town. We stopped to exclaim at the way the vehicles were parked. There was not a square inch of room, and many of the cars were parked so close to each other that drivers must have climbed out through their sunroofs.

We visited the city again with Steve and Maureen in the cool dark of the evening. We found the crowds gone from the place du Palais and instead two South American street musicians were serenading the customers at a pavement café, the haunting strains of their pipes and guitars floated into the night air and echoed from the walls of the palace. A small group of young people were sitting on the Palace steps enjoying the sound of the unusual instruments and we joined them for a time, allowing the music to soothe us after the heat of the day, blending magically with the twilight and the atmosphere of old Avignon.

In the Place de l'Horloge the carousels were now quiet, the street vendors gone, and in their place more street musicians entertained the café crowds. A marionette played a miniature piano, but the sound was drowned by a Maurice Chevalier look-alike serenading the diners as he wandered from café to café. A conjuror gained an attentive audience of two Asian children, whilst behind him skateboarders used the wheelchair ramp of the *Hôtel de Ville* to hone their skills.

Torben was in Avignon with us, but the next day he had again left early. This time we didn't need to rush to catch him up, as there are no locks between here and Arles. Instead we left a little later but whilst the sun was still low in the morning sky, suffusing the air with a red-gold radiance. Our final view of the port was the perfect symmetry of the boats framed by the arch, and all painted in glowing light.

Yesterday we had watched with interest and some apprehension as huge logs, often as big as trees, were swept down the river. This morning we caught up with them, bobbing silently on their way downriver. Fortunately many had drifted out of the channel and we were able to pick our way between the rest.

We found the Rhône to be easily navigable at this time of year; the floating logs were our only hazard. Shipping was light and there was enough room to avoid the monstrous double barges and push-tows.

From this point there are two possible routes to the Mediterranean. There is the Canal du Rhône à Sète that leaves the Rhône north of Arles and travels west for 158 km before entering the Mediterranean. There is also the Rhône itself, which continues on to Port St-Louis where it becomes too shallow for navigation, and pleasure craft must enter a short canal via a lock in order to reach the sea. There are various other small canals, including the Canal d'Arles à Bouc, which on the map looks as though it is a possible route, but again is non-navigable at the seaward end. We were heading for Port St-Louis on the Rhône.

Moving out of the craggy area of Provence into the flatter land of the Rhône delta we saw some industry but it was scattered. Apart from the ugly, smelly sprawl of Tarascon, it was inoffensive. Again there was a smell but it was less repellent and soon left behind.

The current assisted our passage, but wasn't fierce. If I had to travel in the opposite direction I would choose this time of year, when the flow is less. But our fear of the Rhône had gone completely, and I wouldn't be worried about travelling against the current on our return trip, providing we had a reliable engine (and working steerable leg). I had been expecting a raging torrent.

By lunchtime we had reached Arles, an ancient town with which I have had a love affair since my first visit twenty years before. It is the capital of the Carmargue, a strange area of marshy plains, salt pans, lagoons and rice fields, and a paradise for bird watchers and photographers. Flamingoes, black bulls and white horses are found here, as well as painters and petro-chemical plants.

Finding the *port de plaisance* full we moored at a very high quay opposite the town at Les Trinquetailles. Judging by the position of the rings high up on the wall, this was meant for barges, but there was plenty of room. Steve was apprehensive because they once tied up in a similar place and returned to find that a bargee had untied one of their lines and the boat was almost adrift. The quay towered above our heads and we had to get ashore by climbing a very long ladder. Prior to my boating days I would never have dreamt of doing such a thing and been very nervous. But needs must and I have now become quite *blasé* about these ladders.

Once upon a time Arles' tiny *port de plaisance* was entirely occupied by live-aboards of the worst kind, unfriendly and unhelpful to pleasure craft, and abandoned boats took up spaces on the pontoons. This has changed now, but there is still heavy demand on the port and later we were to discover why it was so busy.

Arles is a colourful market town and the largest municipality in France, boasting the largest set of Roman remains outside Italy, including a Roman amphitheatre and a Roman theatre, both still in use. The amphitheatre is used for bullfights and the theatre for open-air rock concerts. The town is also famous for its once resident artist, Vincent van Gogh who decided it was the best place to come for inspiration, as did Cézanne and Chagall.

Because Steve was anxious about the safety of the boats we decided to take it in turns to visit the town. Tossing a coin seemed to be a good way of deciding. John and I won the toss. It would be our turn that evening and Steve and Maureen would go in the morning.

198

That evening as we walked along the quay we looked down a side street and saw a group of men blocking the thoroughfare with six-foot high steel fences of vertical bars, and a sign warned that there would be bulls in the street that evening. My pulse quickened. A small crowd was forming and the young men were grinning with anticipation. A sense of excitement filled the air and continued in the town. Hurrying to discover the source of the sound of circus music we saw a band of musicians marching down the street. The red dresses of the women and white suits of the men providing a colourful picture. The streets were crowded with people and loud with music. We discovered that it was the day of the *corrida*, the bullfight, a big event in Arles. No wonder the *port de plaisance* had been full.

We made our way to the flag-bedecked amphitheatre at the highest point in the town. This is an almost complete building and through the row of open stone arches behind the topmost tier of seats we could see crowds of excited people, and heard their excited roar.

The amphitheatre is huge, seating 21,000 people, and on a previous visit I'd stood in the centre of tiers and tiers of seats which formed a circle round the floor, watching apprentice *razeteurs* practising their skills on a 'bull' which was a hand cart decorated with horns, pushed by another apprentice.

In the street outside the arena today were numerous souvenir stalls, open air eating places and all the trappings of a festival. Round the back was a decorated, flat cart pulled by two caparisoned horses and attended by men in traditional dress, almost like Morris dancers. The blood on the cart made us suspicious that the *mis a mort* is practised here, in spite of what some guide books might say, but on the other hand it could just be for injured bulls not dead ones. In other parts of France they merely take cockades or ribbons from the bull's horns.

Walking back into the centre of the town, seeing the crowds and experiencing the festive atmosphere, John and I felt very sad that

Maureen and Steve were missing it all.

"We must go back for them," John said, "they can't miss this!" I agreed and we retraced our steps to Les Trinquetailles where Maureen & Steve were enjoying a glass of wine in the fading light.

They were grateful to us for returning and agreed that as no barges had appeared to chase us off by now we were probably safe. My own feeling was that the French were so unheeding of regulations generally that no one would bother us.

Back in Arles the bullfight had finished and the crowds were streaming down into the old town. The Boulevard des Lices was particularly crowded, and there was an air of anticipation. We found steel fencing again, and didn't have to wait long before four horsemen appeared, well, three and a horsewoman. They were the cowboys or *Gardiens* who look after the cattle in the Carmargue. They wore cowboy hats with fringed trousers and jackets rather like the American cowboys. The horses had western-type saddles and savage gag-type bits.

After a few minutes they returned, galloping down the street, two in front and the others behind flanking two bulls. The bulls were smaller than I would have expected and completely black. A crowd of youths in red neckerchiefs were chasing after them and it seemed that their aim was to get the cockades from the bulls' horns. The only reason for this seemed to be a display of manhood; survival of the fittest perhaps?

The riders passed out of sight only to return a few minutes later with more bulls. This happened three our four times and in between each passage the crowds spilled across the street, craning their necks to look for the horses' return.

I was worried about a family close to us - two tiny girls in traditional gypsy dress with flowing tiered skirts, accompanied by a young woman in a leather mini-skirt and jacket. The youngest, who couldn't have been more than 3 or 4, was wandering into the street unheeded. Her mother was too engrossed in taking photographs to notice. If the horses and bulls chose to return at that moment,

200

would she get out of the way in time, I wondered? Fortunately her mother did eventually take control and I was able to stop worrying. But no one seemed to be at all afraid, even when, on the third run, the youths not only grabbed the cockades, but got a bull as well. It stopped in the street, the youths holding on to its horns, whilst the horses galloped on. There was a moment of confusion when no one seemed to know what to do. The poor thing seemed frightened and confused, its flanks were heaving and its eyes rolling but it didn't look very fierce. Finally with a toss of its head it shook the youths free and ran off, scattering the crowd in all directions. Now we saw why the barriers were designed as they were - the bars were wide enough for a man or woman to pass through, but not for the bull. The crowd melted through them, some shinned up lamp-posts and others climbed onto vehicles. Yes, there were one or two parked cars here, bearing stickers asking their owners to remove them because of the bulls. I wonder what state they were in the next day?

One youth was injured, and we saw him being helped away, limping and clutching his leg. My sympathies were all with the bull.

Having had enough of this, we retraced our steps to the Place du Forum where we found a fire-eater and street musicians entertaining a crowd which filled the square and almost obliterated the statue of the poet Mistral at its centre. Everyone was in festive mood, laughing, chatting, and greeting friends. They were drinking in bars and at pavement cafés in the square and down the side streets, but there was no sign of drunkenness save for an elderly vagrant fast asleep beneath a tree, alongside a band playing deafening jazz music, a discarded bottle at his feet; and a noisy, but cheerful Englishman outside one of the bars vociferously inviting us to join the singing of 'When the saints come marching in'.

Maureen and Steve decided to return to the boats but John and I needed to find somewhere to eat. We wanted to eat in a side street away from the worst of the noise and found a table at Gigi's, a tiny bar/restaurant seating about thirty people. There was a small bar in one corner and the menu of about eight dishes was chalked on a blackboard on the bare stone wall.

Our meal, which was the nearest we had come to a simple country meal (with *frites!*), was served by Gigi's son, a young man in his late teens with the traditional red neckerchief. He was delighted at my attempts to speak French, and in turn tried out his English, proudly telling us he'd been to England, and visited London and Stratford on Avon.

Later, back across the river, we found bull baiting in progress at Les Trinquetailles. Here there were no *Gardiens*, instead two small black bulls were standing, frightened and confused, in an open space being taunted by several youths, whilst the crowd whistled and jeered. Perhaps this is part of their toughening up process, preparing them for the bullring? Now and again one would paw the ground, toss its head and chase its tormentors across the square, whereupon the youths would shin up the lamp-posts, or squeeze between the barriers.

Sickened and impotent, we returned to *Chefren* determined never ever to eat Arles sausage, which is made from bull meat.

The following day we had a further opportunity for sightseeing which included the Maison de Dieu, the institution where Van Gogh received treatment for his personality problems – now a cultural centre and where we had coffee in the gardens which he painted.

Returning to the boats we prepared for our last short journey. I was looking forward to this with mixed feelings. It would be wonderful to have arrived safely, and to have met the challenge, but sad to have finished the trip which had given us so much pleasure.

CHAPTER 15 – The End of the Journey

Mosquitoes

The river broadens quite considerably after Arles and is very shallow inshore, but there is a well-marked channel and we made good progress. Towards lunchtime we heard Maureen calling on the radio, but they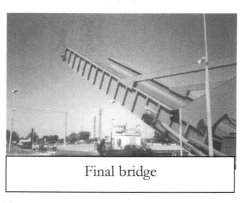

Final bridge

were having problems with transmission and we couldn't make out what she was saying. They were a long way back and we slowed down to allow them to catch up. As they got closer I could see Maureen on the foredeck, waving a towel. Oh dear, trouble, we thought. But she was merely attracting our attention to suggest a lunch stop and a swim. It was not smelly here so we agreed and pulled into the side, out of the current where it was shallow enough to anchor but where our feet didn't touch the bottom. The water was murky and we couldn't see our feet, even the intrepid Steve didn't try to go where he could put his feet down. He probably would have sunk into the silt. But we enjoyed the cool water and kept our heads well in the air to prevent ourselves swallowing it. This spot was in a curve of the river, sheltered by bushes and trees, and would make a good overnight anchorage.

We were now travelling along the edge of the Carmargue. Our view was restricted by the trees which lined the banks, but we did see some ibis, sitting at the water's edge. (We saw flamingos later in the trip calmly feeding in the *étangs* close to the oil refineries – an incongruous sight).

The only sign of humanity here were the ubiquitous small quays for fishermen, none of them in use.

Eventually we arrived at Salin de Giraud, where a smaller canal leaves the main river, leading to the Gulf of Fos in the Mediterranean. This canal is forbidden to pleasure boats.

Carrying on down the main waterway we saw huge pyramids of salt piled high around the salt pans, and a little further on ferries crossing the river at Bac de Bacarin, presumably taking workers to the salt plant on the right bank. A huge ship, registered in Split, was tied up to the quay, taking on salt, and later we saw this same ship locking out into the Mediterranean. Lower down was another ferry which took railway wagons across.

The water here was polka-dotted with seagulls, hundreds of them floating on the surface, heedless of the passage of the boat. Perhaps this was an indication of a fishing area?

Soon a large square tower constructed of ancient bricks became visible on the left bank, surrounded by the low buildings of the town, and a quay where a huge black *péniche* was moored. There was a *port de plaisance* for small boats, and eventually a cut leading to the final lock with a lock basin and another quay. This was Port-St-Louis-du-Rhône - we had finally arrived. But the excitement was not over yet.

Turning into the lock cut we prepared to tie up at the quay, *Chefren* going in first to assess the depth. Suddenly there was a frantic call on the radio. It was *Dolma*. They had gone aground on a shoal and were unable to get themselves off. They needed us to give them a tow. We manoeuvred in close to take their lines and making jokes about negotiating 'terms of salvage'. Maureen threw me a strong rope which I secured to a cleat on *Chefren*'s stern. John put the engine into gear and we pulled away. As we did so, to our horror (and amusement), we saw their rope snaking across their decks before the end of it dropped into the water. It wasn't attached. "What was that about making sure ropes were tied on, Steve?"

A very red faced Maureen re-attached the rope and we tried again, but still failed to budge them. On the third attempt we tried pulling them off backwards instead of forwards and at last succeeded. Now we could moor up and get the kettle on.

This is the last river port at the mouth of the Rhône and is also a seaport. The river isn't navigable here, because of the silt brought down by the river over the centuries. Every year the Grand Rhône sweeps 20 million cubic yards of gravel, sand and mud down to its delta - enough to cover Paris in a silt blanket 25 cm or 10½ in. thick. Some of this is swept away by the sea, but enough remains to extend the delta by 10 to 15m a year.

Boats which want to reach the sea must lock into the Canal St-Louis and we were amazed at the size of the ships which used this route, even huge cruise liners, taking their passengers on a trip up to Arles and Avignon. The lock is very long and wide. It isn't very deep and its main purpose is to provide an interface between the sea and the river. It has regular opening times, as there are virtually no tides which need to be taken into account.

The focus of the town is the canal which is well used and we had a few nervous moments when huge seagoing ships came very close to *Chefren* and *Dolma* as they entered the lock.

The quay here was mainly occupied by fishing boats but there was a section of public quay where there were two fuel pumps and a small rusty crane in front of a much-repaired corrugated iron shed, bearing the notice, *J. L. Messiant, Constructions Navales, Reparations, Ravitaillement, Gazoil, Matage, Carenage, Gardiennage*, together with a telephone number. Another notice behind the diesel pumps advertised a sail loft in the town.

There were three pleasure boats already tied up. A very smart Swiss yacht named *Merlin*, and another two occupied by live-aboards, one of these being only partially completed and little more than an empty hull.

The crew of the Swiss boat, a young couple, were sitting in their cockpit as we arrived, but they didn't come ashore to take our lines, or greet us in any way. We found this surprising but the following day discovered the reason when the skipper came around to say hello. They had recently arrived to pick up a local man who was to crew with them on an Atlantic crossing. When they arrived they were told he had had a fatal heart attack while swimming a day or so before. What a sad thing to happen. They were still in shock.

He also told us that there would be no crane available for another week, due to holidays. They had been hoping to have their mast raised. We would have to get this done in the marina.

Later that first evening we decided to take a walk ashore with Steve and Maureen and explore the town. We had got no further than the lifting bridge which gives access to the canal, 100 yards away, when we became aware that we were surrounded by clouds of mosquitoes - and they were biting. Poor Maureen became enveloped in a fine cloud of them and they seemed to be having a feeding frenzy. I've never experienced anything like it before. We took to our heels and raced back to the boats, closing all the doors and hatches and anointing ourselves with mosquito repellent. Looking out of the windows we could see clouds of them fluttering around the streetlights. Maureen had been bitten far more than any of us, which was a new experience for me, because I'm usually the one they go for.

For the rest of our stay in this part of France we covered ourselves with mosquito repellent whenever we went out. I don't know how the locals cope, although we did learn that this was a particularly bad time of year because of the rice and grape harvests.

Our bikes came in very useful. We used them to cycle down to inspect the two marinas which were our possible laying up places. They were Port Napoleon and Naval Services. The road was little more than a tarmac covered track running alongside the canal and I was reminded of the Manchester Ship Canal at home. This too is set in marshland and surrounded by oil refineries. An unfenced

206

railway line ran alongside the rutted road, used by goods wagons pulled by a noisy steam engine and I recognised one or two names of international firms stencilled on the sides of the wagons. Port-St-Louis is part of the Marseilles complex on the Gulf of Fos, handling products which include hydrocarbons, liquid chemicals, timber and wine.

Apart from the town of Port-St-Louis, and its associated fisheries and the industry, there is nothing here for miles, except the Carmargue. The nearest large towns are Arles and Marseille.

After visiting the marinas, listing their facilities and working out relative costs we decided to leave the boats at Port Napoleon. As well as chandlery, and boat repair sheds, this marina had cars available for hire, a mini-bus for transport to the shops, and a very helpful receptionist who spoke excellent English with a rather odd accent, who would make our travel arrangements for us. (Her odd accent was due to being married to a New Zealander.) Naval Services has excellent dry storage, but no storage in the water, and they charged a daily fee for living aboard. This would add to our expenses, as we wanted to do live aboard and do some more work on *Chefren*, not only in the next week or so but also when we returned in the spring. There was a third marina in the port basin but this had no storage facilities out of the water.

Both Port Napoleon and Naval Services are surrounded by the wild countryside of the Carmargue and as we travelled between the two marinas we passed some animal pens and buildings where the *Guardiens* live. Some small bulls and horses were out in the compounds. The bulls are said to be very intelligent animals, with stamina and sureness of foot, and are used by the *Guardiens* at *ferrades* when they cut out year old steers and drive them for branding. Apart from that they probably spend the first couple of years of their lives here in fairly peaceful seclusion, then one day, wham, they are loaded onto a wagon and find themselves in the middle of Arles, being tormented by noise, horses and human beings. No wonder the ones we saw looked frightened and

207

confused.

Port Napoleon was very busy and unable to make arrangements to lift our boats out of the water for a few days, so we decided to stay tied to the public quay, closer to the shops and it was free.

Our bikes came in useful for a trip to the local *supermarché* on the other side of the port basin. The *supermarché*, unsurprisingly, had lots of anti-mosquito products. There were products to spray in the air, lotions and gels to rub into the skin and candles to keep them away. We stocked up both boats.

We now had time for some sightseeing and went on foot into the town, starting by visiting the tourist office which was on the water front in La Tour St. Louis, the tower which we had seen as we approached. This tower was built in 1737 to defend the mouth of the Grand Rhône. It later became a customs house, and was the last in a series of such buildings. Each time the river changed its bed a new customs house had to be built. It later came into use as a lighthouse.

Two very helpful assistants supplied us with maps and information but were puzzled when I asked for directions to the ancient stone circle, which I had seen on a signboard. They eventually realised that I was asking about the *Cercle des Anciennes*. This was the local Derby and Joan club! I'd thought it was a smaller version of Stonehenge. In France *ancienne* means senior as well as ancient. I returned red-faced to Maureen and Steve to confess my mistake.

On our way into town we had passed a little café building named La Cabane, and built to resemble one of the old cabins of the Carmargue. Outside was a sign saying,

CHICKENS
STOP
PARKING

Wow, do chickens have driving licences now, and are they

208

making a nuisance of themselves by parking here?

The main street of the town runs parallel to the river and at right angles to the port basin. We found an excellent chandlery where we were able to buy one or two necessities for the boat and spent a long time contemplating the purchase of a boarding ladder. In the Mediterranean we would need a good means of access to the water for swimming. We delayed the purchase until next year.

A huge liner was moored in the port basin, and its passengers were taking a walk along the quayside. Port Napoleon is an interesting little town with a population of 10,393 but isn't the sort of place you'd put on the itinerary of a Mediterranean cruise. In fact they had disembarked their passengers for a coach trip to Arles and Avignon.

It was definitely out of season here. Although there were many restaurants and bars, most were closed. There is a campsite nearby, and a pretty Provençal hotel. Tourists must come here in season, presumably for fishing, water sports and sailing, as well as to visit the Carmargue. But the town seemed dead now.

We ended our sightseeing by visiting the restaurant grill, Le Passeport, built in the shape of s ship and advertising itself as a piano bar. It specialised in seafood. We wanted a cooling drink.. The customers were a handful of local people who stared curiously at us as we ordered our drinks, greeting us politely but offering no further conversation. We took our drinks outside to the shade of a brightly coloured awning.

It had been overcast all day and later that evening we heard the roll of thunder and saw flashes of lightning overhead. The rain didn't come until after dark. When it did, it was torrential. One moment the thunder was a few miles away, next it was overhead. It then moved away, only to return later. The rain continued all night, falling in relentless sheets, obliterating the scenery and turning the quayside into a lagoon.

The next morning the rain had lessened and we were contemplating walking into town to find the street market when we

209

became aware of activity on the quay. At first we thought the crane driver had returned because the shed was open and people were sheltering inside, but trestle tables had been set up, and bunches of flowers laid on them alongside bottles of wine and plastic cups. From the sombre faces we realised that it was a wake for the man who should have been crewing on *Merlin*.

By lunchtime the rain had stopped and we ventured out. The market was closing but we managed to get one or two last-minute bargains before the rain began again, the last baguettes and some vegetables. We took refuge in a *salon du thé*, which was more like a snack bar, serving meals as well as tea and coffee.

All around us French workmen were having lunch, and the most popular dish seemed to be the French equivalent of a 'chip buttie' - a *baguette* stuffed with *frites*. It looked and smelled very tempting on this wet day and we debated whether to stay and have lunch ourselves. I remembered I had a packet of frozen *frites* in our fridge and offered to make 'chip butties' for both boats. My offer was accepted. I got the fat temperature just right, and produced several platefuls of hot, golden *frites*, which we packed into the fresh *baguettes* we had bought at the market. Mmmm.

My job in the afternoon was to make a mosquito net to seal off our cabin. We had on board the type of net you see in films, which drapes over a bed. The roof of our cabin is too low for this and the net hung around our faces when we were in bed. We decided to open it out and attach it by Velcro to the open side of our cabin and, together with another mosquito net which we fixed to the main hatch, our cabin became completely mosquito proof. As the cabin is also the saloon of the boat we were then able to entertain in a mosquito-proof environment.

The mosquitoes were worse after dark, so I got into the habit of preparing our evening meal before dusk and we would eat it in the mosquito-free zone. We tried not to emerge again until daylight when the mosquitoes had gone, taking it in turns to dash out with the dirty plates and to make a drink, leaving the washing up until morning.

During the day we did one or two small jobs around the boat, but left the major work until we reached the marina. We watched the fishing boats going out and returning with boxes of strong-smelling fish. Most of these boats seemed to be in dual ownership, with one man using the boat in the morning and the other later in the day. One of them had a pretty partner who came down to help him unload his catch. One day he took a gun with him on his fishing trip, and returned with a dead duck as well as his fish. We also watched the big ships going through the lock. One day there was a huge passenger liner, which needed a tug fore and aft to manoeuvre it. It came down the Rhône and waited alongside our boats until it could enter the lock. It towered over us and the crew peered down at us curiously from their lofty deck. There almost wasn't enough room for this boat in the lock and the forward tug had to go in first turning sideways at the end. The ship came next, and finally the last tug which also had to fit in sideways before the lock could close.

There is a lifting bridge across the end of the lock. This is the only access between the town and the side of the canal on which we were moored, a peninsula known as the Presqu'île du Mazet. There is some industry on this side, some modern housing, a campsite and the hotel, as well as the two marinas. One day, because the bridge was up, a fire engine with lights flashing and bells ringing had to wait 15 minutes before it could cross. What terrible scenes of devastation did it encounter when it arrived at the blaze I wonder?

The lock is opened five times per day to pleasure craft, to minimise inconvenience to the town, and a notice on the lock gives these times. It may open at other times for commercial craft but yachts are not allowed through on these occasions.

Once upon a time the bridge was notorious for breaking down and causing shipping to be held up, sometimes for days, but it has now been replaced by this splendid new turquoise and blue bridge which works beautifully.

We had been there three days when *Gee Bee* arrived. They were going straight through to Port Napoleon so that Steve could use the phone line, and there was only time for a quick cup of tea before the lock opened and they went through in company with three other small boats, all going to the same place.

It was great to meet them again and catch up on their news. We heard all about Steve's back injury which had held them up for about three days, and their quite different experiences of the places we had visited.

They were very glad they had gone straight into the marina, and later in the day we wished we had gone with them because another storm blew up, probably the dreaded Mistral. The thunder and lightning were as bad as the previous day, but now accompanied by winds that strengthened to gale force and agitated the water, producing white-topped waves which rolled in from the direction of the sea. The rain was so heavy that again it restricted our visibility.

We were violently tossed about and only our fenders prevented us from being dashed against the quay.

Dolma, alongside us, together with the other monohulls, were plunging up and down like demented rocking horses. *Chefren*, being a catamaran, has a gentler motion even in a gale like that, but we all passed a very uncomfortable night. Next day the storm had not abated and Steve decided he would like to go through the lock to see if they could find a more sheltered spot on the other side. But always at the time of lock opening the gale renewed its energy making manoeuvring very difficult. Even the fishing boats hadn't gone out. Added to the gale there was always a strong current in the lock, so he decided to remain.

One or two boats were foolhardy enough to venture out, perhaps they had no choice. One of these was a small fibreglass dinghy powered by an outboard motor. At the helm was a man of about thirty-five, with a child cowering in the bow, clad in only the lightest of wet weather gear. We felt sure they would want to come alongside and tie up as they emerged from the lock into the teeth of the gale, but no, they went on, turned right up the Rhône and were lost to view. They were probably heading for the tiny *port de plaisance* just around the corner.

On another occasion a yacht with its mast secured on deck ready for the canals, came out of the lock, and proceeded straight down the non-navigable section of the Rhône in the direction of the sea. The skipper was bent over the helm, muffled to the eyebrows and beyond in his wet weather gear. The weather conditions at the time were so bad that he was quickly lost to view in the curtain of rain. We stared after him in consternation. "Where did he go?" we asked ourselves. "He's going to run aground, and he's travelling fast!" We tried to call him on the radio, but there was no reply, and there was absolutely nothing we could do. To our relief, about 15 minutes later, he returned and went in the right direction.

We passed another uncomfortable night and in the morning discovered that Steve had spent most of it sitting in his cockpit to ensure *Dolma*'s safety.

However the sun came out and the water was calm again. Apart from the huge puddles and the water-filled motorboats tied to the quay, you wouldn't know there had been a storm. Thankfully this was the day we had arranged to go to Port Napoleon.

Whilst we were making preparations to go through the lock another English yacht requested permission to tie alongside. They had been anchored up river, by the ferries, all night because the wind was too strong for them to make any headway in spite of having the current with them. When they turned the corner by the ferries they found themselves in the full teeth of the gale. They had no alternative but to anchor and they too sat up on watch all night. They were feeling pretty shattered.

They had called the lock on the radio, and heard the *éclusier* say they would need to wait an hour and then contact the pilot. We were very puzzled by this piece of information, especially as the lock gates were opening as they spoke.

I called the *éclusier* myself and got no response but I did hear him speaking to another boat, which sounded like a big ship on its way in from the sea. I presumed this was the conversation that the other boat had overheard, and we persuaded him to cast off and lead the way into the lock. The *éclusier* called us then and asked us to be quick as there was someone waiting, and again I heard him on the radio talking about *trois plaisanciers* in the lock – us. The newcomers had obviously heard the instructions about the pilot given to the other boat. Sure enough when we were through the lock there was a huge tug towering above us.

The short journey to Port Napoleon took us first down the canal, passing fisheries and factories, and the cottages of the Carmargaise, as well as one or two fishing hamlets. We passed Naval Services from the canal side, and another smaller *port de plaisance* for local boats.

In no time at all we had reached the breakwater where the Phare de St. Louis marks the seaward end of the canal and we were at sea, in the Mediterranean at last. The welcoming blue water stretched before us.

We had little time to savour the moment turning almost immediately at the lighthouse and passing by a huge mussel bed and on into the Canal St. Antoine l'Hermite heading for Port Napoleon which was clearly identifiable at the end of the broad waterway.

This waterway had a deep marked channel in the centre but shallowed rapidly at the sides, and it was a strange sight to see mussel diggers, waist deep in water, only feet from our boat. We were able to see them shovelling spadefuls of mud into submerged containers, which they then riddled to remove the sand leaving only the shellfish behind. It looked hard, wet work.

Calling the marina on the radio we were allocated a berth and in no time at all we were tied up, connected to the electricity and walking ashore to explore the facilities. The marina was huge with dry standing for at least 300 boats as well as two huge hangars where boats could be stored under cover for an extra charge.

There was every possible convenience, including a snack bar, *le Nautilus*, which served simple meals, and bread was delivered by van every day. We met up again with *Gee Bee* on the next pontoon and called to invite them to join us that evening and celebrate our safe arrival in the Mediterranean.

Panta Rhei was there, already lifted out onto the hard standing and looking somewhat lonely as Riet and Ed had gone home. *Orca* too was laid up in a corner of the yard, but Torben had chosen to lay *Joker* up at Naval Services.

We cracked open a bottle of champagne which Colin had given us to celebrate our arrival. It was appropriate to be drinking his champagne, as he was then included in the group, in spirit if not in body.

EPILOGUE

Port Napoleon Marina, Port-St-Louis-du- Rhone

Tuesday, 21st September, 1999.

We are now safely ashore at Port Napoleon after two months travelling, albeit slowly, through the very heart of France, beginning at St. Valéry-sur-Somme, and ending here at Port-St-Louis-du-Rhone. According to my

Pontoons at Port Napoleon

calculations we have covered 699.6 miles (1166 kilometres), which included 283 locks and 270 hours of travelling in 26 days, with 44 rest days. It has been a fascinating experience and our job now is to prepare the boat for winter lay-up and put right the one or two little problems, and one big problem, which occurred during the trip. We've allowed ourselves two weeks for this.

The two boats, *Dolma* and *Chefren*, were lifted out of the water yesterday. It was a time consuming and boring process involving lots of standing around in the heat, waiting and watching. Each boat had to motor to the lifting bay, and wait until the crane had finished with the previous boat. The crane is a transporter type, with a wheel at each corner which can be manoeuvred independently. It has huge slings which are lowered into the water underneath the boat. The boat is then lifted aloft and hosed down

217

before being taken to its place on the hard standing.

My job after lunch was the cleaning and storage of the fenders whilst John began the overhaul of the engine.

By dusk we had to shut ourselves in our cabin again, behind our mosquito net. The mosquitoes here are BAD.

Friday, 24th September, 1999

Maureen and Steve have been very industrious and did most of their jobs whilst we were tied up outside the Port-St-Louis canal lock, and they went home yesterday. To save cash they decided to go by bus to Avignon, where they'd booked a coach to Paris and from there another to London. This will involve overnight travelling. Rather them than me. I once travelled overnight by coach from Austria to London and I vowed I would never ever do it again. The economy did not make up for the discomfort and I ended the journey with swollen ankles and so tired that I didn't know which way was up.

John and I have decided to fly back. The easyJet airline operates from Nice to Liverpool, which is our nearest airport at home. We were not sure how we would get to Nice from here, and suspected that the cheap fares advertised might all disappear quite quickly. But the helpful receptionist at Port Napoleon made enquiries for us and discovered we could fly home for 459FF each (£46) and the flight would take 2½ hrs. We can take a train to Nice from Arles for 187FF each (£19) which will take 3½ hrs and we can either go by bus, or by taxi, to Arles. We are astonished and very pleased at the low cost and have decided we can afford the taxi to Arles.

The only disadvantage to flying is that we can take so little luggage with us. Normally when we go home from a sailing trip our car is groaning with equipment and luggage, and on this occasion it would have included several bottles of wine, not to mention a few pieces of cheese.

It will be a new experience for us to leave our stuff aboard the boat, and we will have to trust our navigation equipment to the security of the marina.

John and I went over to help bring *Gee Bee* into the dock for lifting out. The boat ahead of them took a very long time to be washed down and transported to its berth, so we spent a lot of time hanging about. I had some washing in the machine so I cycled backwards and forwards keeping an eye on it while we were waiting. On my last trip, as I accelerated away on the gravel, the bike went from under me. I landed with quite a thump in an undignified tangle of bike, arms and legs. Everyone within range came running to assist. Fortunately for me I had a large purse in the hip pocket of my shorts, which cushioned the fall. Apart from minor grazes and a bruise which I expect will develop into a work of art over the next few days, I am unhurt. Lesley rushed aboard *Gee Bee* for their new, unused first aid kit, and returned waving it in the air and making siren-type noises. She was quite disappointed to discover that all I needed was an antiseptic wipe and a cup of tea to restore my equilibrium.

A young couple in a German boat alongside are hoping to leave tomorrow. They have been sailing in the Med for a year but now must return to Germany to work and replenish their bank account. They have given us a whole selection of pilot books for the Med. These are printed in German, but it is quite easy to understand the maps and the harbour plans.

They are selling their boat and have had an offer for it subject to survey and have been waiting for the surveyor to arrive. After waiting around all day, he sent a message to say that his car had broken down and he wouldn't be coming. They are not sure when he will come now. They shared their disgust with us and tell us that this would not have happened in Germany, and from my experience I think they are right. Punctuality and reliability are Teutonic virtues. They ask about efficiency and punctuality in Britain and I am sorry to have to tell them that this sort of thing happens there too, although not as often as it once did. The French do seem much more relaxed about work generally; maybe it's not such a bad thing. It's an interesting debate whether customers expect too much these days and whether we should lighten up a bit and take things as they come.

Saturday, 25th September, 1999

This is the part of owning a boat which makes me ask myself whether it is worth it. I've never given myself an answer, but I haven't given up, so I suppose that's an answer in itself.

Chefren now looks more like a 'project' than a home, with boxes of tools and pots of glue and paint littering the main cabin, the cushions covered with dust sheets, and in the midst of it all I am trying to maintain some semblance of 'gracious living', not to mention hygiene.

Half filled dry-bags stand waiting to consume bedding and clothes as these are used for the last time, and washed and dried.

All those little jobs we've been promising to do over the past weeks are now under way. They include putting an extra screw in the gunwale; repairing minor damage to the hull; changing the engine oil; and making new tops for the cockpit lockers.

Most days I am likely to be found on my knees with my arms in a bucket of soapy water, cleaning out lockers, or squeezed into an impossible space with a wet sponge in my hand, sweat oozing from every pore. John kneels in the cockpit with his head in the battery compartment making modifications to the boat electrics, or his arms in the engine compartment, covered with grease.

When he isn't doing this he is to be found underneath the boat correcting the problem we had with the steerable leg. It appears to have been a pin, worn and bent over years of use. He thinks he has sorted it – let us hope so.

The weather continues very warm. By afternoon it has reached 30 degrees and working becomes slow and difficult. I feel the heat pinning me to the deck. By five we are ready for cool showers and the security of our mosquito-proof cabin.

During the day we usually get one or two bites, often on the way to the showers, or at the snack bar. Surprisingly John is getting badly bitten for the first time in his life. We have no idea why, and he has been unscathed throughout the trip until now. The mosquitoes are cheeky too. Several times I have felt the prick of a bite and see the little so and so still feasting away. It takes a very firm blow to detach them from your skin. Ugh!

There is quite a strong wind today, which cools everything down and makes the temperature bearable outside. Inside the heat is stifling. Working in this heat, with the need to retreat from the mosquitoes by late afternoon is slowing the work down.

We leave on Thursday with a taxi collecting us at 10h00. There will be time for another look around Arles and our last French meal for a while. I don't want to go home, I have come to love life aboard, and enjoy being in France, but we will return at the start of the next sailing season.

Monday, 27th September, 1999

The temperature has dropped! Until last night we were sleeping with just a sheet to cover us and the hatch above our berth wide open, but during the night, at some point we needed the sleeping bag over us.

Yesterday the temperature was lower and it was easier to work. I found the energy to clean out the heads and the bilges in there, and have sprayed everywhere with mildew deterrent.

Later in the day I coated the new locker tops and the cockpit table, as well as our deckchair, with Hydrosol, a wood preservative. They look very smart and John will fit the locker tops this morning.

Washing our clothes is something of a problem as I want to leave everything clean and there is only one washing machine and one dryer for the whole site. There are over 300 boats, most of which are being laid up, like ours, for the end of the season. You can imagine the demand for the one machine. You have to place your bag of washing in a queue, and even then, if you are not there when the previous person takes their load away, you might lose your place. So I end up cycling backwards and forwards to try to get there at the right time. I've worked out that each wash takes 45 minutes.

Tomorrow I'll take a book and sit by the washer until it's my turn. I'm just dreading the machine breaking down under the strain. The tumble dryer has already packed up, but fortunately in this heat we can manage without. When I want a new washer at home I will definitely consider getting this make, it must be made of stern stuff.

Yesterday was a day for *Les Chevaliers du Carmargue* and there was a festival of blessing and an open-air meal in Port St. Louis. The *Guardiens* of the Carmargue were there with their horses parading through the streets. Lesley and Steve went in at lunchtime and their remaining impression was the cruelty of one of the riders towards a very nervous horse. His method of training was apparently to punch it in the face. The French are definitely not sentimental about animals.

Looking back over the journey I wouldn't have missed any of it, except perhaps the gale at the end, and I would definitely have taken more time to explore some of the wonderful little places we passed through. Even so, we have seen a lot of France which the tourists don't usually see, eaten and (dare I say it) drunk very well, become very fit and made lots of new friends.

The Channel crossing was uneventful, and we found our way into St.-Valéry via the buoyed channel without difficulty.

French officialdom was nothing to be worried about, and other than wanting to see our licence to use the canals and the ship's papers we haven't been asked to produce any paperwork. But this might have been a different story if we had been involved in an accident.

We got the hang of the locks and are in fact quite proud of the way we handled most of them, however I'm glad we only had the one sloping-sided one, but even these can be handled well, with practice.

Navigation on the Rhône was no problem, and the only thing

that bothered us there was the strong wind on the first day. We escaped the dreaded Mistral which funnels down the valley and cuts through you like a knife. The current assisted us and the channel was clearly identifiable.

The barges and *péniches* were not a particular hazard and we found their skippers courteous and friendly. Yes, it is possible to get stuck behind them in the narrow waterways, but, *c'est la vie*, they have a job to do and we are on holiday.

The only thing we would do differently is to buy our *Navicartes* or *Vaignon* guides before we left England so we knew exactly what to expect at each step of the way and could find the mooring places and identify the lock cuts more easily

I am looking forward to coming back next year, starting to explore the Mediterranean, and to having a wonderful reunion with all the friends we have made.

UPDATE CHAPTER

We return from Greece

We were delayed in our return to Port St. Louis to continue our sail to Greece because just as we were beginning to prepare for our return I was diagnosed with breast cancer. I had to remain at home for treatment, although we did manage a two week stay aboard *Chefren* in June, in between my courses of chemotherapy. We cleaned her up and serviced the engine. All our friends had already sailed away, but we made some new ones, had several lovely meals in a smart new restaurant which had replaced the snack bar, and acted like tourists visiting lots of wonderful places in Provence in a hire car.

I love Provence and this visit lifted my spirits enormously. We had time to visit Aigues-Mortes, Sts Maries-de-la-Mer and Les Baux-de-Provence amongst other places and it increased my determination to beat the disease and be back aboard the following year, which we were.

We sailed *Chefren* to Greece via Corsica and Italy and spent every summer for the next three years in the Ionian Islands, and one year sailed round the Peleponnese, the most southern tip of Greece, coming back through the Corinth canal. It was all very wonderful. We had worked and planned for this for so long.

But as the years went on we had to acknowledge that Greece had changed; it was getting busier, the lovely unspoilt harbours and anchorages we remembered from our flotilla days were getting crowded and polluted. Not only that, sailing is really quite hard work, hoisting and lowering the sails, anchoring and mooring, and all of this done in very high temperatures. A consequence of my cancer treatment was that I could not cope with heat and was extremely uncomfortable. We had to rethink. Greece had been our goal for many years, and whilst it is important to have a goal it is also important to recognise that goals may alter as circumstances change. So it was with us. We had loved the French canals on our trip down and had said to each other, "One day we will come back". Now we were on our way back and by the middle of 2004 we were back at Port-St-Louis and heading up the Rhône. We said that if we enjoyed the journey back as much as we had enjoyed the journey down we would sell *Chefren* and buy a motor cruiser to explore the inland waterways of France.

We set off back in early September which was an ideal time. August would have been just as good. In Spring the melt-water from the Alps swells the river, and similarly Autumn rains contribute to a very fierce current, and we would be travelling against the flow this time. We knew that two years previously floods had washed away the marina pontoons at Arles and Avignon. Would our 18 hp engine be man enough for the job, we wondered? What about the Mistral? No one knows when this cold, unrelenting, north wind will blow, or how long it will last when it does. It can make life difficult for small boats.

We had the mast removed in the marina at Port Napoleon, and tied on every fender we possessed, fastening wooden planks outboard to protect the hull in the locks and tunnels and were ready to set off.

Passing through the sea lock at Port-St-Louis on September 6th, just before 09h00, we were delighted to find that we only had 1kn. of current against us. We made a speed of 4.1kn. over the ground which augured well. The sun was shining and we began to relax and to admire the herons, cormorants and egrets which were using channel markers as vantage points from which to spot their prey.

We motored along under a blue sky in temperatures of 32 degrees C with all the windows and hatches open, waving cheerily to some yachts coming the other way and pulling to the side of the channel when we spotted a laden barge heading towards us. As it passed we fell foul of its considerable wash and were tossed about, dipping our nose into the trough of its wake and scooping up water across the foredeck. I rushed into the cabin to close the fore-hatch but too late, I was met by a huge wave which completely swamped the saloon.

Thankfully it was fresh water and it was so warm that by the time we reached Arles we had dried everything but the carpet. From that point we were more careful when passing the huge push tows and barges.

We re-visited Arles and were disappointed that we were no longer able to moor at Les Trinquetailles, but instead found a berth alongside what had once been the marina where twisted and broken pontoons lay abandoned on the bank, testimony to the devastating flood of 2002. However there was water and electricity and easy access ashore, and we spent a pleasant evening in this lovely old Roman city, eating savoury crêpes in the Place du Forum.

Waking next morning I was delighted to see a tiny bright blue kingfisher using our pulpit as a vantage point from which to get his breakfast from the river below.

As we reached the first huge lock of the Rhône we dutifully put on our *gilets de sauvetage*, but did not see anyone else doing the same. One new thing we noticed was small pontoons very close to the gates of every lock. At first glance we saw they had 'No Parking' signs on them, but closer inspection revealed a notice, in French, saying *sauf plaisanciers* (except for pleasure boats). These pontoons were very useful as we sometimes had to wait up to half an hour and they helped us keep out of the way of commercial traffic. But we had to be brave and get quite close to the lock gates before we discovered the waiting pontoon.

At Avignon all traces of the well-equipped marina had gone, another victim of the flood. Apparently the water was so high that the pontoons floated off the upright posts to which they were attached. But the harbour master's office, and showers, in the converted barge were still there, and we were able to tie up to the quay, in company with many live aboard *péniches* and some yachts.

All the boats we had encountered so far had been travelling south but here we met two who were going north and suggested travelling together to make it quicker negotiating the locks. They were happy to do this and one boat continued with us to St-Etienne-des-Sorts, and the other came as far as Mâcon, on the Saône, forming another of the nautical friendships which we had encountered on our way down and adding to the enjoyment of this kind of life. This was John and Jane who were time-sharing their boat *Conspiracy* and had six weeks in which to enjoy their holiday.

The sun-bleached village of St-Étienne-des-Sorts had changed a little. It still had its small pontoon[5] but the wonderful *auberge* where we had enjoyed a splendid meal was closed, and in its place a more modern café. The cave too was changed, probably for the better. It now had a new shop selling wine by the bottle and by the case, and there were smart new pumps dispensing Côtes du Rhône, and Côtes du Rhône Villages *en vrac*. We were able to buy enough wine to last us the rest of that trip and at less than €1 litre.

Leaving St-Etienne we were dreading the Donzère Mondragon gorge because here the river is funnelled through concrete sides and the current can be quite fierce. When we arrived we found the sides littered with debris left by the spring floods. It was strange to see huge tree trunks 7 metres above water level as we steered a slalom course between more tree trunks and patches of weed, which diverted our attention from the impressive 100m cliffs above.

At the head of the gorge we pulled into Viviers again. The little marina, run by the local yacht club had been extended and improved, and had showers and toilets. It was no longer necessary to moor to the high quay we had used on our previous visit. We stayed a couple of nights and enjoyed again the lovely old town which has been frozen in time.

---

[5] This pontoon also became the victim of floods later and had still not been replaced by 2012.

We dined with our new friends in the town square, and were served a memorable meal. *Escalopes Florentine* turned out to be turkey in a mouth-watering mushroom sauce, served with crisp, golden frîtes, and a pitcher of the local wine.

It was a long trip to our next stop, Valence, but worth the extra kilometres for the facilities offered by l'Epervière marina which has been greatly enlarged and the entrance channel dredged. The fuel pontoon was out of action because it was being moved but was due to re-open shortly.

The trip to Tournon next day was magical. On every side vistas of mountains and valleys opened up across to the Alps. Smaller rivers branched temptingly off the main channel between wooded banks; bearing notices "*Sauf plaisanciers*". The many smaller motor boats which had left the marina with us that morning had disappeared into these and I imagined them fishing, picnicking and swimming in the clear waters somewhere beyond the bend.

Tournon is on the opposite bank to Tain l'Hermitage a famous wine area where the vineyards cover the sun-lit slopes, dominated by the hermit's chapel which gives the area its name. We had not stopped here on the way down but our friends encouraged us to stop for a couple of nights and take a trip on the Vivarais narrow gauge railway which makes a spectacular journey following the river Doux through deep gorges on the edge of the Massif Centrale to Lamastre, a gourmet town. We joined them on the trip but were disappointed to find that the famous street market was just closing as we arrived – surely bad timing? But we had enjoyed the trip looking down into the deep gorges and watching the water swirling below.

In contrast to l'Epervière the small marina at Tournon had not been dredged or maintained for some time, and although we draw less than 1 metre we could not get in and had to tie up to some piles at the entrance intended for larger boats. As we realised we could not get into the marina John shouted "Quick, get lines on!" I managed to get the forward rope onto one of the piles and then had to balance along a short beam to the shore, run to the stern of the boat and balance along another beam to take a line from John before the stern swung away from the quay. I felt like a gymnast and all the time I was doing this I was conscious of the interested gaze of a crowd of tourists who were leaning on the railings above me, waiting for a coach. I was quite proud of my agility and speed in tying us up and turned to the spectators and made a little bow, whereupon they burst into applause.

In Tournon we also visited the museum, housed in the 16th century chateau, where one room was given over entirely to exhibits relating to the river and the efforts made to turn the raging torrent that was the Rhône into the navigable waterway of today. We saw a model of a paddle steamer with a wheel in place of keel, that could be lowered for the purpose of 'gripping' the river bed; and an oil-painting depicting a team of more than fifty wild-eyed and sweating horses hauling a commercial boat through the torrent.

We moored the next night in the well kept marina at Les-Roches-de-Condrieu which is famous for its white wines and also its waterway traditions. Bargemen were recruited from here and the town still hosts boat jousting tournaments. Behind the marina is a lake for swimming and wind surfing.

We had the wind against us the next day which took 2kn. off our speed and at times we were reduced to 3 knots. We hoped it was not the beginning of the Mistral. We were approaching Lyon where industry is more noticeable, but there are still woods in between each factory, and the first fingers of autumn were beginning to paint the leaves. Swans and herons fished at the water's edge. We tied up to the same quay we had used before which now bore a sign saying that it was reserved for pleasure boats[6].

---

[6] There is now a marina in Lyon, off the Rhône beyond the junction.

It was useful to be still in company with *Conspiracy* when we reached Lyon as we were able to take turns 'minding' the boats whilst we went to re-visit the traboules and the old town.

We breathed a sigh of relief to have navigated the Rhône to this point. Now we were turning into the Saône where the current would be a little gentler.

As we moved on we noticed that several new pontoons between Collonges au Mount D'Or, (PK 12), and St. Germaine (PK23.5). These included Fontaines sur Saône, and one opposite Port du Val de Saône. They would have been a useful and secure place from which to visit Lyon.

We by-passed Neuville-sur-Saône this time as I was very keen to spend a night or two in Trevoux just a little further north. Here we found a pontoon where boats were allowed to stay free for a limited period. It was either a new pontoon or we had missed it on our trip down. By sheer luck we had arrived at the time of the patrimonial festival and when walking into the lovely old town that evening we encountered stalls set up at the sides of the cobbled streets demonstrating old crafts such as basketry, clog making and ironwork. People on another stall were making French toast, and most of the stall holders were dressed in traditional costume.

The town had once been a principality with its own parliament and a governor and minted its own currency. A landmark on the quay was a huge tower with a sugar-sprinkler roof. This was once part of the ramparts but has now been incorporated into a hospital. The hospital was originally built for lepers, but in 1686 the local grand dame, the Duchess of Montpensier, sovereign of the Dombes, established it as a hospital. The pharmacy of the hospital, together with many old buildings in the town, was open for visitors and we were able to view the banks of drawers and big blue and white jars which had once housed the powders and potions, including leeches, used by the early pharmacists.

The main street of Trevoux, rue Casse-Cou, or break-neck street, is cobbled and a stream runs down the centre. It is bordered by timbered houses and shops and climbs straight up the hill from the bridge. From the top you can enjoy a wonderful view over the Saône valley.

Old hospital and tower, Trevoux

We said good-bye to *Conspiracy* at Trevoux. They were heading to Mâcon where they were planning to leave their boat in the marina, and left a day earlier than ourselves. As we travelled we noticed several sand quarries which we had not noticed on our way down, and which were not marked in the guide book. We had to slow down for sand barges several times and use our horn as warning. We passed through breathtaking scenery and colour washed villages bright with flower beds. The journey took us 6½ hours

'Our' pontoon close to the bridge in Mâcon was occupied by three boats. No one poked their heads out and invited us to tie alongside so we crossed the river and found a low concrete quay on the edge of a small park where the water was only 1 metre deep. From here we walked into town and along the way noticed signs exhorting the citizens to clean up after their dogs and maintain civic pride. Bins were provided and we actually saw someone use one. This is a first. That night the park bench close to the boat was used as accommodation by an old man with a grizzled beard and a woolly hat but he caused us no trouble.

The 14th century bridge in the town is the townspeople's pride and joy and when the Saône was being widened to meet European gauge standards for river traffic it was too low and therefore threatened with destruction. This was vigorously opposed and eventually a by-pass canal was constructed.

Since our previous visit I had taken an examination back in Britain and obtained my Inland Waterways Certificate (CEVNI). I found it very useful, particularly on the next day when we encountered a dredger in mid-stream. I was able to identify the red flag on one side (do not pass this side), and the red and white flag on the other (pass this side but make no wash). I felt very proud of myself.

Our next stop was Tournon where we tied up to the same pontoon as before, and had rabbit stew from the local charcuterie for our tea. Nothing seems to have changed, and when we reached Chalon-sur-Saône it too seemed the same. We stayed two days and the helpful staff at the Office du Tourism helped us make plans for our return to Britain. It seemed the best way would be to take the train to Paris and then use one of the cheap air lines to fly to our home airport of Liverpool.

Before leaving Chalon we had to visit a dentist. John had had trouble with a broken tooth before we left home and our dentist had made a temporary crown. On the first night in Chalon the cap broke up leaving him with a metal post protruding from his gum. At first he thought he could manage but by lunch time the post was causing him to have a very sore lip. On our way into town we had passed the local hospital and decided to call in and enquire as to whether they had a dental department. They did not, but the very helpful assistant asked us to call back in an hour when the lunch-time was over and she would phone and locate a dentist for us. Can you imagine this happening in Britain? On our return the assistant took out the Yellow Pages and started ringing dentists until she found one who could see us that day.

We made our way to a dentist in the middle of the town where the surgery was located on the first floor of an old building with an ancient lift in a wire cage. The dentist was young man who had no receptionist. He answered the door himself and whilst he was working on John he had to answer the door again and take a phone call. The crown cost €30 and has lasted much better than the English one.

We phoned ahead from Chalon and arranged a winter berth in the marina at H₂O in St-Jean-de-Losne which we reached two days later. Next day I used the computer in the Office du Tourism to book our flights home and walked into town to the NCF *boutique* to buy our train tickets to Paris and was very pleased with myself as I made most of the arrangements in French.

After readying *Chefren* for the winter it was hard to say good-bye but we packed our bags and headed for the taxi which was to take us to the station, looking forward to our return the following year.

FINAL CHAPTER

Bringing Chefren home

B y the time we returned to France we had already had a trip to Holland and found a canal cruiser we wanted to buy. We hoped to get *Chefren* back to England as quickly as possible, travelling all day and every day as long as the locks were open. It was May and the weather was still quite cool.

John with Liberty, our canal boat

We arrived at the boat late in the evening having taken the train to Dijon and taxi to St. Jean-de-Losne. We were planning to sleep aboard as the bedding had been left in dry bags and was usually fine to use after unpacking, but not this time. As I climbed aboard and stepped into the cockpit I stepped into water, uh uh! As I opened the cabin door I became aware of reflections on water in the darkness of the cabin. John fumbled for the torch which we keep by the door for such eventualities and shone it into the cabin. It was a foot deep in black smelly water. The berth cushions which I stand on end to air were now standing in the water, and a pair of sandals was floating forlornly on the surface.

We set to with buckets to remove the water and when we were able to step inside we set up our electric bilge pump. At this point I went to find a member of the marina staff and was feeling very angry that they had allowed our boat to get into this state. One of the directors arrived with a huge pump but by that time we had emptied out most of the water and his only contribution was to suggest that we spend the night in a hotel. When I enquired whether the marina would pay for this his response was "Why should we?" and when I replied. "Because we've been paying you to look after this boat" he just walked away.

We had no idea where the hotel was and as it was getting late and we were worried that it might be closing. We set off in search of it, wheeling our luggage behind us. Finding a lady at her open kitchen window, we enquired as to the whereabouts of the hotel. She told us we had crossed the canal bridge instead of the river bridge, but she not only phoned the hotel to ask them to stay open but took us there in her car. The helpfulness of French people never ceases to amaze me. The proprietor even provided a 'cold collation' for us despite the lateness of the hour. Pâté and cheese with a baguette, quiche, apple tart and a bottle of wine. As we had not eaten since breakfast this was a feast indeed.

We spent the next few days drying and cleaning *Chefren*. It appeared that the cockpit drains had blocked with leaves and seeds from the nearby trees. The secondary drains had taken over but that left 2.5 cm. of water in the cockpit which had seeped into the bilges and when they were full had risen into the central cabin. The accommodation in the side hulls was untouched. Fortunately I had taken a steam cleaner in our luggage in order to give *Chefren* a good clean preparatory to putting her up for sale. John had complained about the weight of this throughout the journey but we were glad of it now. The cleaner together with three or four days of beautiful sunshine helped us to get the boat habitable again. Our CD player and our heater would never work again and our berth cushions needed replacing but everything else cleaned up well, and we were assisted by a local boat upholsterer, Catherine. Our insurance company were wonderful and had an assessor with us by the first working day. He gave us the go-ahead to replace those things which were immediately necessary and we would sort out the rest of the claim when we got home.

Cleaning up the boat took us a week and as we left the weather began to deteriorate. We missed our heater as the nights were particularly cold and there was ice on the decks in the early morning. We breakfasted under way but had to stop for lunch because of the new European directive on working hours which restrict the *éclusiers* to a 35 hour working week. We were glad of this break, taking the opportunity to have a good lunch and rest before moving on.

The first thing we noticed as we left the Saône was that lock at Heuilley before the Canal de la Marne à la Saône had been made smaller. It had been reduced to a quarter of its previous size. But the *éclusier* was still there and we bought some honey from him as we had previously.

We used the same stopping places and were delighted when reaching Chaumont to find that our goat-herd *éclusier* was still there. At first we did not recognise him as he had on a baseball cap and waterproofs and seemed much younger. But when we reached his lock-keeper's cottage and asked about the goats, we identified him. I told him he was mentioned in my book and this cleared up a mystery for him as he said lots of British people had been asking about the *éclusier* who kept goats and wondered why. He no longer has the goats as the veterinary regulations had become too stringent for him, and he had given up his dream of a farm in Galway as the land prices had started to soar. But he seemed happy with a new partner. I gave him a signed copy of my book.

He again travelled with us through several locks and I was very disappointed to miss the bread van at one of them and he offered to buy me a baguette on his way to the next lock. He also cleared up a mystery about a tiny little house close to a lock at

237

Riaucourt, which we had seen on our previous visit. It had now been turned into a pretty mooring spot. He told us it had once been the dove-cote of a chateau whose grounds had been bisected by the canal, isolating the dove-cote. After standing empty and unused it was now having a new lease of life.

We did not encounter the 'monkey-man' *éclusier* but did stop at his quay, Donjeux, and found that the grassy, neglected quay of our previous visit had become a smart new concrete one with water and electricity. A French family were living aboard a barge permanently moored there. The children came and chatted to us and told us they went to the local school.

We found that many of the pontoons on this stretch of the canal had been improved by the addition of electric points, and several new pontoons had been added.

We began to find that our planks outboard of such a large boat with fenders were more of a liability than a help. On one occasion the edge of the plank caught on the metalwork of the lock gates as we inched through and snapped the rope. We attached them with stronger rope and the result was that the next time this happened the plank itself snapped. On one dreadful occasion we even bent the struts holding the handrail of the lock gate. After that we removed the planks, although they had been useful on the Rhône to prevent our fenders getting trapped in the indentations where the floating bollards and ladders were.

After Langres we were accompanied by a cyclist who stopped to photograph *Chefren*. He then travelled with us for the whole of that day. Every time we pulled into a lock he was there with his camera and was beginning to be intrusive. We forgave him however when he approached us and asked if we had an email address as he would like to send us a copy of the photographs. Some of his wonderful shots will be seen in this book.

At St. Dizier we met two young men, Alain and Daniel in a smart canal cruiser, a Nichols, with an inside steering position. Our boats travelled together, very slowly, behind a *péniche* which was taking up the whole waterway. After spending the night tied up behind the it close to the lock, Daniel enquired of the *éclusier* as to whether the *péniche* skipper would allow us to go into the lock first that morning. She told us that he was a very awkward man and was insisting on his right to have priority. However he got his 'just deserts' after the lock when he went aground. Of course this held us up still further as the *éclusier* had to fill and re-fill the lock to let water through to refloat the *péniche*. We decided to wait and let him get well ahead, especially as we learned that he was travelling along the same route. Alain and Daniel invited us for lunch. They took pity on us standing outside in our wet weather gear in cold, wet conditions as we helmed the boat, whilst they were snug at their inside steering position. For the next few days whenever we were held up we were invited to get warm inside their centrally heated boat.

It was Sunday and we expected the canals to be quiet, but far from it., as we moved into the Canal Lateral à la Marne we encountered twelve *péniche*s travelling together. As this section of the waterway was quite narrow we had to pull right into the side and practically stop to allow them to pass.

We stayed that night at Orconte where there was also a small, beautifully maintained, shower block. We sat outside in the warmth of the evening sun, sipping our French wine. Daniel and Alain pushed on to Vitry-le-Francois and when we met up with them again later they reported that showers had been added to the lovely little marina there.

We said good-bye to them at Chalons-sur-Marne where our paths diverged. We carried on up the Canal de l'Aisne à la Marne following our previous route whilst they went on to Paris.

We found few other changes as we made our way north apart from what appeared to be an increase in commercial traffic. From Longueil-Annel onwards we were meeting *péniche*s regularly, although as this was a wider stretch of the canal and there was room for us to pass without slowing down. Another evidence of increased commercial traffic was the empty town quay at Péronne. The *péniches* were gone, and were likely to have found work..

John wanted to fill our fuel tanks and we had seen a sign for a filling station just by the marina. We found a berth on a pontoon close to the entrance where it was not so shallow. The marina offices were also the reception for a large camp site sprawling away from the river. They had lots of facilities but did not seem to have bread on sale. Whilst John filled his fuel cans, taking a trolley to the filling station, I set off in search of a supermarket which the attendant said was five minutes walk away. After I had been walking for 15 minutes, I asked a passer by who said the supermarket was another 10 minutes further on. The prospect of another 10 minutes walk and uphill at that, plus a 25 min walk on my return was too much. I gave up on the idea of fresh bread for lunch and retraced my steps. John would have been wondering where I was and anxious to be on our way.

Reaching the river Somme we were surprised to find a row of yellow buoys apparently blocking the entrance. We knew the Somme had been closed for a year sometime since our last visit because of bank erosion but our understanding was that it was now open. We carried on up the Canal du Nord as it looked as though we might have to travel to Calais before crossing to Britain. We tied up outside the next lock where several *péniches* were already waiting. Some of the skippers were standing on the towpath chatting, so I took my courage in both hands and approached them to ask about the closure of the river. I did not expect them to speak English and they did not. But we understood each other.

"The river is not closed" one said, looking puzzled.

"But what about those yellow buoys?" I asked.

They had a consultation amongst themselves until the light dawned.

"Ah," said one, "it is where the river is too shallow."

He then took out a pencil and paper and drew me a map of where the shoal was, and where the channel went to get round it. I thanked them and returned to John with a big grin on my face.

Greatly relieved we negotiated the buoys and entered the river. Soon we came to a lock which was open but there was no sign of an *éclusier*. There was a cottage a little way from the lock and I walked up to the door and knocked. An elderly lady hurried to the door with many apologies and came to operate the lock for us. It was Sunday after all.

As we passed out of the lock we saw a sign to our left which gave a telephone number to call in order to have the next bridge lifted. It came as such a surprise and we were past it so quickly I did not have time to note it down and when we came to the bridge I had to find the telephone number of the last lock from the guide book and phone to ask for the number.

After a long wait a young man arrived and as well as opening the bridge for us he gave us some literature about the river, where we could moor and what places of interest there were. It seemed to suggest that we would be given a mobile phone with speed dial numbers to call when we wanted a lock or a bridge opening. But I guess that was just for the hire boats, of which there are many.

We then had to telephone at every lock and bridge, it seemed to take a very long time and there were no more *éclusiers* in residence. We wondered why they didn't just phone ahead for us as they had done in other parts of France. We moored in all the same places as we had on our previous trip and found few changes except that the restaurant boat was gone from the quay at Abbéville, leaving behind an untidy tangle of electricity cables covered with a battered tarpaulin, and the remains of its *passerelle* jutting out over the river. The wooden surface of the quay was slimy with rain and verdigris and as I leapt ashore with our lines my Wellington boots slipped on the greasysurface. My life passed before my eyes as I found myself falling towards the edge of the quay. With a great effort I altered my centre of gravity and managed to fall sideways. Fortunately nothing was hurt but my pride.

Along its length the river had not been dredged to the charted depth of 1.80m and we touched bottom a few times but it was only mud and not a problem.

There was a round, sloping-sided lock still in use on our first trip, but this had gone, converted like all the others by the addition of an extra chamber. The round basin was still there, but it was permanently open.

The only other problem we encountered was the current which was very fierce at places where a deviation canal joined or left the river to give access to a lock. It was difficult to hold the boat against the current if we were waiting for a lock or bridge at this point.

When we reached St. Valéry we moored close to the boatyard and went to arrange to have the mast replaced. The patron told us he was too busy to do it for a few days, but suggested we went through the sea lock into the marina where there was now a new crane.

The tide was coming in and the lock was to be open in an hour so we took the opportunity to go through into the estuary, tied up at the marina and made arrangements for our mast to be re-fitted there.

We now had to wait for the tide and the weather for our channel crossing. We took the opportunity to do some shopping on our folding bikes. John's bike has pedals with a mind of their own. They often fold up just when you want to put your foot on them. They did this in St. Valéry with the result that John pitched over the handle-bars and landed on his face in the roadway. I looked round when I heard the clatter and saw him picking himself up with blood streaming down his face and shins. Fortunately I had lots of sticking plasters in my rucksack and was able to patch him up, and we were grateful to the lady motorist who stopped to offer help, even though we did not need it.

Every day the capitaine would put the weather forecast on the notice board and we scanned it eagerly waiting for the right conditions. It usually went up before lunch but on the very day when we thought we might be able to leave on the morrow he did not do this. We wanted to make our preparations and, desperate for the information, we phoned a friend in Wales who went on the Internet and then phoned us back with the information that conditions did look good for the following day. He added that a weather system was on its way from the east and if we did not leave the next day we might miss the opportunity for several days.

At 06h00 the following morning we cast off our lines and made our way out into the estuary to follow the buoyed channel in the reverse direction this time and into the English Channel for our trip to England where we were to put our dear boat *Chefren* into brokerage. It was the end of a very wonderful phase of our lives with *Chefren* and we were very sad, but having already bought our Dutch motor cruiser we were looking forward to the next phase.[7]

---

[7] Floating Through Holland; (2008) Davison, Brenda

Glossary and Information

Exchange rate

I have used a rough exchange rate of 10 FF to £1.

Distances and sizes

All distances and sizes are given in metric measurements, kilometres and metres.

1 mile = 1.6 kilometres

1 foot = 0.3 metres.

I have given examples of the capacity of some of the locks by comparing it with how many double-decker buses it could accommodate. I have taken the size of a bus to be 10.5m long, by 3m wide and 4.5m high.

Sailing Terms

Aft – Near the stern, towards the stern

Aground – Touching the bottom

Alongside – Lying side by side with another vessel, or at a jetty or quay

Autohelm – Automatic steering mechanism

Beam – Widest point of vessel, or on the side.

Berth – Sleeping accommodation. Place where boat is tied up at a quay, dockside etc.

Bief – a stretch between canal locks

Bollards – Mooring post

Boom – 1. A spar to which a sail is fastened to control its position relative to the wind.

2. A floating barrier across a waterway

Bow – Front of vessel

Bridge deck – That part of a catamaran spanning the two hulls

Catamaran – Vessel with two hulls

Cleat – A device consisting of two hornlike prongs projecting horizontally in opposite directions from a central base, used for securing lines on boats, quays, etc.

Coach roof – Top of the cabin, usually a sliding cover.

Cockpit – Part of the boat from where the boat is steered and where the crew work

Course – Direction in which the vessel is being steered

Crosstrees – Horizontal bar towards the top of the mast

Dan buoy – Floating marker with flag for 'man overboard'

Davits – Means of suspending dinghy over side or stern of boat

Dinghy – Small open boat

Draft – Depth of vessel from waterline to keel

Dolphins – Tall mooring posts where big ships can wait prior to going in to port

Fender – Object tied onto outside of vessel to protect against rubbing by another vessel, quay wall etc. Usually made of plastic, or rope, sometimes wood

Fend off – To push away

Foresail – The sail at the front of the boat

Foul – Opposite of clear, e.g. a foul wind, to get the propeller fouled in a rope

Furl – To gather the sail on or round a spar or stay

Galley – Cooking area

Guardrail – Rails, wires or ropes attached to stanchions round edge of deck

Grapnel – A small anchor with several claws or arms

Halyards – Lines used for hoisting sails

Heads – Toilet

Helm – Means of steering

Hull – Main part of boat

In-boom furling – Sail rolled inside the boom

Keel – A structure of the boat underneath the water which provides stability

Monohull – Vessel with one hull

Moor – To tie up a vessel

Passerelle – gang plank or footbridge.

Pontoon – Floating walkway to which boats are moored

Port – Left-hand side of the boat facing forward

Pulpit – Metal guardrail at the bow

Rafting – Vessels moored alongside each other

Roller furling – Sail furled around a wire or foil

Rond – A small stake (or hook) for attaching a line to the bank.

Rubbing strake or gunwale (gunn'l) – Sacrificial strip of wood, metal or rubber attached to outside of vessel

Shackle – A staple like link, closed with a pin

Shoals – Shallow part of river or sea

Spinnaker – A large, light triangular racing sail set from the foredeck, usually brightly coloured and patterned

Stanchion – Upright metal post fixed at intervals around edge of deck

Starboard – Right-hand side of the boat facing forward

Underway – Moving through the water

Warp (verb) – To tow with rope

Warp (noun) – Heavy rope for towing or mooring

<u>**French words**</u>

A demain – Until tomorrow

Auberge – Inn

Au'voir, or Au revoir – Good bye

Baguette – Long thin loaf of French bread

Banque – Bank

Bateau – Boat

Brave gars – Brave guys

Boeuf – Beef

Bonjour – Good day

Bon voyage – Good journey

Boulangerie – Bread shop

Bureau – Office

Cadeau – Gift

Canard – Duck

Carenage – Cleaning of hull

Chateau – Stately home, castle

Chomages – Repairs and closures to the canals

Confiture des groseilles – Redcurrant jam

Corrida – Bull fight

Crottins de chien – Dog excrement

Defilé – Gorge

Deshabillé – State of undress

Droite – Right

Eau – Water

Écluse – Lock

Éclusier – Lock keeper *En panne* – Broken down

En vrac – Unbottled

Étang – Small lake, lagoon

Ferme (Fermer) – Closed (to close)

Gardiennage – Care (of boats)

Gare – Station

Gilets de sauvetage – Life jackets

Gîte – Holiday cottage

Horloge – Clock

Il fait chaud – It is hot

Il n'est pas bon – It isn't good

J'envois – I send

Mairie – Mayor's office

Matage – Masts removed and replaced

Mis a mort – To the death

Morceau – Piece

Non – No

Oui – Yes

Petit(e) – Small

Phare – Lighthouse

Plaisancier – Pleasure boat

Plaisanciers – Pleasure boat users

Poisson – Fish

Poireau(x) Leek(s)

Port de Plaisance – Marina for pleasure boats

Potager – Vegetable garden

Presqu'il – Peninsula

Probleme – Problem

Ravitaillement – Refuelling

Razateurs – Bull fighters (the French, non-killing kind)

Reparations – Repairs

Salon du Thé – Tea shop

Sauvetage – Safety

Supermarché – Supermarket

S'il vous plaît – Please

Tout(e) – All

Trois – Three

Voie – Way

Appendix:

Addresses

Releve de Balisage (positions of buoys in Baie de la Somme)
Direction Departement de l'Equipment de la Somme obtainable
from Voies Navigables de France.

Leaflet of costs and addresses, obtainable from French Tourist
Office in London, or from VNF - Direction du Développement,
175 Rue Ludovic Boutleux - B.P. 820 - 62408 Béthune.
www.vnf.fr
Cedex - Tel:03 21 63 24 54. Fax: 03 21 63 24 42.

Boat yard at St. Valéry.

E.M.T.C.M., Quay Jules Verne, 80230 St. Clery S/Somme.
Tel: 03 22 26 82 20
Fax: 03 22 26 82 52
NB Masts can now be removed and replaced at St-Valéry marina.

Navicarte guides for the French canals, and *Guides Vagnon.*

Detailed chart guides for each canal.
These are now being published under the name **Fluviacarte**
Catalogue available from
Imray Laurie Norie & Wilson, Wych House, The Broadway St.Ives
Huntingdon, Cambridgeshire PE17 4BT, England
Tel: 01480 462114. Fax: 01480 496109

Or

Fluvial,
2 Rue des Consuls,
C.S. 30031
34973 Lattes cedex,
France
www.librarie.fluvial.com

Licence to use French waterways.
This can be purchased in France at selected outlets. Our first places
would have been Compeigne, or Reims. You can also get one at
Le Havre, Calais and Dunkerque.

Or by post from
French Tourist Office in London,
or from VNF - Direction du Développement, 175 rue Ludovic
Boutleux - B.P. 820 - 62408 Béthune.
Cedex - Tel:03 21 63 24 54. Fax: 03 21 63 24 42.
Or on line at
www.vnf.fr

Bibliography:

Bowskill, Derek (1995) *The Channel to the Med, A guide to the main routes through the French Canals*, Opus Book Publishing.

Bristow, Philip (1994) *Through the French Canals*, Adlard Coles Nautical.

Davison, Brenda; Edgar, Roger; and Harwood, Margaret – editors
(2012) *Cruising the Inland Waterways of France and Belgium*, Cruising
Association, London.

Davison, Brenda (2008) *Floating Through Holland (and Belgium)*,
www.lulu.com.

Edwards-May, David (1991) *Inland Waterways of France*, Imray, Laurie,
Norrie and Wilson Ltd.

Provence and Cotes d'Azur, European Regional Guide (1993), published by
the AA.